GENOCIDE AND CRIMES AGAINST HUMANITY

This book explores the ambiguities of the French law of genocide by exposing the inexplicable dichotomy between a progressive theory and an overly conservative practice. Based on the observation that the crime of genocide has remained absent from French courtrooms to the benefit of crimes against humanity, this research dissects the reasons for this absence, reviewing and analysing the potential legal obstacles to the judicial use of the law of genocide before contemplating the definitional impact of this judicial reluctance and the consequent confusion between the two crimes. Whilst it uses the French law of genocide and related case law on crimes against humanity as its focal points, the book further adopts a more general standpoint, suggesting that the French misunderstandings of the crime of genocide might ultimately be symptomatic of a more widespread misconception of the crime of genocide as a crime perpetrated against 'a group'.

Studies in International and Comparative Criminal Law: Volume 13

Studies in International and Comparative Criminal Law

General Editor: Michael Bohlander

Criminal law had long been regarded as the preserve of national legal systems, and comparative research in criminal law for a long time had something of an academic ivory tower quality. However, in the past 15 years it has been transformed into an increasingly, and moreover practically, relevant subject of study for international and comparative lawyers. This can be attributed to numerous factors, such as the establishment of ad hoc international criminal tribunals and the International Criminal Court, as well as to developments within the EU, the UN and other international organisations. There is a myriad of initiatives related to tackling terrorism, money laundering, organised crime, people trafficking and the drugs trade, and the international 'war' on terror. Criminal law is being used to address global or regional problems, often across the borders of fundamentally different legal systems, only one of which is the traditional divide between common and civil law approaches. It is therefore no longer solely a matter for domestic lawyers. The need exists for a global approach which encompasses comparative and international law.

Responding to this development this new series will include books on a wide range of topics, including studies of international law, EU law, the work of specific international tribunals, and comparative studies of national systems of criminal law. Given that the different systems to a large extent operate based on the idiosyncracies of the peoples and states that have created them, the series will also welcome pertinent historical, criminological and socio-legal research into these issues.

Volume 1: The German Criminal Code: A Modern English Translation
Michael Bohlander

Volume 2: Principles of German Criminal Law
Michael Bohlander

Volume 3: Crime, Procedure and Evidence in a Comparative and International Context
Essays in Honour of Professor Mirjan Damaska
Edited by John Jackson, Maximo Langer and Peter Tillers

Volume 4: The Criminal Responsibility of Senior Political and Military Leaders as Principals to International Crimes
Hector Olasolo

Volume 5: Transnational Organised Crime in International Law
Tom Obokata

Volume 6: Sentencing in International Criminal Law: The Approach of the Two ad hoc Tribunals and Future Perspectives for the International Criminal Court
Silvia D'Ascoli

Volume 7: OLAF at the Crossroads
Constantin Stefanou, Simone White and Helen Xanthaki

Volume 8: Principles of German Criminal Procedure
Michael Bohlander

Volume 9: Hybrid and Internationalised Criminal Tribunals
Sarah Williams

Volume 10: The Defendant in International Criminal Proceedings: Between Law and Historiography
Björn Elberling

Volume 11: Counsel Misconduct before the International Criminal Court
Professional Responsibility in International Criminal Defence
Till Gut

Volume 12: The Concept of Mens Rea in International Criminal Law: The Case for a Unified Approach
Mohamed Elewa Badar

Genocide and Crimes Against Humanity

Misconceptions and Confusion in French Law and Practice

Caroline Fournet

·HART·
PUBLISHING
OXFORD AND PORTLAND, OREGON
2013

Published in the United Kingdom by Hart Publishing Ltd
16C Worcester Place, Oxford, OX1 2JW
Telephone: +44 (0)1865 517530
Fax: +44 (0)1865 510710
E-mail: mail@hartpub.co.uk
Website: http://www.hartpub.co.uk

Published in North America (US and Canada) by
Hart Publishing
c/o International Specialized Book Services
920 NE 58th Avenue, Suite 300
Portland, OR 97213-3786
USA
Tel: +1 503 287 3093 or toll-free: (1) 800 944 6190
Fax: +1 503 280 8832
E-mail: orders@isbs.com
Website: http://www.isbs.com

British Library Cataloguing in Publication Data
Data Available

ISBN: 978-1-84946-334-8

Typeset by Hope Services, Abingdon
Printed and bound in Great Britain by
MPG Books Ltd

In loving memory of my uncle

ACKNOWLEDGEMENTS

Much has been written on crimes against humanity and on genocide, whether as part of international criminal law projects or as analyses of domestic systems – including the French one.[1] In that sense, the present work might appear redundant if it wasn't for the fact that it aims at answering a question which, although fairly simple, seems never to have been raised, namely, why – in the French context – have individuals involved in the destruction of the European Jews[2] been prosecuted for crimes against humanity, and not for genocide?

The question first arose in my mind while I was still a high school student, lucky enough to follow the History classes of a passionate and committed teacher, M. Frédéric Fouletier, professeur agrégé at the lycée international in Lyon. This book, and probably my choice of profession, owe a lot to him and I would like to take this opportunity to thank him for conveying his dedication to teaching about the atrocities perpetrated during the Second World War, and for having been such an inspiration.

This was at the beginning of the nineties, a time marked by a renewed interest for international criminal law and a revival of international criminal justice as the two ad hoc international criminal tribunals were being set up to respond to the crimes perpetrated in the war that was raging in the former Yugoslavia as well as to the destruction of Tutsis in Rwanda. From a French perspective, this was in the immediate aftermath of the trial of Klaus Barbie, an event that would impact both domestic and international law and which still constituted a vivid memory in my home town of Lyon, where Barbie had been tried and where, under the Nazi occupation, he had also earned his chilling nickname, The Butcher. The beginning of the nineties also witnessed the trial of the first French man, Paul Touvier, for complicity in crimes against humanity perpetrated in Rillieux-la-Pape, a small town near Lyon. While I was totally ignorant of the law, one element did strike me: as I was studying the destruction of the European Jews, I rapidly became puzzled by the fact that, although there was of course no question that this event constituted genocide, these two men – Barbie and Touvier – tried for their participation in the genocide, had been charged with and tried for crimes against humanity, not for genocide. Not only was I unable to find a clear explanation for this, but it also seemed that no one was actually raising the issue.

[1] In particular, see the excellent analyses in KE Smith, *Genocide and the Europeans* (Cambridge, Cambridge University Press, 2010).

[2] The expression, used throughout the present work, is of Raul Hilberg. See R Hilberg, *The Destruction of the European Jews*, 3rd revised edn (New Haven, Yale University Press, 2003).

As I moved on in my studies, I was once again fortunate, in having the privilege to write my PhD thesis under the supervision of a renowned international law expert and a truly admirable man, Professor Malcolm N Shaw QC from the Faculty of Law at the University of Leicester. I will always be grateful to him for his kindness and infallible support throughout the years. While I was conducting research on international crimes, the unanswered French issue was becoming a disconcerting matter; one that was merely highlighted in my thesis for lack of available academic considerations and answers.[3] Later choosing this unexplored question as the focal point of a book chapter, I tentatively tried to provide an explanation as to why these participants in genocide had instead been tried for crimes against humanity.[4] Faced once again with an absence of satisfactory resources, this work dissected the research question and only suggested an explanation, which I further elaborated upon in a second monograph on the law of genocide.[5] At this stage however, faced with fruitless research, what was initially a perplexing observation was turning into a blatant lack of understanding: why would the crime of genocide be tried as a crime against humanity? Why – in the French context – have genociders been prosecuted for crimes against humanity, and not for genocide? And, even more strikingly, why had this question never been raised?

After years of incomprehension, I finally decided to take the time to exclusively focus on the French trials for crimes against humanity and to attempt to answer these questions. In this respect, I would like to express my most sincere thanks to Professor Michael Bohlander, Professor of Criminal Justice in Durham Law School, for accepting to include this monograph within the series 'Studies in International and Comparative Criminal Law' he is editing with Hart Publishing, where Rachel Turner and Richard Hart's incredible patience has been an inestimable help. Professor Bohlander's constant encouragements and support since the very beginning of my academic career have been invaluable in the pursuit of this research and in the completion of this work.

This research was also made possible thanks to a grant awarded by the British Academy, which enabled me to spend essential time at the *Mémorial de la Shoah, Centre de documentation juive contemporaine* (Paris, France) and to consult there the precious archives, original transcripts and published and unpublished works. It also gave me the opportunity to meet with Annette Wieviorka (director of research, CNRS), whose magisterial work on the Shoah needs no further introduction. Her kind interest for my work, her warm welcome and willingness to answer my questions made my encounter with her an unforgettable experience.

[3] C Fournet, *International Crimes – Theories, Practice and Evolution* (London, Cameron May, 2006).

[4] C Fournet, 'Reflection on the separation of powers: The law of genocide and the symptomatic French paradox' in R Henham and P Behrens (eds), *The Criminal Law of Genocide- International, Comparative and Contextual Aspects*, International and Comparative Criminal Justice (Aldershot, Ashgate, 2007) 211–22.

[5] C Fournet, *The Crime of Destruction and the Law of Genocide: Their Impact on Collective Memory*, International and Comparative Criminal Justice Series (Aldershot, Ashgate, 2007).

Acknowledgements

I started writing this book while I was still working at the Law School at the University of Exeter, and completed it at the Department of Criminal Law and Criminology of the University of Groningen, two institutions which rightly deserve my further thanks and gratitude.

As always, my deepest thanks go to my family for their continuous and infallible love and support.

Caroline I Fournet
May 2012

CONTENTS

TABLE OF ABBREVIATIONS

AFDI	Annuaire Français de Droit International
AJIL	American Journal of International Law
BYBIL	British Yearbook of International Law
cass crim	Cour de Cassation, Chambre Criminelle (France)
CCL N° 10	Allied Control Council Law N° 10
ECHR	European Convention for the Protection of Human Rights and Fundamental Freedoms, Council of Europe, 1950
EJIL	European Journal of International Law
Elements of Crimes	Report of the Preparatory Commission for the International Criminal Court, Part II: Finalized Draft Text on the Elements of Crimes, 2 November 2000, PCNICC/2000/1/Add.2
ESCOR	Economic and Social Council Official Records
GA	General Assembly of the United Nations
GAOR	General Assembly Official Records
Genocide Convention	Convention for the Prevention and Punishment of the Crime of Genocide, United Nations, 1948
HRLJ	Human Rights Law Journal
HRQ	Human Rights Quarterly
ICC	International Criminal Court
ICC Statute	Rome Statute of the International Criminal Court, 17 July 1998, UN Doc A/CONF.183/9
ICCPR	International Covenant on Civil and Political Rights, United Nations, 1966
ICJ	International Court of Justice
ICLQ	International and Comparative Law Quarterly
ICTR	International Criminal Tribunal for Rwanda
ICTR Statute	Statute of the International Criminal Tribunal for Rwanda, in Security Council Resolution 955
ICTY	International Tribunal for the Prosecution of Persons Responsible for Serious Violations of International Humanitarian Law Committed in the Territory of the Former Yugoslavia since 1991 (also referred to as the International Criminal Tribunal for the Former Yugoslavia)

ICTY Statute	Statute of the International Criminal Tribunal for the Former Yugoslavia, in Security Council Resolution 808
ILC	International Law Commission
ILC 1954 Draft Code of Offenses	1954 International Law Commission Draft Code of Offenses Against the Peace and Security of Mankind, 28 July 1954, [1954] II *ILC Yearbook*
ILC 1991 Draft Code of Crimes	1991 Draft Code of Crimes Against the Peace and Security of Mankind, 19 July 1991, [1991] II (2) *ILC Yearbook*
ILC 1996 Draft Code of Crimes	1996 International Law Commission Draft Code of Crimes Against the Peace and Security of Mankind, 6 May–26 July 1996, [1996] II (2) *ILC Yearbook*
ILM	International Legal Materials
ILR	International Law Reports
IMT	International Military Tribunal at Nuremberg
IMT Charter	Charter of the International Military Tribunal, in Agreement for the Prosecution and Punishment of the Major War Criminals of the European Axis, 8 August 1945, 82 UNTS 279
IMTFE	International Military Tribunal for the Far East
JICJ	Journal of International Criminal Justice
LJIL	Leiden Journal of International Law
National Prosecutions	Post-World War II prosecutions held in different states predicated on the Law of the IMT Charter, but based on national legislation and conducted before military tribunals, special tribunals and ordinary courts
Nuremberg Judgment	Trial of the Major War Criminals before the International Military Tribunal (TMWC), 42 volumes, Nuremberg, 1947–1949
Nuremberg Principles	Principles of International Law Recognized in the Charter of the Nürnberg Tribunal and in the Judgment of the Tribunal, [1950] II *ILC Yearbook*
Nuremberg Subsequent Proceedings	Proceedings by the Allied Powers held pursuant to Control Council Law N° 10. In [1950] Trials of War Criminals before the Nuremberg Military Tribunals Under Control Council Law No. 10, 15 volumes, Washington: US department of the Army, Government Printing Office, 1946–1949

PCIJ	Permanent Court of International Justice
RCADI	Recueil des Cours de l'Académie de Droit International
RGDIP	Revue Générale de Droit International Public
RIDC	Revue Internationale de Droit Comparé
SCOR	Security Council Official Records
Tokyo Charter	Charter of the International Military Tribunal for the Far East, 19 January 1946, *United States Treaties and Other International Acts Series* 1589
Tokyo Trials	Trial of the Major War Criminals, Proceedings of the International Military Tribunal for the Far East at Tokyo
Torture Convention	Convention against Torture and Other Cruel, Inhuman or Degrading Treatment or Punishment, United Nations, 1984
UDHR	Universal Declaration of Human Rights, United Nations, 1948
UN	United Nations
UN Convention on Statutory Limitations	Convention on the Non-Applicability of Statutory Limitations to War Crimes and Crimes Against Humanity, United Nations, 1968
UNTS	United Nations Treaty Series
Whitaker Report	Review of Further Developments in Fields with which the Sub-Commission has been Concerned, Revised and updated report on the question of the prevention and punishment of the crime of genocide prepared by Mr. B. Whitaker, United Nations Economic and Social Council, Commission on Human Rights, Sub-Commission on Prevention of Discrimination and Protection of Minorities, Thirty-eighth session, E/CN.4/Sub.2/1985/6, 2 July 1985
Yale L J	Yale Law Journal

TABLE OF CASES

European Commission on Human Rights

European Court of Human Rights

International Court of Justice

International Criminal Tribunal for the former Yugoslavia

International Criminal Tribunal for Rwanda

Canada

France

TABLE OF LEGISLATION

Treaties, Conventions and Other International Instruments

Introduction

> Yes, the criminal madness of the occupier was seconded by Frenchmen, by the French State. Fifty-three years ago, on 16 July 1942, 450 French policemen and gendarmes, under the authority of their superiors, acceded to the Nazis' requests.
>
> On that day, in the capital and its suburbs, nearly ten thousand Jewish men, women and children were arrested in their homes, in the early hours of the morning, and assembled at police stations. . . .
>
> France, country of Human Rights and Enlightenment, land of refuge and asylum, France, on that day, committed the irremediable. Failing to honour its words, it abandoned its children to their torturers.[1]

In making this speech, 53 years after the infamous *rafle du Vel d'Hiv*, and 50 years after the Second World War had finally come to an end, President Chirac acknowledged the responsibility of the French State in the perpetration of the Nazi genocide. His 1995 speech was the first official French recognition of this responsibility, notwithstanding the trials of Frenchmen before French courts in the direct aftermath of the war, and also earlier in the nineties, when Paul Touvier, an agent of the French *Milice*, was finally brought to justice and made to answer for his wartime crimes. In these instances, the responsibility of Vichy France had never been recognised.[2] Indeed, to the contrary, one of the lower courts in the

[1] J Chirac, 'Allocution, le dimanche 16 juillet 1995, lors des cérémonies commémorant la grande rafle des 16 et 17 juillet 1942' in J Chirac, *Discours et Messages de Jacques Chirac, Maire de Paris, Premier Ministre, Président de la République, En hommage aux Juifs de France victimes de la collaboration de l'Etat français de Vichy avec l'occupant allemand* (Paris, Fédération des Fils et Filles des Déportés Juifs de France, 1998) 22–23. Translation by the author. The original version reads as follows: 'Oui, la folie criminelle de l'occupant a été secondée par des Français, par l'État français. Il y a cinquante-trois ans, le 16 juillet 1942, 450 policiers et gendarmes français, sous l'autorité de leurs chefs, répondaient aux exigences des nazis. Ce jour-là, dans la capitale et en région parisienne, près de dix mille hommes, femmes et enfants juifs furent arrêtés à leur domicile, au petit matin, et rassemblés dans les commissariats de police . . . La France, patrie des Lumières et des Droits de l'Homme, terre d'accueil et d'asile, la France, ce jour-là, accomplissait l'irréparable. Manquant à sa parole, elle livrait ses protégés à leurs bourreaux.'

[2] The interchangeable expressions 'Vichy France' or 'Vichy government' designate the French political regime which actively collaborated with the Axis Powers from 10 July 1940, the date on which, following the French defeat, Maréchal Philippe Petain was awarded full authority to rule over France, until 20 August 1944. To reinforce its authority and attempt to effectively quash any form of resistance, the Vichy government disposed of its own paramilitary force – known as the French *Milice* – which started operating on the French territory from 30 January 1943, perpetrating summary executions, arbitrary murders and zealously committing torture. See generally J Delperrie de Bayac, *Histoire de la Milice 1918–1945* (Paris, Le Cercle du Nouveau Livre d'Histoire, Arthème Fayard, 1969).

Touvier case had justified a dismissal of the charges on the basis that no precise ideology had reigned in Vichy, that Vichy had been 'a constellation of "good intention and political animosities"'.[3]

While it is correct that 'a trial is held to try a criminal, not to understand a historical event',[4] such a finding from the Paris Court of Appeals remains highly illustrative of the judicial reluctance to adjudicate atrocities perpetrated by Frenchmen in the name of the French State. The disinclination of the French courts was all the more disconcerting insofar as it stood in complete contradiction to France's political attitude and legislative actions, on both the international and the domestic scenes, with respect to the recognition and prosecution of the crimes perpetrated during the Second World War. France was not only among the prosecutors at the Nuremberg trial, it was also one of the first signatory parties to the Genocide Convention.[5] At the domestic level, important legislative steps had been taken to allow for the prosecution of such crimes. In particular, since 1964 France has recognised the non-applicability of statutory limitations to crimes against humanity,[6] and was even a pioneer in enacting a law expressly prohibiting the denial of the crimes as defined in the Nuremberg Charter, the famous loi Gayssot.[7] More recently, French legislation caused great controversy – both within and outside its borders – by providing for the recognition and punishment of the Armenian genocide.[8]

[3] Arrêt du 13 avril 1992, Première Chambre d'accusation de la Cour d'appel de Paris, 1992. Translation by the author. The original reads as follows: 'à Vichy ne régnait pas une idéologie précise'; Vichy was 'une constellation de "bonnes intentions" et d'animosités politiques'. See A Klarsfeld, *Touvier, Un crime français* (Paris, Fayard, 1994) 31.

[4] J Sémelin, *Purifier et Détruire – Usages politiques des massacres et génocides* (Paris, Editions du Seuil, 2005) 383. Translation by the author. The original version reads as follows: 'un procès est fait pour juger un criminel, non pour comprendre un événement historique'.

[5] France signed the Convention on the Prevention and Punishment of the Crime of Genocide (Genocide Convention) on 11 December 1948 – that is, only two days after its adoption by the General Assembly of the United Nations. It subsequently ratified the Convention on 14 October 1950.

[6] Loi n° 64-1326 tendant à constater l'imprescriptibilité des crimes contre l'humanité (26 December 1964).

[7] Loi n° 90–615 tendant à réprimer tout acte raciste, antisémite ou xénophobe dite Gayssot (13 July 1990): 'Il est ainsi inséré, après l'article 24 de la *Loi du 29 juillet 1881 sur la liberté de la presse*, un article 24*bis* ainsi rédigé : Art. 24bis. – Seront punis des peines prévues par le sixième alinéa de l'article 24 ceux qui auront contesté, par un des moyens énoncés à l'article 23, l'existence d'un ou plusieurs crimes contre l'humanité tels qu'ils sont définis par l'article 6 du Statut du tribunal militaire international annexé à l'accord de Londres du 8 août 1945 et qui ont été commis soit par les membres d'une organisation déclarée criminelle en application de l'article 9 dudit statut, soit par une personne reconnue coupable de tels crimes par une juridiction française ou internationale.' The official bulletin of the Justice Ministry specified that only those crimes against humanity perpetrated during the Second World War were the subject of the loi Gayssot. Bulletin Officiel du Ministère de la Justice N° 39 (30 September 1990) Circulaire CRIM 90-09 F1 (27 August 1990) 'Application de la *Loi n°90-615 du 13 juillet 1990 tendant à réprimer tout acte raciste, antisémite ou xénophobe*'.

[8] Loi n° 2001–70 relative à la reconnaissance du génocide arménien de 1915 (29 January 1990). This law, which contains only one article, is phrased straightforwardly in the following terms: 'la France reconnaît publiquement le génocide arménien de 1915' ['France publicly recognises the 1915 Armenian genocide']. This law was interpreted by the Tribunal de Grande Instance de Paris as prohibiting the denial of this genocide. See *Cdca et autres v Editions Robert Laffont, Encyclopédies Quid*, Tribunal de Grande Instance de Paris, 17e chambre civile, Jugement, 6 July 2005. More recently however, a law expressly prohibiting the denial of all the instances of genocide as defined by the New Penal Code and

Why then this judicial reluctance? Was it due to a judicial concern that recognition of the crimes perpetrated by French agents of the Vichy regime might turn into a trial of Vichy France's policy as a whole? It is very true that, in such cases as crimes against humanity and genocide, there is a risk of confusing between the criminal responsibility of the individual sitting in the dock, and that of the state, which more often than not supported, if not initiated, the crimes. It is also true that courts are not here to try history, and such considerations on the part of the French courts could be understandable. Yet, while this argument is tempting, it fails to convince. First, because French courts had no such *états d'âme* when they tried German-born Klaus Barbie for the crimes he had perpetrated in the name of Nazi Germany, qualified by the French Cour de cassation as 'a state practising a policy of ideological supremacy'.[9] Second, because French courts have constantly shown their willingness and ability to punish genocide denial without trying to impose a particular version of the historical truth.[10] And third, because courts were never asked to try the Vichy regime as a whole: they were requested to adjudicate acts which particular criminal nature ignores the passage of time.[11] In the words of Annette Wieviorka,

> History is the study of specificities – and thus of the specificity of genocide. In this it differs both from the political sciences' approach which aims at establishing models and from the legal perspective which deals with issues of qualification *to make individuals accountable for their crimes but not to account for history*.[12]

After years of ongoing judicial proceedings and vicissitudes, accompanied by unjustifiable modifications of the definition of crimes against humanity, French courts finally undertook to simply fulfil their role and 'to make the individuals accountable for their crimes', not without committing errors on the way. One

recognised as such under French law – see Proposition de loi visant à réprimer la contestation de l'existence des génocides reconnus par la loi, texte adopté n° 813, Assemblée nationale (22 December 2011) and texte adopté n ° 52, Sénat (23 January 2012) – was deemed unconstitutional by the Conseil Constitutionnel . See Decision n° 2012-647 DC (28 February 2012).

[9] *Fédération Nationale des Déportés et Internés Résistants et Patriotes et Autres c Klaus Barbie*, cass. crim., 20 December 1985. Reprinted in (1986) RGDIP 90, 1024 and in (1986) ILR 78, 125.

[10] A close reading of the rulings issued by French courts regarding genocide denial indeed reveals that, far from being willing to impose a form of historical truth, French courts merely sanction the confusion between historical knowledge and a messianic, propagandist discourse. In other words, French courts do not impose a particular vision of history, but rather 'obligations of prudence, objective caution and intellectual neutrality' on historians. *Affaire Faurisson, Ligue internationale contre le racisme et l'antisémitisme et autres c R Faurisson*, Tribunal de Grande Instance de Paris, 8 July 1981. Incidentally, it is worth noting that the judiciary, proving proactive, did not wait for the loi Gayssot to be enacted to punish Holocaust denial. See D Salas, 'Le droit peut-il contribuer au travail de mémoire?' in Association française pour l'histoire de la Justice, Commission nationale consultative des droits de l'homme, Ecole nationale de la magistrature , *Colloque La lutte contre le négationnisme Bilan et perspectives de la loi du 13 juillet 1990 tendant à réprimer tout acte raciste, antisémite ou xénophobe* (Paris, La Documentation française, 2003) 36, 41.

[11] See M Zaoui, *Mémoires de justice – Barbie, Touvier, Papon* (Paris, Editions du Seuil, 2009) 19.

[12] Interview with the author. Translation by the author: 'l'Histoire est l'étude des spécificités – et donc de la spécificité du génocide – contrairement à l'approche politiste qui correspond à une recherche de modèles et à l'approche juridique qui s'occupe de la qualification *pour rendre justice mais non pour rendre compte de l'histoire*' (emphasis added).

such mistake, and not the least, was the qualification of the acts perpetrated against the Jews as crimes against humanity, and not as genocide.

Klaus Barbie, chief of the Gestapo in Lyon, and Aloïs Brunner, Adolf Eichmann's assistant, were both tried and convicted of crimes against humanity, while the French Paul Touvier, member of the French *Milice*, and Maurice Papon, a high-ranking civil servant in charge of the Jewish section of the *préfecture de Gironde* during the war, who subsequently remained in charge of some of the country's most important functions, including those of Préfet de Police from 1958 to 1967 and Budget Minister from 1978 to 1981, were found guilty of complicity in crimes against humanity. Why this choice of characterisation of the crimes, to the detriment of the qualification of genocide?

To attempt to answer this question, the following study will first analyse the different French courts' decisions in these four cases; decisions which simultaneously reveal an impeccable command by the French judiciary of the law of crimes against humanity – the *Barbie* and *Touvier* findings still have, decades later, an impact on the case law of the ad hoc international criminal tribunals – as well as a visible willingness to minimise the responsibility of Vichy France and of its agents, as exemplified by clever twists in the interpretation of the definition of the crimes. If French courts have shown an expert understanding in their apprehension of the law of crimes against humanity, they however have failed to even consider the law of genocide in instances where precisely all the accused were brought to justice to answer for crimes perpetrated in the context of the Shoah. Voluntary omission? Ignorance of the law? The answer can only be tentative; what remains certain however is that the law of genocide would have been applicable to all these instances – as the second part of this research will demonstrate.

Just as the regrettable current tendency to use 'the magic word, genocide . . . to spice up the charges',[13] the 'g-word' having undoubtedly acquired an unfortunate 'rhetorical power',[14] only empties the crime of its meaning and specificity, failing to qualify the real crime of genocide as genocide similarly deprives it of its essence and uniqueness. By not qualifying the respective crimes perpetrated by Klaus Barbie, Paul Touvier, Maurice Papon and Aloïs Brunner against the Jews as genocide, French courts ultimately misinterpreted the facts and misread the law.

French courts ignored the distinction between crimes against humanity and genocide, and operated a merging of the two notions; a confusion which was to stay in French law insofar as, while it recognises genocide as a self-standing incrimination, the French New Penal Code still includes it under the heading of crimes against humanity.[15] If this amalgam is to remain, French law and case law would not only deviate problematically from international criminal law norms, but would also persistently fail at grasping the specificity of the crime of genocide.

[13] W Schabas, *Unimaginable Atrocities – Justice, Politics, and Rights at the War Crimes Tribunals* (Oxford, Oxford University Press, 2012) 100.

[14] *ibid* 103.

[15] See art 211–1 of the New Penal Code (France).

There is absolutely no intention here to devalue the seriousness of crimes against humanity, to depreciate the utmost gravity of such crimes. To the contrary, it is only precisely when the qualifications of crimes against humanity and genocide are used adequately that the extreme horror of the acts can be properly recognised and reflected in the judgments. Genocide and crimes against humanity do not stand in competition or in opposition; they are simply different crimes. When a group is targeted for destruction, when whole families are destined for annihilation because they belong to this group, when children are sent to their deaths with their parents, genocide is occurring, and nothing else.

By not using the qualification of genocide when they could – and should – have done so, by persistently refusing to assert the responsibility of Vichy France in the destruction of the Jews, by even going as far as to rule that Maurice Papon, one of Vichy's high civil servants who signed and authorised the deportations, was unaware of the Nazi genocidal plan, French courts not only erred in law, they also issued judgments in bad faith. If Papon admittedly could not have conceived the unimaginable horror of the Nazi concentration and extermination camps, he simply cannot not have known of the despicable conditions of detention in the French transit camps, which alone proved fatal for thousands of victims, he simply cannot not have guessed the fate that was awaiting those being put in these trains under *his* authorisation. The victims themselves were not so naïve. On their respective cards, thrown from the deportation wagons, 10-year-old Marcel Rozenbaum, arrested with his mother, had written to the rest of his family: 'We are in the train and glad that you are not with us',[16] while nine-year-old Jeannette Gryf, arrested with her mother and her three brothers, wrote to her aunt:

> If you get a letter from Papa, tell him of our unhappiness, and I don't know if we'll see each other again. Aunt dear, it would be very kind of you to send this letter to Papa. Papa, we say hello to you for always, a hello from us all and thank you for everything.[17]

Marcel Rozenbaum and Jeannette Gryf did not come back.[18]

[16] Marcel was deported on 9 September 1942. Translation available at www.holocaust-history.org/klarsfeld/French%20Children/html&graphics/T1164.shtml. The original version reads: 'Nous sommes dans le train et contents que vous ne soyez pas avec nous.' S Klarsfeld, *Adieu les enfants (1942–1944)* (Paris, Mille et une nuits, 2005) 105.

[17] Maurice was 7 years old, Simon was 5 years old and Léon just one year old. After their arrest, they were transferred from Bordeaux to the camp of Drancy and deported on 7 September 1942. Translation available at www.holocaust-history.org/klarsfeld/French%20Children/html&graphics/T0760.shtml. The original version reads: 'Si tu reçois une lettre de papa, dis-lui le malheur de nous. Papa on te dit bonjour pour toujours. Un bonjour de nous tous et merci pour tout.' Klarsfeld, *Adieu les enfants (1942–1944)* (2005) 106. See also A Klarsfeld, *La Cour, Les Nains et Le Bouffon* (Paris, Editions Robert Laffont, 1998) 146.

[18] On the murder of the children, see generally the work of Serge Klarsfeld and, in particular; S Klarsfeld, *Les enfants d'Izieu, une tragédie juive* (Paris, AZ Repro, 1984); S Klarsfeld, *La Shoah en France – Le mémorial des enfants juifs déportés de France* (Paris, Librairie Arthème Fayard, 2001).

Part 1

Crimes Against Humanity: From Nuremberg to Lyon . . . And Back Again

France, together with the United States, the United Kingdom and Soviet Russia, was one of the original parties to the London Charter which provided for the establishment of the International Military Tribunal set up at Nuremberg.[1] France was thus one of the countries which, in the direct aftermath of the Second World War, showed its early attachment to punishing the crimes perpetrated by the Nazis, and contributing to the definition and judicial application of the novel concept of crimes against humanity, at least as far as these were used at the international level to try and punish Nazi criminals for the

> murder, extermination, enslavement, deportation, and other inhumane acts committed against any civilian population, before or during the war, or persecutions on political, racial or religious grounds in execution of or in connection with any crime within the jurisdiction of the Tribunal, whether or not in violation of the domestic law of the country where perpetrated.[2]

The situation was quite different at the national level and, while it would be a mistake to assert that the crimes perpetrated by French people in France, during what undoubtedly constitutes one of the darkest pages in French history, had gone unnoticed before the 1970s,[3] these crimes failed to be qualified as ones against humanity. Numerous trials occurred, and what is referred to as the '*épuration*', or purge, was in many ways rigorous.[4] As Olivier Wieviorka reports, the

[1] Charter of the International Military Tribunal, Annex to Agreement for the Prosecution and Punishment of Major War Criminals of the European Axis, London, 8 August 1945, 82 UNTS 279. Reprinted in (Supp. 1945), AJIL 39, 257. Hereafter referred to as the London Charter, the Nuremberg Charter or the Charter of the IMT.

[2] See art 6 (c) of the London Charter.

[3] In this respect, Henry Rousso distinguished what he referred to as the first *épuration*, based on a form of transitional justice, from the second one, which coincides with memorial justice. See H Rousso, *Vichy – L'événement, la mémoire, l'histoire* (Paris, Éditions Gallimard, Collection folio histoire, 2001) 35.

[4] O Wieviorka, *La Mémoire Désunie – Le souvenir politique des années sombres, de la Libération à nos jours* (Paris, Editions du seuil, 2010) 54.

wartime behaviour of nearly 1 per cent of the French population came under scrutiny.[5] Yet, these trials failed to draw upon the then recent legacy of Nuremberg, in terms of the categories of crimes with which the individuals were charged, to the benefit of the qualifications of treason and intelligence with the enemy,[6] qualifications which emphasised the French dependence on the Nazi occupier, rather than the autonomy of a French dictatorship.[7]

More specifically, there was nothing in the qualifications of treason and intelligence with the enemy that expressly encompassed anti-Semitism, persecutions, crimes against humanity or genocide,[8] lacunae which impeded the competent courts to actually grasp the specific nature of the crimes that had been committed against the Jews under the Vichy regime. If such crimes were not completely absent from the courtrooms, and if the sufferings inflicted on the Jews by the Vichy regime were judicially considered,[9] the fact still remains that the lack of precise and specific legal dispositions prohibiting and punishing anti-Semitism led to serious problems in practice as the courts found themselves unable to directly address these crimes as self-standing offences.[10] As a result, the crimes linked with the Shoah were never tried as such.

French judicial efforts were short-lived, and were soon followed by the subsequent enactment of amnesty laws, thereby imposing legal forgetfulness and impeding any judicial action.[11] The first amnesty law, promulgated in 1951,[12] applied to the less serious crimes[13] but the second amnesty law, passed by a vote of

[5] ibid.

[6] Art 75 of the French Penal Code. Henry Rousso observed that numerous low-ranking individuals were charged with 'acts harmful to national defence' (*actes nuisibles à la défense nationale*) under art 83 of the Penal Code. In practice, this difference in the charges had a considerable impact insofar as, unlike treason and intelligence with the enemy, the death penalty did not apply to acts harmful to national defense. See Rousso, *Vichy – L'événement, la mémoire, l'histoire* 674–75.

[7] See ibid 459–60.

[8] Henry Rousso however noted one exception embodied in the *ordonnance* of 26 August 1944 which defined the crime of national indignity (*indignité nationale*) as notably encompassing the publication of articles, brochures or books or the presentation of conferences in favour of the enemy, of collaboration with the enemy, of racism or of totalitarian doctrines, and which thereby singled out racism as a specific – and prohibited – ground of commission. Yet, as further explained by Rousso, this only related to ideological opinions, and not to actions, which were rather leniently repressed by national degradation. See Rousso, *Vichy – L'événement, la mémoire, l'histoire* 638. See also article premier, Ordonnance du 26 août 1944, *Journal officiel de la République française* (28 August 1944).

[9] See Rousso, *Vichy – L'événement, la mémoire, l'histoire* 670. For an excellent analysis of these trials, see notably pp 443–49 on the respective trials of Maréchal Philippe Pétain and of Pierre Laval; 650–53 on the trials of the civil servants in charge of the 'Jewish Question'; 653–57 on the trials of Drancy's gendarmes; 657–62 on the *Bousquet* case.

[10] Rousso, *Vichy – L'événement, la mémoire, l'histoire* 672.

[11] ibid 371–72.

[12] *Journal officiel* (6 January 1951). This law was voted by 327 votes in favour and 263 against, a vote which clearly showed the opposition of communists and of the majority of socialists. See Rousso, *Vichy – L'événement, la mémoire, l'histoire* 374.

[13] As Henry Rousso explained, '[t]his law granted amnesty to all those who had committed acts for which the punishment involved loss of civil rights [*dégradation nationale*] and a prison sentence of less than fifteen years. The law also provided for individual remedies for those who had been forcibly conscripted, minors below the age of twenty-one, and those who had already served most of their time. Though broad in principle, this law did not apply to grave crimes or to decisions of the Haute Cour,

394 to 212 in 1953, provided for total amnesty. As observed by Henry Rousso, the first article of this law did 'little to hide the Assembly's paramount concern with justification' and, breaking 'with customary practice and [setting] forth the legislators' grounds', reflected 'the law's ambiguities and the deputies' misgivings'.[14] It read:

> The French Republic pays homage to the Resistance, whose combat both inside and outside our borders saved the nation. It is out of fidelity to the spirit of the Resistance that the Republic today wishes to grant clemency. Amnesty is neither rehabilitation nor revenge, nor is it a criticism of those who, in the name of the nation, bore the heavy burden of judgment and punishment.[15]

As Rousso further wrote, '[i]t therefore took less than a decade for the ostracism to end', 'the amnesty was a missed opportunity for the nation to remember.'[16] The amnesty laws notwithstanding, as 1965 approached, and with it the spectrum of statutory limitations and their 20-year benchmark, France unanimously adopted a law providing for the non-applicability of statutory limitations to crimes against humanity as defined in the Nuremberg Charter.[17] Despite appearances, these two legislative actions did not stand in contradiction to each other: at the time the 1964 law was adopted, not one of the French deputies, all voting in its favour, would have thought this law could one day be applicable to French individuals. The 1964 law on the non applicability of statutory limitations to crimes against humanity aimed at ensuring that German criminals would not go unpunished, not at trying French individuals for their participation in the crimes perpetrated against the Jews.[18] None of these deputies could at the time have foreseen that Jean Leguay,[19] a former civil servant under the Vichy government, or René Bousquet, former secretary general of Vichy's police – who both died before being tried – would be charged with crimes against humanity; or that Paul Touvier, member of the *Milice* or Maurice Papon, former high civil servant under Vichy, would actually stand trial for, and be convicted of, such crimes.[20]

It is therefore the 1964 law on the non-applicability of statutory limitations to crimes against humanity which prompted such crimes, as defined in the Nuremberg

which had been abolished along with the other *cours de justice* the previous year' (footnote omitted). H Rousso, *The Vichy Syndrome – History and Memory in France since 1944* (Cambridge, MA, Harvard University Press, 1991) 51.

[14] ibid 53.

[15] *Journal officiel* (7 August 1953). Translation available in Rousso, *The Vichy Syndrome* 53. He noted: 'The first sentence, included at the behest of the Communist deputies (who voted against the law), was voted on separately and unanimously approved.' Ibid.

[16] Rousso, *The Vichy Syndrome* 54.

[17] Loi n° 64-1326 tendant à constater l'imprescriptibilité des crimes contre l' humanité (26 December 1964).

[18] See Rousso, *Vichy – L'événement, la mémoire, l'histoire* 416–18.

[19] It is noteworthy that Jean Leguay, responsible for the deportation of large numbers of Jews from France, was charged with crimes against humanity, rather than with genocide.

[20] See Rousso, *Vichy – L'événement, la mémoire, l'histoire* 542–43. It is in this respect interesting to note that none of these trials were set into motion through the public prosecution: all were due to the initiatives of the victims as *parties civiles*. See ibid 699.

Charter, to finally be used by the French judiciary in proceedings engaged against both German and French nationals. As mentioned above, Jean Leguay died on 2 July 1989, before he could actually stand trial, just as the investigation had been completed and the case was about to be sent to a Paris court. Yet, this missed judicial event unexpectedly gave the opportunity to the court to point to the would-have-been defendant's guilt. In a break with judicial custom, the statement declaring the case closed by virtue of the defendant's death explicitly alluded to Leguay's *guilt* in the following terms: 'The investigation established that Leguay, Jean, did participate in crimes against humanity committed in July [the Vel d'Hiv round-up], August, and September 1942.'[21] As Henry Rousso pointed out, '[t]he prosecutor's final report to the court, submitted on 26 July 1989, included no fewer than thirty-three pages detailing the charges against the deceased.'[22]

Due to Leguay's death, and perhaps in an ironic turn of events, it was a German national – Klaus Barbie – who was the first to be found guilty of crimes against humanity by French courts, in 1987. This was however purely coincidental and, as observed by Michel Zaoui, the chronology of the trials was mainly due to chance, as both Paul Touvier and Maurice Papon had been charged before Barbie actually was. As further observed by Zaoui, chance probably played a beneficial role, as it is most likely that, had the trials followed the chronology of the indictments, this could have led to a 'gigantic judicial uproar' ('*une gigantesque cacophonie judiciaire*'),[23] France arguably being at the time unable to deal with crimes against humanity perpetrated by Frenchmen. If this observation is beyond any possible verification, one could also argue that the *Leguay* precedent could have brought hope to the contrary. Further, one could also argue that the *Touvier* and *Papon* trials, both held after that of Barbie, were not far from 'judicial uproars'.

[21] Tribunal de grande instance de Paris, 'Writ of dismissal issued by Judge Jean-Pierre Getti' (11 September 1989) 3.

[22] Rousso, *The Vichy Syndrome* 151. Here referring to Tribunal de grande instance de Paris, Parquet du procureur de la République, 'Réquisitoire définitif aux fins de constatation de l'extinction de l'action publique' (26 July 1989).

[23] Zaoui *Mémoires de justice – Barbie, Touvier, Papon* 7.

1

Trying Klaus Barbie: Setting a Precedent?

The trial of Klaus Barbie was the first ever trial held in France to deal directly with the genocide perpetrated in France during the Second World War.[24] If Barbie, chief of the Gestapo in Lyon and also known as 'the butcher of Lyon', owed his sinister reputation to his fierce and relentless struggle against *Resistance* fighters, he was also responsible for the deportation of Jews and an extremely active participant in the Shoah.[25] He was nonetheless ultimately charged with crimes against humanity and not with genocide.

On 23 February 1983 the prosecutor made public the indictment against Barbie, which listed eight counts of crimes against humanity, all involving the arrest, torture and deportation of civilians, in particular Jews, and excluding crimes perpetrated against *Resistance* fighters:

> Not included under the head of crimes against humanity are acts alleged to have been committed by Klaus Barbie against the person of members of the Resistance . . . These acts were war crimes for which the statute of limitations is now in effect, and they do not appear to constitute *crimes against humanity*, that is, massacres, murders, and deportations inflicted on civilian populations during the Occupation, *including acts of genocide* and hostage taking . . . Because resistance fighters fought against the Vichy regime and the army of occupation, they are considered to have been volunteer combatants, as they themselves have always forcefully insisted and as the law has recognised . . . Legally, therefore, they cannot be confused with the civilian population that endured the kinds of treatment described in the charter of the International Tribunal of Nuremberg.[26]

This indictment calls for a series of remarks. First, as it explicitly states, acts of genocide were covered by the definitional scope of crimes against humanity. Put differently, French law at the time had not fully emancipated the crime of genocide

[24] See A Wieviorka, 'La France et le Procès de Nuremberg' in A Wieviorka (ed), *Les procès de Nuremberg et de Tokyo* (Paris, Editions Complexe, 1996) 69, 81.

[25] Klaus Barbie had already been tried by French courts *in absentia*. He was tried in 1952 and again in 1954 and sentenced to death for his part in more than 4,000 killings and in the deportation of more than 7,000 Jews to the concentration camps. Barbie managed to evade justice for nearly 40 years, supported by American intelligence officers who sought his assistance in anti-Soviet intelligence. In 1951, he emigrated to Bolivia and, under and the name Klaus Altmann, acquired Bolivian citizenship in 1957. After being discovered by Serge and Beate Klarsfeld in 1971, Barbie was extradited to France. His trial lasted from 11 May 1987 to 4 July 1987. He was sentenced to life imprisonment and died in prison on 25 September 1991.

[26] Translation available in Rousso, *The Vichy Syndrome* 203–204 (emphasis added).

from the category of crimes against humanity, a dependence which probably stemmed from the law of Nuremberg itself. Indeed, if the indictment at Nuremberg did charge the defendants with 'deliberate and systematic genocide',[27] the Nuremberg Charter itself did not expressly list genocide among the crimes over which the International Military Tribunal could exercise its jurisdiction, although it was most probably implicitly included therein within the wider category of crimes against humanity.[28] Although it is clear that, according to contemporary international criminal law, '[g]enocide . . . is different from other crimes against humanity',[29] the fact that genocide finds its roots in the very concept of crimes against humanity seems equally clear. The ICTR has unequivocally found that the 'crime of genocide is a type of crime against humanity', and that its definition 'was based upon that of crimes against humanity, that is, a combination of "extermination and persecutions on political, racial or religious grounds"',[30] while the ICTY has explicitly qualified genocide as 'the most abhorrent crime against humanity'.[31] In this respect therefore, the French indictment and its understanding of crimes against humanity stood perfectly within the Nuremberg tradition.

This inclusion of genocide within crimes against humanity, even if in line with the Nuremberg precedent, was however not without consequences. And indeed, the second remark that the indictment against Barbie calls for is that it drew – and rightly so – a clear distinction between crimes committed against *Resistance* fighters and crimes committed against Jews. As the Lyon Court of Appeals acknowledged this distinction, it logically established two separate qualifications for these two distinct types of crimes. Yet, it is precisely in its legal qualifications of the crimes that the court arguably erred and that the case started on an erroneous basis. And indeed, as the Court of Appeals qualified crimes against *Resistance* fighters as war crimes, and crimes against Jews as crimes against humanity, the debate that ensued focused on the distinction between these two sets of crimes. Far from being purely theoretical, this distinction had a dramatic consequence in practice: the qualification of war crimes entailed the application of statutory limitations and thus the impossibility of trying Barbie for his crimes against *Resistance* fighters.[32] The popular outrage at what was felt to be an illegitimate and unaccept-

[27] *France et al v Goering et al*, 22 IMT 203 (1946) 45–46.

[28] See art 6 of the Nuremberg Charter.

[29] *The Prosecutor v Clément Kayishema and Obed Ruzindana* (Trial Chamber Judgment) ICTR–95–1–T (21 May 1999) para 89.

[30] ibid.

[31] *The Prosecutor v Zoran Kupreškić , Mirjan Kupreškić, Vlatko Kupreškić, Drago Josipović, Dragan Papić, Vladimir Santić* (Trial Chamber Judgment) IT–95–16 (14 January 2000) para 751. See also *The Prosecutor v Dragan Nikolić* (Trial Chamber Initial Indictment) IT–94–2 (4 November 1994) para 24; *The Prosecutor v Radislav Krstić* (Trial Chamber Judgment) IT–98–33 (2 August 2001) para 684.

[32] For an analysis of the reasoning of the French Cour de cassation on the reasons for the applicability of statutory limitations to war crimes under French law, see A Lyon-Caen, 'De Nuremberg au Procès Barbie' in Centre de droit international de l'Institut de Sociologie de l'Université Libre de Bruxelles (Centre Henri Rolin), Fondation Auschwitz-Stichting (Centre d'Etudes et de Documentation), *Le Procès de Nuremberg – Conséquences et actualisation, Actes du Colloque international, Université Libre de Bruxelles, Brussels, le 27 mars 1987* (Brussels: Editions Bruylant, Editions de l'Université de Bruxelles, 1988) 47, 55–56.

able impunity did not go unnoticed by the Court of Appeals, which subsequently struggled to apply the distinction it had itself created. The inherent limits of this distinction rapidly emerged when the Court had to qualify the crimes perpetrated by Barbie against a Jewish *Resistance* fighter, Professor Gompel, and thus had to assess whether such crimes had been committed against a Jew, and therefore punishable as crimes against humanity, or against a *Resistance* fighter, thereby constituting war crimes and subject to statutory limitations. In a vain attempt at being convincing, the Court here explained that:

> Barbie could have thought that he was a Resistance fighter and, therefore, the presumption of innocence must apply here. We must consider, by presumption, that he was a non-innocent Jew and that the tortures Gompel had to endure fell within the statutory limitations applicable to war crimes.[33]

In other words, pushing its distinction to the extremes, the Court, in order to exclude all *Resistance* fighters from the scope of application of crimes against humanity, defined Jews who were also members of the *Resistance* as 'non-innocent' Jews. If it does appear from a close reading of the case, that the court equated 'innocent' with 'inoffensive', and 'non-innocent' with 'offensive', the least that can be said is that the choice of terminology is most unfortunate.[34] Faced with such an unsustainable distinction between Barbie's victims, the Cour de cassation famously quashed the decision of the lower court and, by a ruling of 20 December 1985, put an end to the debate by extending the notion of crimes against humanity to encompass crimes committed against fighters of the *Resistance,* which would thereby:

> constitute crimes against humanity immuned from any statutory limitation, according to article 6(c) of the Charter of the International Military Tribunal at Nuremberg, appended to the London Charter of 8 August 1945, and even if they also qualify as war crimes, according to article 6(b) of this same text, inhumane acts and persecutions which have been systematically committed, in the name of a state practising a policy of ideological supremacy, against individuals by reason of their belonging to a racial or religious community as well as against the adversaries of this policy, whatever the form of their opposition – whether armed or not.[35]

With this finding, not only did the Cour de cassation break with the more restrictive interpretation which had so far prevailed, extending crimes against humanity

[33] The original version reads as follows: 'Barbie a pu penser qu'il était résistant, par conséquent la présomption d'innocence qui joue en sa faveur doit jouer là, et l'on doit considérer, par présomption, que c'était un juif non-innocent et que les tortures qu'on a fait subir à ce malheureux Gompel étaient couvertes par la prescription des crimes de guerre'. Lyon-Caen, 'De Nuremberg au Procès Barbie' 55.

[34] See ibid.

[35] Translation by the author. The original version reads as follows: 'Attendu que constituent des crimes imprescriptibles contre l'humanité, au sens de l'article 6(c) du Statut du Tribunal militaire international de Nuremberg annexé à l'accord de Londres du 8 août 1945, alors même qu'ils seraient également qualifiables de crimes de guerre, selon l'article 6(b) de ce texte, les actes inhumains et persécutions qui, au nom d'un Etat pratiquant une politique d'hégémonie idéologique, ont été commis de façon systématique, non seulement contre des personnes en raison de leur appartenance à une collectivité raciale ou religieuse, mais aussi contre les adversaires de cette politique quelle que soit la forme de leur opposition – autrement dit forme armée ou forme non-armée'. See Lyon-Caen, 'De Nuremberg au Procès Barbie' 56.

to cover those civilians who had taken up arms against the oppressor, it also introduced the concept of a 'state practising a policy of ideological supremacy', which could be seen as coming within the ambit of article 6 of the Nuremberg Charter, which gave the Tribunal the authority to punish persons '*acting in the interests of the European Axis countries*, whether as individuals or as members of organizations'.[36]

As a result of this ruling, Barbie was ultimately tried under five counts,[37] not limited to the crimes perpetrated as part of the Nazi Final Solution, and which notably included the lethal acts of torture inflicted upon Professor Gompel as well as the arrest and deportation of the 44 Jewish children of Izieu, a village where they had found refuge.[38] These counts did not distinguish between Jews and Resistance fighters: for the French court, it was the nature of the acts perpetrated, not the identity of the victims, which qualified a crime as one against humanity – a reasonable finding in the law of crimes against humanity, but one which seems to contradict the law of genocide. As will be emphasised later in this research, had both the law of crimes against humanity and the law of genocide been applied – as arguably should have been the case – the identity of the victims would have been awarded a preponderant role, precisely to distinguish between the two types of offences. To the contrary, by applying the same legal qualification to both crimes perpetrated against Jews and crimes committed against fighters of the *Resistance*, this decision blurred the distinction between these two crimes. If crimes against *Resistance* fighters were undoubtedly crimes against humanity, crimes against Jews were – equally undoubtedly – genocide and, by failing to differentiate between the crimes through the use of distinct qualifications, the Cour de cassation here reached a questionable decision, which it was to repeat in both the *Touvier* case and the *Papon* case, thus yet again failing to adequately qualify the destruction of the European Jews as genocide.

If the qualification of genocide was regrettably left aside, the Cour de cassation's finding still remains interesting with respect to the definition it gave of crimes against humanity. Although the court explicitly referred to the definition contained in article 6(c) of the Nuremberg Charter, it is noticeable that it simultaneously adapted it to the specific case pending before it. The definition of crimes against humanity given by the Cour de cassation indeed recognised three legal ingredients to these crimes, which were not in the Nuremberg Charter as such.

[36] See art 6 of the IMT Charter. Emphasis added.

[37] Barbie, sentenced to life imprisonment for the perpetration of crimes against humanity, died in custody in 1991.

[38] Barbie was also charged with the arrest and deportation of 84 persons following the round-up of the Union Générale des Israélites de France (UGIF) in Lyon. The UGIF was the French Jewish council, established by law 'to ensure the representation of Jews with public authorities. Translation by the author. The original version reads as: 'd'assurer la représentation des Juifs auprès des Pouvoirs publics'. See loi instituant une Union générale des Israélites de France (29 November 1941) *Journal officiel* 2 December 1941. Barbie was further charged with the arrest and deportation of the five adults caring for the 44 children in Izieu, the deportation of approximately 650 persons from Lyon, further deportations of members of the Resistance and the deportation of the Lesèvre family.

First, it brought all types of crimes against humanity (both homicide crimes and crimes of persecution) to the same level, whether they were committed because of specific characteristics of the victims or because of their political engagement and/or actions and therefore made grounds for commission relevant for all of these acts. Second, it only considered as crimes against humanity those acts which had been 'systematically committed, in the name of a state practising a policy of ideological supremacy, against individuals by reason of their belongings to a racial or religious community as well as against the adversaries of this policy'. Third, with regards to the *mens rea*, it only qualified crimes as ones against humanity if the individual had been willing to participate in the state's systematic policy of ideological supremacy.[39]

If it is arguable that the Cour de cassation's definition remained within the spirit of Nuremberg, the import of this definition – formulated in 1985 – can only be fully appreciated in light of contemporary international criminal law, and of the most recent definition as embodied in article 7(1) of the ICC Statute, thereby allowing for an assessment of its impact on the international scene. Article 7(1) of the ICC Statute reads as follows:

> For the purpose of this Statute, "crime against humanity" means any of the following acts when committed as part of a widespread or systematic attack directed against any civilian population, with knowledge of the attack:
>
> (a) Murder;
> (b) Extermination;
> (c) Enslavement;
> (d) Deportation or forcible transfer of population;
> (e) Imprisonment or other severe deprivation of physical liberty in violation of fundamental rules of international law;
> (f) Torture;
> (g) Rape, sexual slavery, enforced prostitution, forced pregnancy, enforced sterilization, or any other form of sexual violence of comparable gravity;
> (h) Persecution against any identifiable group or collectivity on political, racial, national, ethnic, cultural, religious, gender as defined in paragraph 3, or other grounds that are universally recognized as impermissible under international law, in connection with any act referred to in this paragraph or any crime within the jurisdiction of the Court;
> (i) Enforced disappearance of persons;
> (j) The crime of apartheid;
> (k) Other inhumane acts of a similar character intentionally causing great suffering, or serious injury to body or to mental or physical health.[40]

[39] See generally Lyon-Caen, 'De Nuremberg au Procès Barbie' 58–59.

[40] Rome Statute of the International Criminal Court, adopted by the United Nations Diplomatic Conference of Plenipotentiaries on the Establishment of an International Criminal Court on 17 July 1998, UN Doc A/Conf.183/9, 1998. Entry into force 1 July 2002. Hereafter referred to as Rome Statute or ICC Statute.

1.1 Crimes Against Humanity and the Victimisation of the Individual

Unlike the different international definitions of crimes against humanity which have all characterised such crimes as committed 'against any civilian population',[41] the French definition refers to 'individuals', victims because of their race (*sic.*), religion or political opinions. The French Cour de cassation indeed unequivocally found that both inhumane acts and persecutions constituted crimes against humanity 'if systematically committed, in the name of a state practising a policy of ideological supremacy, against individuals, by reason of their belonging to a racial or religious community as well as against the adversaries of this policy', thus making racial, religious or political grounds relevant for all crimes against humanity and not only for persecutions, thereby departing from both the Nuremberg definition and the most current understanding of the crimes as embodied in the Rome Statute.

The Nuremberg Charter indeed listed two sets of crimes – murders and persecutions – making the motive of the perpetrator relevant only in the case of the latter, and thus indicating that, while some acts were so heinous and destructive as to be crimes per se, other acts were criminal because the perpetrator had acted against the victim based on specific grounds, whether political, racial or religious.[42]

If the Statute of the Yugoslavia Tribunal followed on from the path drawn at Nuremberg, thereby making grounds for commission relevant only for persecutions, and not for the other acts listed such as murder or extermination,[43] the Tribunal nonetheless departed from its founding instrument. In the *Tadić* case, the Trial Chamber indeed held that the term 'population' implied that *all* the acts enumerated – and not only persecutions – had to be committed on discriminatory grounds to qualify as crimes against humanity,[44] a finding all the more surprising considering that neither international customary law nor the Statute of the Tribunal itself required such a narrow understanding. In reality, this new judicially created requirement stemmed from a Report of the United Nations's

[41] See art 6(c) of the IMT Charter, art II(c) of CCL No 10, art 18 of the ILC 1996 Draft Code of Crimes, [1996] II (2) *ILC Yearbook* 47, art 5 of the ICTY Statute, art 3 of the ICTR Statute, art 7(1) of the ICC Statute.

[42] It is worth noting here that, although substantially the same as the Nuremberg definition, the one enshrined in art 5(c) of the Tokyo Charter did not list religious grounds among the prohibited grounds for commission.

[43] See art 5 of the ICTY Statute. This was arguably in line with the general understanding of crimes against humanity prevailing at the time. Indeed, while in art I of the 1954 Draft Code of Offences, the International Law Commission had made clear that grounds for commission were highly relevant for all crimes against humanity, its 1996 Draft Code went back to the 'bifurcation' contained in the Nuremberg Charter and only kept this requirement for 'persecutions' and 'institutionalized discrimination'. [1996] II (2) *ILC Yearbook* 47.

[44] See *The Prosecutor v Dusko Tadić* (Trial Chamber Opinion and Judgment) IT–94–1–T (7 May 1997) paras 650–52.

Secretary-General, which – to paraphrase Theodor Meron – the Chamber inexplicably regarded as 'gospel',[45] and which stated that:

> Crimes against humanity refer to inhumane acts of a very serious nature, such as wilful killing, torture or rape, committed as part of a widespread or systematic attack against any civilian population on national, political, ethnic, racial or religious grounds.[46]

Overruling the Trial Chamber's decision, the ICTY Appeals Chamber went back to the terms of the Statute, unequivocally finding that:

> The ordinary meaning of Article 5 makes it clear that this provision does not require all crimes against humanity to have been perpetrated with a discriminatory intent. Such intent is only made necessary for one sub-category of those crimes, namely 'persecutions' provided for in Article 5(h).[47]

If the ICTY Statute indeed does not require grounds for commission for the qualification of all crimes against humanity, this is not the case of its Rwanda counterpart, in which the definition of crimes against humanity specifically requires that there be discrimination in the form of an 'attack against any civilian population on national, political, ethnic, racial or religious grounds',[48] thereby narrowing the scope of crimes against humanity through the extension of the grounds for commission requirement to all offences.[49] This statutory limitation notwithstanding, the ICTR Appeals Chamber nonetheless ruled that 'Article 3 . . . does not require that all crimes against humanity . . . be committed with a discriminatory intent'.[50]

The Rwanda Statute was in any event to remain a temporary deviation at the international level, and the ICC Statute went back to the Nuremberg distinction, requiring grounds for commission only in the case of persecutions. Thus, all the other acts listed can be deemed crimes against humanity even if they are committed without any specific motive. It must however be stressed that Article 7(1)(h) marks a step backwards in the definition of persecutions as it requires that persecutions be made 'in connection with any act referred to in this paragraph or any crime within the jurisdiction of the Court', thus adding a requirement which did not previously exist. With this formulation, the Court will thus not be able to prosecute persecution per se, as it is not, in itself, considered in its Statute a self-standing crime against humanity.

[45] T Meron, 'War Crimes Law Comes of Age' (1998) 92 *AJIL* 462, 465.

[46] Report of the Secretary-General Pursuant to Paragraph 2 of Security Council Resolution 808 (1993), UN Doc S/25704, para 48, 32 ILM 1173.

[47] See *The Prosecutor v Tadić* (Appeals Chamber Judgment) IT–94–1–A (15 July 1999) para 283. See also *The Prosecutor v Tihomir Blaškić* (Trial Chamber Judgment including Declaration of Judge Shahabuddeen) IT–95–14 (3 March 2000) paras 244 and 260; *The Prosecutor v Dario Kordić and Mario Čerkez* (Trial Chamber Judgment) IT–95–14/2 (26 February 2001) para 186; *The Prosecutor v Stevan Todorović* (Trial Chamber Judgment) IT–95–9/1 (31 July 2001) para 113.

[48] Art 3 of the ICTY Statute.

[49] See T Meron, 'International Criminalization of Internal Atrocities' (1994) 89 *AJIL* 554, 557.

[50] *The Prosecutor v Jean-Paul Akayesu* (Appeals Chamber Judgment) ICTR–96–4–A (1 June 2001) para 469. See also *The Prosecutor v Laurent Semanza* (Trial Chamber Judgment) ICTR–97–20–T (15 May 2003) para 332: 'There is no requirement that the enumerated acts other than persecution be committed with discriminatory intent'.

This consideration notwithstanding, this deviation from international criminal law did not prevent the 1985 ruling from having a very significant import in practice. More than a decade later, both ad hoc international criminal tribunals were to explicitly refer to the *Barbie* definition in their consideration of crimes against humanity and of their scope of application to civilians and combatants.[51] In particular, Trial Chamber I of the ICTY in its *Vukovar Hospital* Decision used the definition set forth in the *Barbie* case to find that crimes against humanity applied equally whether the victims were members of a resistance movement or civilians:

> Although according to the terms of Article 5 of the Statute of this Tribunal combatants in the traditional sense of the term cannot be victims of a crime against humanity, this does not apply to individuals who, at one particular point in time, carried out acts of resistance. As the Commission of Experts, established pursuant to Security Council Resolution 780, noted, "it seems obvious that Article 5 applies first and foremost to civilians, meaning people who are not combatants. This, however, should not lead to any quick conclusions concerning people who at one particular point in time did bear arms . . . Information of the overall circumstances is relevant for the interpretation of the provision in a spirit consistent with its purpose."[52]

In the subsequent *Akayesu* judgment, the ICTR concurred with this conclusion, finding that it was 'supported by case law'[53] and expressly recalling the French Cour de cassation's definition in the *Barbie* case:

> 'inhumane acts and persecution which, in the name of a State practising a policy of ideological hegemony, were committed systematically or collectively not only against individuals because of their membership in a racial or religious group but also against the adversaries of that policy whatever the form of the opposition' could be considered a crime against humanity.[54]

Perhaps more extensively, the *Tadić* Trial Chamber relied heavily on the *Barbie* precedent in its determination of 'which individuals of the targeted population qualify as civilians for purposes of crimes against humanity':[55]

> Precisely this issue was considered in the case of *Fédération Nationale des Déportés et Internés Résistants et Patriotes and Others v. Barbie* (*Barbie* case). In this case the *Chambre d'accusation* of the Court of Appeal of Lyons ordered that an indictment for crimes against humanity be issued against Klaus Barbie, head of the Gestapo of Lyons during the Second World War, but only for 'persecutions against innocent Jews', and held that prosecution was barred by the statute of limitations for crimes committed by Barbie against combatants who were members of the Resistance or whom Barbie thought were members of the Resistance, even if they were Jewish, because these acts

[51] See *The Prosecutor v Jean-Paul Akayesu* (Trial Chamber Judgment) ICTR–96–4–T (2 September 1998) paras 569–76.

[52] *The Prosecutor v Mile Mrkšić et al* (Trial Chamber Review of the Indictment Pursuant to Rule 61 of the Rules of Procedure and Evidence) IT–95–13–R61 (3 April 1996) para 29. For the report of the Commission of Experts, see UN Doc S/1994/674, para 78.

[53] *Akayesu* Trial Judgment para 576.

[54] ibid, quoting Cass Crim 20 December 1985.

[55] *Tadić* Trial Judgment para 639.

> could only constitute war crimes and not crimes against humanity. The order of the examining magistrate along the same lines was confirmed by the *Cour d'Assises* and an appeal was lodged. On appeal the *Cour de cassation* quashed and annulled the judgment in part, holding that members of the Resistance could be victims of crimes against humanity as long as the necessary intent for crimes against humanity was present. As the court stated, '[n]either the driving force which motivated the victims, nor their possible membership of the Resistance, excludes the possibility that the accused acted with the element of intent necessary for the commission of crimes against humanity.' Thus, according to the *Cour de cassation,* not only was the general population considered to be one of a civilian character despite the presence of Resistance members in its midst but members of the Resistance themselves could be considered victims of crimes against humanity if the other requisite elements are met.[56]

Explicitly citing both the *Barbie* judgment and the *Vukovar Hospital* Decision, which had also relied on *Barbie,* to support its definition of 'civilian' which included soldiers *hors de combat,* the ICTY Trial Chamber here also found that the presence of *Resistance* fighters amongst civilians did not change the character of the population as civilian and that they themselves could be considered victims of crimes against humanity:

> Despite the limitations inherent in the use of these various sources, from Common Article 3 to the *Barbie* case, a wide definition of civilian population, as supported by these sources, is justified. Thus the presence of those actively involved in the conflict should not prevent the characterization of a population as civilian and those actively involved in a resistance movement can qualify as victims of crimes against humanity. As noted by Trial Chamber I of the International Tribunal in its Review of the Indictment Pursuant to Rule 61 of the Rules of Procedure and Evidence in *The Prosecutor v. Mile Mrkšić, Miroslav Radić, and Veselin Šljivančanin* ('*Vukovar Hospital Decision*'), although crimes against humanity must target a civilian population, individuals who at one time performed acts of resistance may in certain circumstances be victims of crimes against humanity. In the context of that case patients in a hospital, either civilians or resistance fighters who had laid down their arms, were considered victims of crimes against humanity.[57]

Although the *Tadić* judgment here proceeded with caution, suggesting, rather than affirming, that crimes against humanity *can* be committed against members of a resistant movement and that 'individuals who *at one time* performed acts of resistance *may in certain circumstances* be victims of crimes against humanity',[58] the fact is that the *Barbie* case, a decade-old domestic precedent, had an unquestionable impact on the interpretation of crimes against humanity at the international criminal level, and this in spite of its noticeable difference in its consideration of grounds for commission.

Why the Cour de cassation required grounds for commission for both murder-type crimes against humanity and persecutions, thereby offering a different

[56] ibid, para 641 (footnotes omitted).
[57] ibid, para 643 (footnotes omitted).
[58] ibid (emphasis added).

definition than the one existing at the international level even at the time, remains unclear. One could tentatively suggest that this might be due to the fact that the French definition does not apply to a civilian population as such but rather to individuals belonging to a particular community, whether racial, religious or political, and that the focus on individuals thus required specific grounds for commission to qualify the crimes as ones against humanity. One might also be tempted to establish a link between the absence of the terms 'civilian population' in the definition and the French tradition of refusing to recognise the presence of minorities on the French territory, the Republic being indivisible,[59] and group rights being incompatible with the constitutional and republican principles of individual rights. Perhaps the most convincing explanation however might simply be that the Cour de cassation, eager to put a definite end to the debate that surrounded the lower courts' decisions and their failed attempts to adequately distinguish between crimes perpetrated against Jews and those committed against *Resistance* fighters, opted for a definition that did not discriminate either between the nature of the acts or between the victims, and that focused instead on the systematic aspects of these crimes all committed in the name of a state practising a policy of ideological supremacy. This most probable explanation is supported by a later judgment of the Cour de cassation in the *Barbie* case, in which the Court held that:

> The fact that the accused, who had been found guilty of one of the crimes enumerated in Article 6(c) of the Charter of the Nuremberg Tribunal, in perpetrating that crime took part in the execution of a common plan to bring about the deportation or extermination of the civilian population during the war, or persecutions on political, racial or religious grounds, constituted not a distinct offence or an aggravating circumstance but rather *an essential element of the crime against humanity, consisting of the fact that the acts charged were performed in a systematic manner in the name of a State practising by those means a policy of ideological supremacy.*[60]

1.2 Systematic Crimes 'in the Name of a State Practising a Policy of Ideological Supremacy'

As mentioned earlier, the *Barbie* decision made central to the definition of crimes against humanity the fact that the criminal acts must have been 'systematically committed in the name of a State practising a policy of ideological supremacy', an element which remained within the spirit of Nuremberg and which may be considered, at least partially, as compliant with the contemporary understanding of crimes against humanity.

[59] See art 1 of the 1958 French Constitution: 'La France est une *République indivisible*, laïque, démocratique et sociale' (emphasis added).

[60] *Fédération Nationale des Déportés et Internés Résistants et Patriotes et Autres c Klaus Barbie* (emphasis added). This extract of the judgment was also quoted in the *Akayesu* Trial Judgment, in which this translation can be found, *Akayesu* Trial Judgment para 570.

1.2.1 Pushing Nuremberg's Nexus Requirement Too Far?

If article 6(c) of the Nuremberg Charter provided the first definition of crimes against humanity, a critical compromise was nonetheless made therein, as such crimes were linked both to the armed conflict and to the other crimes over which the Tribunal had jurisdiction, namely, crimes against peace and war crimes. Article 6(c) thus expressly and solely covered crimes against humanity committed 'before or during the war' and 'in execution of or in connection with any crime within the jurisdiction of the Tribunal'.[61]

Interestingly, the initial phrasing of article 6(c) included a semicolon rather than a comma after the word 'war', which meant that there were two types of crimes against humanity: some which could be qualified as such without any relationship with the two other crimes mentioned, and some – namely, persecutions – which could only be qualified as such if committed in relation to them. Nearly two months after the signature of the Charter, a difference was discovered between the Russian text – which had a comma after the word 'war' – and the English and French ones, which showed a semicolon after this same word. On the basis of the Berlin Protocol of 6 October 1945, it was recognised that the proper version was the one with a comma. Such grammatical detail might seem rather trivial but, in reality, this substitution was of a great importance as the Nuremberg Tribunal then used it to give a restrictive interpretation of the notion of crimes against humanity: the requirement that these crimes be connected to some other crime within the jurisdiction of the Tribunal became a limitation on all forms of crimes against humanity, and not only on persecutions. Thus, it was beyond any doubt that the qualification 'in execution of or in connection with any crime within the jurisdiction of the Tribunal' applied to the whole paragraph. As a consequence therefore, and unlike crimes against peace and war crimes which were both granted an independent existence, crimes against humanity were 'accompanying' or 'accessory' crimes[62] to the first two and were punishable only if committed in connection with or in execution of the crimes of aggressive war or violations of the laws and customs of warfare. This nexus requirement was further interpreted as overruling the 'before or during the war' clause in article 6(c), which saw its scope limited to crimes perpetrated after 1939:

> The Tribunal therefore cannot make a general declaration that the acts before 1939 were crimes against humanity within the meaning of the Charter as it has not been satisfactorily proved that they were done in execution of, or in connection with, any crime within the jurisdiction of the Tribunal.[63]

[61] Art 6(c) of the Nuremberg Charter.

[62] See J Robinson, 'The International Military Tribunal and the Holocaust – Some Legal Reflections' (1972) 7 *Israel Law Review* 1.

[63] MC Bassiouni, *Crimes Against Humanity in International Criminal Law* (The Hague, Martinus Nijhoff Publishers, 1992) 31.

Objectionable as this finding might be, it is now admitted that this limitation was purely jurisdictional rather than definitional. Already in 1962, Robert Woetzel observed that the Nuremberg definition merely limited the Tribunal's jurisdiction to crimes perpetrated after 1939:

> The fact that the court only considered crimes committed in the period from 1939 to 1945 does not mean that only acts occurring during wartime can be considered crimes against humanity. It must be concluded that the court merely felt itself generally limited in its jurisdiction to cases occurring in connection with or during the war. It did not mean to qualify the nature of the acts, however, by stating this proviso.[64]

Justice Röling, who sat as a judge in the Tokyo Tribunal, also considered the war nexus requirement to be jurisdictional rather than definitional, and that 'the connection did not restrict the scope of the crime, but only the scope of our jurisdiction'.[65]

The inconsistencies generated by the nexus requirement did not go unnoticed,[66] and the fact that crimes against humanity could only be tried and punished if committed during the war and in connection with other international crimes proved controversial. This jurisdictional limitation was to be lifted soon after, and Allied Control Council Law No 10, under which the Allies prosecuted – or oversaw German prosecutions of –Nazi leaders did not mention the expression 'in execution of or in connection with any crime within the jurisdiction of the Tribunal';[67] an omission which does offer some evidence that the Allies did not regard this nexus as necessary as a matter of custom. Yet, if the nexus was not expressly included therein, the preamble of the law specified that it was meant to 'give effect' to the Charter, while its article I fully integrated the London Agreement. Reading too much into this law, at the time it was enacted, might thus prove erroneous, and the legal conflict intrinsic to this instrument resulted in antagonistic case law. Some decisions suggested that the nexus requirement had not been removed in practice. For instance, in the *Flick* case, the court acquitted the defendant of crimes against humanity for his acquisition of Jewish property

[64] RK Woetzel, *The Nuremberg Trials in International Law With a Postlude on the Eichmann Case* (London: Stevens & Sons Limited, 1962) 180.

[65] A Cassese (ed), *B.V.A. Röling, The Tokyo Trial and Beyond, Reflections of a Peacemonger* (Cambridge, Polity Press, 1993) 56. The Tokyo Charter also expressly included the nexus requirement. See art 5 of the IMTFE Charter: 'The Tribunal shall have the power to try and punish Far Eastern war criminals who as individuals or as members of organizations are charged with *offences which include Crimes against Peace*' (emphasis added).

[66] See Robinson 'The International Military Tribunal and the Holocaust – Some Legal Reflections' 1.

[67] See art II(c) of Law No 10 of the Control Council for Germany, promulgated on 20 December 1945 by the Control Council of the four Occupying Powers in Germany. Unlike the Nuremberg Charter, this law was made pursuant to the supreme legislative authority of the Allies over Germany in view of that country's unconditional surrender. It was not intended to be an international instrument but merely national legislation. In their respective zone of occupation, the Allies could thus also apply their own military laws. Under this law, 12 more trials, known as the 'Subsequent Proceedings of Nuremberg', of 185 important Nazi criminals were held at Nuremberg from 1946 to 1949. In the French zone of occupation, several trials of war criminals were also held at Rastatt by virtue of this law. See e.g. *Roechling* case, National Prosecutions, in 14 *Nuremberg Subsequent Proceedings* 1097–1143.

before the war, finding itself without jurisdiction.[68] In the *Ministries* case, the court discussed Ernst Wilhelm Bohle's activities against the Ha'avara Agreement – also known as the 'transfer agreement' which, signed on 25 August 1933, organised the emigration of German Jews to Palestine, first stripping them of all their assets– and unequivocally stated:

> We are unable to see . . . that these transactions, which started in 1937, and were concluded in March 1938, were *so connected with the aggressive war and crimes against peace* as to render it reasonably certain that the measures had this in view.[69]

Based on this inability to see the connection between Bohle's acts and the world conflict, the court dismissed the charge of crimes against humanity against officials in the Nazi Foreign Ministry and other bureaucracies, noting that the Allied Control Council Law No 10 was not meant to go any further than the Charter itself, which codified international law.[70]

Adopting the opposite stand, other cases suggested that the removal of the nexus requirement allowed for prosecution of crimes not committed during the war. Thus, in the *Einsatzgruppen* case, the court convicted the defendants of the large-scale execution of Jews in occupied Europe and in the Soviet Union,[71] without making any distinction as to *when* the murders occurred and held that:

> The International Military Tribunal, operating under the London Charter, declared that the Charter's provisions limited the Tribunal to consider only those crimes against humanity which were committed in the execution of or in connection with crimes against peace and war crimes. The Allied Control Council, in its Law No. 10, removed this limitation so that the present Tribunal has jurisdiction to try all crimes against humanity as long known and understood under the general principles of criminal law.[72]

Likewise, in the *Justice* case, although the defendants were charged only with crimes committed during the war, the court noted the omission of the nexus language, and seemed to suggest in dicta that it was legally unnecessary.[73]

The uncertain legacy of these trials notwithstanding, the post-Nuremberg Charter legal developments subsequently emancipated crimes against humanity from any dependence on other crimes[74] and, in this respect, article 5 of the ICTY Statute constitutes a legal oddity insofar as it expressly maintained the nexus by requiring that the acts be 'committed in armed conflict, whether international or

[68] *United States v Flick et al*, Case No 5, Military Tribunal IV, 6 *Nuremberg Subsequent Proceedings* 1213.

[69] See *United States v Von Weizsaecker et al*, Case No 11, Military Tribunal IV, 12-14 *Nuremberg Subsequent Proceedings* 1–1096 (emphasis added).

[70] ibid, 112–17 (emphasis added).

[71] *United States v Ohlendorf et al*, Case No 9, Military Tribunal II, 4 *Nuremberg Subsequent Proceedings* 499.

[72] ibid, 664.

[73] *United States v Altsoetter et al*, Case No 3, Military Tribunal III, 3 *Nuremberg Subsequent Proceedings* 973-4 and 979–82.

[74] See art I of the ILC's 1954 Draft Code of Offenses, UN Doc A/1316; art 18 of the ILC's 1996 Draft Code of Crimes, [1996] II(2) *ILC Yearbook*.

internal in character' in order to qualify as crimes against humanity.[75] Considering however the temporal limitation to which the Tribunal is subjected,[76] it is true that the Security Council did not have to address a broader definition and that the nexus was probably

> not intended to reflect a general definition of crimes against humanity or alter the fact that such crimes may be committed in time of war or in time of peace. Rather, it was intended to make the crime specific to the Yugoslav context: an armed conflict which could, at different times, be characterized as being international, internal, or a combination of the two.[77]

As a matter of fact, the UN Secretary-General stressed that crimes against humanity are prohibited 'regardless of whether they are committed in an armed conflict, international or internal in character', thus suggesting that this limitation was not definitional but merely jurisdictional;[78] a suggestion subsequently upheld by the ICTY Appeals Chamber in the *Tadić* case:

> It is by now a settled rule of customary international law that crimes against humanity do not require a connection to international armed conflict. Indeed, as the Prosecutor points out, customary international law *may not require* a connection between crimes against humanity and any conflict at all. Thus, by requiring that crimes against humanity be committed in either internal or international armed conflict, the Security Council *may have defined* the crime in Article 5 more narrowly than necessary under customary international law.[79]

More unequivocal was the finding by the same Appeals Chamber that:

> The Prosecution is . . . correct in asserting that the armed conflict requirement is a *jurisdictional* element, not 'a substantive element of the *mens rea* of crimes against humanity' (i.e. not a legal ingredient of the subjective element of the crime).[80]

[75] Art 5 of the ICTY Statute. This is not the case of the ICTR Statute, which is totally silent on the matter and the nexus to armed conflict does not appear at all in its art 3. It is however true that the ICTR only has jurisdiction over crimes committed in 1994, that is over crimes de facto linked to the armed conflict. As Theodor Meron recalled, 'the Statute for Rwanda is predicated on the assumption that the conflict in Rwanda is a noninternational armed conflict', predication which could explain the absence of the nexus requirement in the Statute as it would be an unnecessary redundancy. Meron, 'International Criminalization of Internal Atrocities' 556. According to Mariann Meier Wang, 'the Statute's starting date of January 1, 1994, is artificially late given the explicit goal expressed by the Statute . . . to punish the perpetrators', even if 'the Tribunal may be able to introduce as evidence acts of planning, organization, and even implementation that occurred outside the period of January 1 to December 31, 1994, but that are nonetheless connected to crimes which were perpetrated during the Statute's designated time period'. M Meier Wang, 'The International Tribunal for Rwanda: Opportunities for Clarification, Opportunities for Impact' (1995) 27 *Columbia Human Rights Law Review* 177, 196–97.

[76] See art 8 of the ICTY Statute: as the Tribunal was created by the Security Council as an enforcement measure, its jurisdiction is limited to the events occurring during the restoration of international peace and security.

[77] LD Johnson, 'The International Criminal Tribunal for Rwanda' in MC Bassiouni (ed), *International Criminal Law, Volume III: Enforcement*, 2nd edn (Ardsley, Transnational Publishers, 1999) 556.

[78] See Report of the Secretary-General Pursuant to Paragraph 2 of Security Council Resolution 808 (1993) UN Doc S/25704 and Annex (3 May 1993) para 47.

[79] See *The Prosecutor v Dusko Tadić* (Appeals Chamber Decision on the Defence Motion for Interlocutory Appeal on Jurisdiction) IT–94–1–AR72 (2 October 1995) para 141 (emphasis added).

[80] ibid, para 249.

Also considering the nexus requirement as purely jurisdictional, the *Blaškić* Trial Chamber held that '[a]n armed conflict is not a condition for a crime against humanity but is for its punishment by the Tribunal'.[81]

Still, the ICTY case law revealed the impact the nexus requirement could have on effective prosecution. For instance, in the *Tadić* case, the Trial Chamber interpreted very widely this connection to the armed conflict, and read into it additional elements than the ones expressly stated in its Statute. Not only did the Chamber expressly require proof between the motives of the acts and the conflict, but also proof that the defendant had acted on the basis of non-personal motives. As Beth Van Schaack explained, this new requirement meant that 'the act and the conflict must be related or, to reverse this proposition, the act must not be unrelated to the armed conflict, must not be done for purely personal motives of the perpetrator';[82] a requirement that 'threatens to revive the war nexus requirement by repackaging it in terms of the motivational state of the defendant'.[83] Fortunately, the *Tadić* Appeals Chamber overturned the Trial Chamber's finding, and held that

> there is nothing in Article 5 to suggest that it contains a requirement that crimes against humanity cannot be committed for purely personal motives . . . except to the extent that this condition is a consequence or a re-statement of the two conditions mentioned [i.e. 'that the acts of the accused must comprise part of a pattern of widespread or systematic crimes against a civilian population and that the accused must have known that his acts fit in such a pattern'].[84]

If it was clear that the nexus requirement in article 5 of the ICTY Statute was not definitional, the Rome Statute of the ICC cast doubt on the matter by expressly defining, in article 7(2)(a), the term 'attack' contained in its definition of crimes against humanity[85] as 'a course of conduct involving the multiple commission of acts referred to in paragraph 1 against any civilian population, pursuant to or in furtherance of a State or organizational policy to commit such attack';[86] a definition which could revive the nexus to armed conflict if interpreted to strictly.[87]

By introducing the condition that crimes against humanity be 'systematically committed in the name of a state practising a policy of ideological supremacy', the French Cour de cassation admittedly merely interpreted the nexus requirement as embodied in article 6(c) of the Nuremberg Charter, and in this sense remained respectful of the spirit of the Charter. Where its finding is more questionable is in

[81] *Blaškić* Trial Judgment para 66.

[82] B Van Schaack, 'The Definition of Crimes Against Humanity: Resolving the Incoherence' (1999) 37 *Columbia Journal of Transnational Law* 787, 832–33. See *Tadić* Trial Judgment para 634.

[83] Van Schaack, 'The Definition of Crimes Against Humanity: Resolving the Incoherence' 840.

[84] See *Tadić* Appeals Judgment paras 248, 255, 271 and 272.

[85] See art 7(1) of the ICC Statute, which requires that crimes against humanity be part of 'a widespread or systematic attack'.

[86] Art 7(2)(a) of the ICC Statute.

[87] It is however worth noting here that, if such was the case, this might only be jurisdictional rather than definitional, art 7(1) expressly specifying that its definition of crimes against humanity is '[f]or the purposes of this Statute'.

its very strict reading of the law of Nuremberg which led to the confinement of the concept of crimes against humanity to acts perpetrated by the Axis Powers.[88] If contemporary international criminal law appears to remain hesitant with respect to the connection to armed conflict, it at least emancipated the crimes from the Second World War. Where the *Barbie* definition arguably proved more progressive is in its requirement that crimes against humanity be '*systematically* committed in the name of a State practising a policy of ideological supremacy'.[89]

1.2.2 Envisioning the International Criminal Law Understanding of Crimes Against Humanity?

1.2.2.1 Anticipating the Systematicity Requirement

By requiring that, to constitute crimes against humanity, the crimes must have been 'systematically committed', the 1985 *Barbie* definition elaborated on article 6(c) of the Nuremberg Charter which does not expressly mention systematicity as such. In doing so however the French understanding pre-empted the evolution of the crimes' definition at the international level. And indeed, according to contemporary international criminal law, to qualify as crimes against humanity, the acts must be committed on a widespread or systematic basis.

As previously mentioned, according to the Nuremberg Charter, crimes against humanity had to be committed against 'any civilian population',[90] a terminology which arguably contained within itself the premises of the subsequent requirement that the crimes be either widespread or systematic insofar as it meant that either their scale or their method qualified the nature of the atrocities. Similarly to the Charter, the Allied Control Council Law required that crimes against humanity, in order to qualify as such, be committed 'against any civilian population'.[91] Subsequently, the 1996 Draft Code of Crimes expressly employed the terms 'in a systematic manner or on a large scale', thus understanding these requirements as non-cumulative.[92] Both Statutes of the International Criminal Tribunals as well as that of the International Criminal Court follow the majority of the post-Charter

[88] With the entry into force of the New Penal Code, crimes against humanity under French law have now been completely emancipated from any war nexus. It is worth noting here that the French position as held in the *Barbie* case was not an exception at the national level. The majority of domestic systems retained the temporal nexus to armed conflicts. For instance, the 1946 Chinese Statute criminalised several acts other than war crimes but with the requirement that they be committed 'before or during a period of hostilities against the Republic of China', thus suggesting a linkage to the war. See art II(3) of the Chinese Statute. The 1988 Australian War Crimes Statute required that crimes against humanity be connected with an armed conflict to be qualified as such. See s 9 of the War Crimes Act. See G Triggs, 'Australia's War Crimes Trials: All Pity Choked' in TLM McCormack and GJ Simpson (eds), *The Law of War Crimes, National and International Approaches* (The Hague, Kluwer Law International, 1997) 127. The United Kingdom's War Crimes Act of 1991 also maintained the nexus to the Second World War.

[89] Emphasis added.

[90] Art 6(c) of the IMT Charter.

[91] Art II(c) of Allied Control Council Law No 10 (CCL No 10).

[92] Art 18 of the ILC 1996 Draft Code of Crimes, [1996] II (2) *ILC Yearbook* 47 (emphasis added).

developments by requiring that these crimes are to be committed 'against any civilian population'.[93]

Interestingly, if article 5 of the ICTY Statute does not explicitly mention the conditions that the crimes be widespread or systematic, this did not stop the different Trial Chambers from considering them as legal ingredients of crimes against humanity.

In fact, Trial Chamber I of the ICTY, in the *Nikolić* case, defined crimes against humanity very narrowly by requiring that each type of crime against humanity be directed against any civilian population, that each be organised *and* systematic, and not the work of an isolated individual, and that the crimes, considered as a whole, be of a certain scale and gravity.[94] Adopting a contrary view, Trial Chamber II, while interpreting the UN Secretary-General's Report on Article 5 of its Statute[95] in the *Tadić* case, held that the requirement that acts be directed against a civilian population can be fulfilled if the acts were *either* widespread *or* systematic.[96] Subsequently, Trial Chamber II, again reading these requirements disjunctively, specified that the widespread or systematic requirement was to be appreciated on a case-by-case basis:

> The widespread or systematic nature of the attack is essentially a *relative notion*. The Trial Chamber must first identify the population which is the object of the attack and, in light of the means, methods, resources and result of the attack upon this population, ascertain whether the attack was indeed widespread or systematic.[97]

The *Tadić* precedent was subsequently confirmed by Trial Chamber I in the *Blaškić* case:

> The 'widespread or systematic' character of the offence does not feature in the provisions of Article 5 of the Statute which mention only acts 'directed against any civilian population'. It is appropriate, however, to note that the words 'directed against any civilian population' and some of the sub-characterisations set out in the text of the Statute imply, both by their very nature and by law, an element of being widespread *or* organised, whether as regards the acts or the victims.[98]

It therefore reached the conclusion that

> there can be no doubt that inhumane acts constituting a crime against humanity must be part of a systematic *or* widespread attack against civilians.[99]

In the *Krstić* case, Trial Chamber I re-confirmed the *Tadić* ruling and affirmed that the attack must be 'widespread *or* systematic';[100] a finding subsequently

[93] Art 5 of the ICTY Statute; art 3 of the ICTR Statute; art 7(1) of the ICC Statute.

[94] *The Prosecutor v Dragan Nikolić* (Trial Chamber Review of the Indictment Pursuant to Rule 61 of the Rules of Procedure and Evidence) IT–94–2–R61 (20 October 1995) para 26.

[95] UN Doc S/25704, para 48 (1993).

[96] *Tadić* Trial Judgment para 646.

[97] *The Prosecutor v Dragoljub Kunarac, Radomir Kovac and Zoran Vuković* (Trial Chamber Judgment) IT–96–23 and IT–96–23/1 (22 February 2001) para 430 (emphasis added).

[98] *Blaškić* Trial Judgment para 202 (emphasis added).

[99] ibid (emphasis added).

[100] *Krstić* Trial Judgment para 482. See also *Kunarac* Trial Judgment para 410.

upheld by the Appeals Chamber, which specified that 'only the attack, not the individual acts of the accused, must be widespread or systematic'[101] and reaffirmed that:

> The requirement that the attack be 'widespread' or 'systematic' comes in the alternative. Once it is convinced that either requirement is met, the Trial Chamber is not obliged to consider whether the alternative qualifier is also satisfied.[102]

Adopting a more explicit approach than its Yugoslav counterpart, the ICTR Statute expressly provides that the acts be committed 'as part of a widespread or systematic attack',[103] and the Tribunal accordingly read the requirement of widespread or systematic action disjunctively, while making it an essential element of the offence.[104] As expressed by the *Akayesu* Trial Chamber, 'it is a prerequisite that the act must be committed as part of a widespread or systematic attack and not just a random act of violence'.[105] Here again casting doubt on the matter, the ICC Statute, while also requiring that the acts be committed 'as part of a widespread *or* systematic attack directed against any civilian population',[106] subsequently defines the term 'attack' as 'a course of conduct involving the multiple commission of acts referred to in paragraph 1 against any civilian population, pursuant to or in furtherance of a State or organizational policy to commit such attack'.[107] According to William Schabas, '[i]t seems, therefore, that the term attack has both widespread *and* systematic aspects';[108] an alteration of the definition which could have serious consequences in practice in terms of prosecution of the crimes.

1.2.2.2 Foreseeing the State Policy Requirement

The inclusion within the definition of crimes against humanity embodied in the ICC Statute of the requirement that the acts be committed 'pursuant to or in furtherance of a State or organizational policy to commit such attack'[109] is not without reminder of the phrase 'in the name of a state practising a policy of ideological supremacy' contained in the *Barbie* definition. In this respect also, the finding of the French Cour de cassation may have proved visionary.

Yet, state involvement in the commission of the acts remains a critical matter: if such involvement seems to have an objective reality in practice, it is however doubtful that it should be considered as a legal ingredient of crimes against

[101] *The Prosecutor v Dragoljub Kunarac, Radomir Kovac and Zoran Vuković* (Appeals Chamber Judgment) IT–96–23 and IT–96–23/1–A (12 June 2002) para 96.

[102] ibid, para 93.

[103] Art 3 of the ICTR Statute.

[104] *Akayesu* Trial Judgment paras 579–81, and *Kayishema and Ruzindana* Trial Judgment para 123.

[105] *Akayesu* Trial Judgment para 579.

[106] Art 7 (1) of the ICC Statute. Emphasis added.

[107] Art 7 (2) (a) of the ICC Statute.

[108] WA Schabas, *An Introduction to the International Criminal Court*, 4th edn (Cambridge, Cambridge University Press, 2011) 111 (emphasis added).

[109] Art 7 (2) (a) of the ICC Statute.

humanity. As Cherif Bassiouni explained, international crimes are either 'the product of "state-action" or the result of a "state-favoring policy" by commission, or as a result of a lack of state enforcement, that ranges from permissiveness to purposeful omission'.[110] As he however also added:

> In all cases, individuals commit crimes. What is called 'state action' and 'state-favoring policy' does not alter the fact that one or more individual authors are involved. The characterizations of 'state action' and 'state-favoring policy' refer to collective decision-making and actions by individuals who develop a policy or who execute a policy or carry out acts which constitute international crimes under color of legal authority. Decision-makers are usually few in comparison to the entire apparatus of government, let alone to the entire population of a state . . . The invocation of the concept of state responsibility is, however, a symbolic act by the international community to stigmatize regimes that engage in internationally proscribed policies and conduct, irrespective of the effective results of the stigmatization in altering the internationally proscribed behavior.[111]

The idea that only individuals can commit crimes can be found as early as 1923, when the Permanent Court of International Justice held that 'States can act only by and through their agents and representatives'.[112] In the same vein, Justice Jackson, in his opening statement at Nuremberg, stated:

> While it is quite proper to employ the fiction of responsibility of a state or corporation for the purpose of imposing a collective liability, it is quite intolerable to let such a legalism become the basis of personal immunity.[113]

At Nuremberg, the Tribunal also famously stated that '[c]rimes against international law are committed by men, not by abstract entities, and only by punishing individuals who commit such crimes can the provisions of international law be enforced'.[114] Ruling solely on the basis of individual criminal responsibility,

> 'Nuremberg' focused on individual criminal responsibility for conduct that was the product of state policy and for which collective responsibility and state responsibility could have been assessed. Those who established the IMT were careful to avoid the notions of state and collective responsibility, except with respect to criminal organization, namely the S.S., S.D., and S.A. The simple reason is that these governments did not want to establish a principle that could one day be applied to them.[115]

[110] MC Bassiouni (ed), *International Criminal Law, Vol I: Crimes*, 2nd edn (Ardsley, Transnational Publishers, 1999) 27.

[111] ibid, 27–28.

[112] *German Settlers in Poland*, PCIJ No 6, 22 (1923). Cited in Bassiouni, *Crimes Against Humanity in International Criminal Law* 269.

[113] RH Jackson, *The Nürnberg Case* (New York, Cooper Square Press, 1972) 88–89.

[114] *Judgment of the International Military Tribunal for the Trial of German Major War Criminals*, Part 22, 447. The full transcript of the Nuremberg Judgment is available at avalon.law.yale.edu/subject_menus/judcont.asp.

[115] MC Bassiouni, 'The Nuremberg Legacy' in Bassiouni (ed), *International Criminal Law, Vol III: Enforcement*, 2nd edn (1999) 210.

The Tribunal neither denied nor admitted the criminal responsibility of states, yet '[t]he victorious allies in both world wars treated the defeated states as criminal entities':[116]

> Despite the impossibility of placing the German state in the dock at Nuremberg, Germany was on trial with its major war criminals. There can be no doubt that the allies intended to punish the German nation as well as its captured leaders. The Yalta Conference meetings, declarations, and documents are replete with references to the 'dismemberment of Germany', sizeable reparations, and enforced disarmament.[117]

In the *Eichmann* case, the District Court of Jerusalem was less cautious, and unequivocally stated that '[a] State that plans and implements a "final solution" cannot be treated as *par in parem*, but only as a gang of criminals'.[118]

From a purely historical point of view, facts clearly indicate that, hitherto, the commission of crimes against humanity has primarily relied on the state apparatus, or on an organisation which has shared the same features as the state apparatus. As early as the First World War, in their joint declaration of 1915, the Allies acknowledged this reality by condemning the 'new crimes of Turkey', and by stating that members of the government or their responsible agents would be tried.[119] In a similar vein, the Nuremberg Charter acknowledged the perversion of state apparatus and bureaucracy by the Axis powers by giving the Tribunal the authority to punish persons '*acting in the interests of the European Axis countries*, whether as individuals or as members of organizations'.[120] The subsequent Allied Control Council Law remained silent on the matter, although it may still be noted that the majority of the individuals tried under it were governmental officials. In the cases of the German industrialists who took advantage of the Nazi policies however, the American courts adopted a looser standard to find defendants guilty, based on their conduct towards the victims without requiring any connection with state policy.[121]

This looser standard seems since to have been the one adopted in international criminal law. The ICTY Statute does not mention state policy in its definition of crimes against humanity.[122] Yet, this has not prevented the *Nikolić* Trial Chamber to include state policy within the 'three distinct components' of crimes against humanity:

[116] RA Friedlander, 'Problems of Enforcing International Criminal Law' in MC Bassiouni (ed), *International Criminal Law, Vol III: Enforcement* (Ardsley, Transnational Publishers, 1987) 15.

[117] ibid.

[118] *Attorney-General of the Government of Israel v Eichmann*, 36 ILR 46 (Israel District Court – Jerusalem, 1961). See E David, 'L'actualité juridique de Nuremberg' in Centre de Droit International de l'Institut de Sociologie de l'Université Libre de Bruxelles (Centre Henri Rolin) et Fondation Auschwitz – Stichting (Centre d'Etudes et de Documentation) 89, 144. The Israeli Court here rejected the act of state doctrine which lies in the principle *par in parem non habet jurisdictionem*, and according to which a sovereign state cannot prosecute another sovereign state.

[119] See E Schwelb, 'Crimes Against Humanity' [1946] *BYBIL* 178–81.

[120] See art 6 of the IMT Charter (emphasis added).

[121] See generally *Nuremberg Subsequent Proceedings.*

[122] Art 5 of the ICTY Statute.

> the crimes must, to a certain extent, be organised and systematic. Although they need not be related to a policy established at State level, in the conventional sense of the term, they *cannot* be the work of isolated individuals alone.[123]

In the *Tadić* case, the Trial Chamber stated that crimes against humanity need not be associated with a formal state policy against a civilian population. Yet, it also held that proof of an informal policy carried out by non-state actors was sufficient,[124] and reached the conclusion that crimes against humanity could be committed by non-state entities in de facto control of a particular territory.[125] Even if the Trial Chamber here specified that 'it need not be the policy of a state',[126] that 'such a policy need not be formalized and can be deduced from the way in which the acts occur',[127] and 'if the acts occur on a widespread or systematic basis that demonstrates a policy to commit those acts, whether formalized or not',[128] it still found that crimes against humanity could only be committed when there was a policy to commit such acts.

Such findings were nevertheless overturned by the ICTY Appeals Chamber, which reached the conclusion that the existence of a plan or policy did not constitute a legal element of crimes against humanity, but rather an evidentiary tool which can be used in order to prove that the acts were directed against any civilian population or that the attack was widespread or systematic. In the *Kunarac* Appeal Judgment, the Appeals Chamber unequivocally held that:

> neither the attack nor the acts of the accused needs to be supported by any form of 'policy' or 'plan'. There was nothing in the Statute or in customary law at the time of the alleged acts which required proof of the existence of a plan or policy to commit these crimes. As indicated above, proof that the attack was directed against a civilian population and that it was widespread or systematic, are legal elements of the crime. But to prove these elements, it is not necessary to show that they were the result of the existence of a policy or plan. It may be useful in establishing that the attack was directed against a civilian population and that it was widespread or systematic (especially the latter) to show that there was in fact a policy or plan, but it may be possible to prove these things by reference to other matters. Thus, *the existence of a policy or plan may be evidentially relevant, but it is not a legal element of the crime.*[129]

Supporting the ICTY Appeal Chamber's position is the fact that the Statute of the Rwanda Tribunal makes no reference to state action in its definition of crimes against humanity.[130] In this instance, this implies that, although many crimes were committed by persons not associated with a state, the Security Council – most

[123] *Nikolić* Review of Indictment para 26 (emphasis added).
[124] See *Tadić* Trial Judgment paras 653–54.
[125] ibid, para 654.
[126] ibid, para 655.
[127] ibid, para 653.
[128] ibid.
[129] *Kunarac* Appeals Judgment para 98 (emphasis added). It may be noted here that this position of the Appeals Chamber had been largely foreseeable since the *Jelisić* genocide case. See *The Prosecutor v Goran Jelisić* (Appeals Chamber Judgment) IT–95–10–A (5 July 2001) para 48.
[130] Art 3 of the ICTR Statute.

probably evidencing state practice[131] – considered that these individuals still had to be tried for crimes against humanity. Although the events in Rwanda clearly showed that some form of organisation was needed in order to perpetrate the crime, and that the criminal factions had de facto control over the country's institutions and media, the wording of the ICTR Statute nonetheless acknowledges the fact that state action is not to be considered as a definitional element of crimes against humanity.

Nevertheless, it is doubtful that the decision reached by the ICTY's Appeals Chambers finds any support in the work of the International Law Commission which has a settled – and different – position on the issue. Indeed, the 1954 Draft Code made state action highly relevant, and so did the 1996 Code which mentioned acts 'instigated or directed by a government or by any organization or group'.[132]

More importantly, the Rome Statute of the ICC also departed from the ICTY case law and became the first legal instrument to require a 'state or organizational policy' in the definition of crimes against humanity;[133] a regrettable requirement, insofar as it might indeed contain the risk that massive human rights violations committed by non-state actors would fall outside the definitional scope of crimes against humanity. Even if it may be argued that the use of the term 'organizational' prevents such an absurd result from occurring,[134] the formulation of the Preparatory Commission in the 'Elements of Crimes' is in this respect all the more confusing. Indeed, while the Commission introduced yet another restriction by interpreting 'policy to commit such attack' as requiring 'that the State or organization *actively promote or encourage* such an attack against a civilian population',[135] in a footnote attached to its interpretation of article 7, the Commission also provided that '[s]uch a policy may, in exceptional circumstances, be implemented by a deliberate failure to take action, which is consciously aimed at encouraging such attack'.[136]

This aspect of the Rome Statute is to be highly regretted as, not only was the conclusion reached by the ICTY Appeals Chamber legally correct, it is also the most reasonable. While it is very true that, more often than not, crimes against humanity will need the state apparatus for their commission as only the state – or

[131] However, see *Regina v Finta* [1994] 1 Supreme Court Reports 701. In this case, the Supreme Court of Canada found that the national statute implied the connection between crimes against humanity and governmental action.

[132] Art 18 [1996] II(2) *ILC Yearbook* 47.

[133] Art 7(2)(a).

[134] Some authors however held that the term 'organizational' is ambiguous and, if interpreted as a *mens rea* requirement, contains the risk of limiting prosecution to high level perpetrators. In this context, culpability for crimes against humanity would then depend on the perpetrator's knowledge that he or she is acting pursuant to a policy. See eg, M McAuliffe deGuzman, 'The Road from Rome: The Developing Law of Crimes Against Humanity' (2000) 22 *HRQ* 335, 371.

[135] Report of the Preparatory Commission for the International Criminal Court, Part II: Finalized Draft Text of the Elements of Crimes (2 November 2000) PCNICC/2000/1/Add 2 (Elements of Crimes), art 7, Introduction (3) (emphasis added).

[136] ibid.

another organisation usurping the functions of a state – will have the means and resources necessary to perpetrate them,[137] the element of state action should be dealt with great caution and should be considered as an evidentiary element and not as a definitional one. The drafters of the Rome Statute should have considered the *Barbie* definition's emphasis on a 'state practising a policy of ideology supremacy' which, if in line with the Nuremberg Charter and with the most recent definition of crimes against humanity, unduly enclosed the concept of crimes against humanity to specific perpetrators over a limited period of time and had deplorable consequences in practice.[138]

1.3 Perceiving the Knowledge Requirement

By putting the emphasis on a 'state practising a policy of ideological supremacy', the French Cour de cassation in the *Barbie* case also hinted at the *mens rea* of the perpetrator, who must not only have intended the perpetration of the acts but also must have known of the wider context in which they were committed, thereby posing a knowledge requirement which was to be subsequently confirmed in other domestic cases and the one retained by contemporary international criminal law.[139] As ruled by the *Kordić and Čerkez* Trial Chamber:

> Part of what transforms an individual's act(s) into a crime against humanity is the inclusion of the act within a greater dimension of criminal conduct; therefore an accused should be aware of this greater dimension in order to be culpable thereof. Accordingly, actual or constructive knowledge of the broader context of the attack, meaning that the accused must know that his act(s) is part of a widespread or systematic attack on a civilian population and pursuant to some sort of policy or plan, is necessary to satisfy the requisite *mens rea* element of the accused.[140]

[137] See Bassiouni, *Crimes Against Humanity in International Criminal Law* 248–49: crimes against humanity are 'collective crimes which cannot be committed unless they are part of a given state's policy because their commission requires the use of the state's institutions, personnel and resources in order to commit, or refrain from preventing the commission of, specific crimes described in Article 6(c)'.

[138] See below.

[139] See art 7(1) of the ICC Statute, which offered the first definition expressly posing the knowledge requirement, although it had already emerged in the case law of the ad hoc international criminal tribunals. See eg *Tadić* Appeals Judgment para 271; *Kunarac* Appeals Judgment paras 102 and 410; *The Prosecutor v Dario Kordić and Mario Čerkez* (Appeals Chamber Judgment) IT–95–14/2–A (17 December 2004) paras 99–100. See also below.

[140] *Kordić and Čerkez* Trial Judgment para 185. See also *Kayishema and Ruzindana* Trial Judgment para 133: 'The perpetrator must knowingly commit crimes against humanity in the sense that he must understand the overall context of his act'; *Tadić* Appeals Judgment para 248: 'it may be inferred from the words "directed against any civilian population" in Article 5 of the Statute that the acts of the accused must comprise part of a pattern of widespread and systematic crimes directed against a civilian population and that the accused must have *known* that his acts fit into such a pattern'; *The Prosecutor v George Rutaganda* (Trial Chamber Judgment) ICTR–96–3–T (6 December 1999) para 71; *The Prosecutor v Goran Jelisić* (Trial Chamber Judgment) IT–95–10–T (14 December 1999) para 56: 'The accused must . . . be aware that the underlying crime which he is committing forms part of the widespread and systematic attack'; *The Prosecutor v Alfred Musema* (Trial Chamber Judgment) ICTR–96–13–T (27 January

The consideration of the *mens rea* of crimes against humanity by French courts was to be further developed in the respective trials of Paul Touvier and Maurice Papon, in which the courts elaborated on the notion of complicity of crimes against humanity – a judicial exercise which, although criticisable in that it arguably followed a political rather than a legal agenda, seems however to have anticipated the developments on the international criminal justice scene.

2000) para 206; *Blaskić* Trial Judgment para 247: 'The accused must first have knowledge of the general context in which his acts occur and then of the nexus between his action and that context'; *The Prosecutor v Georges Ruggiu* (Trial Chamber Judgment) ICTR–97–32 (1 June 2000) paras 19–20; *The Prosecutor v Ignace Bagilishema* (Trial Chamber Judgment) ICTR–95–1A (7 June 2001) para 94; *The Prosecutor v Milorad Krnojelac* (Trial Chamber Judgment)) IT–97–25 (15 March 2002) para 59; *Kunarac,* Appeals Judgment para 102: '[T]he accused must have had the intent to commit the underlying offence or offences with which he is charged, and that he must have known "that there is an attack on the civilian population and that his acts comprise part of that attack, or at least that he took the risk that his acts were part of the attack"'; *The Prosecutor v Eliezer Niyitegeka* (Trial Chamber Judgment) ICTR–96–14 (16 May 2003) para 442.

2

Trying Paul Touvier and Maurice Papon: Twisting the Precedent

Considering its impact on the international criminal justice scene, one could have legitimately thought that the *Barbie* definition would have remained an authoritative precedent before French courts. This however was not to be the case, and when Paul Touvier – a Frenchman – faced charges of crimes against humanity, the requirements posed in *Barbie* proved problematic. And indeed, according to the *Barbie* precedent, so as to try Touvier for crimes against humanity, it had to be proven that, as an agent of the French Milice, Touvier had acted in pursuance of a 'state practising a policy of ideological supremacy'. Put differently, it had to be demonstrated that Vichy France was such a state,[1] an idea that quickly proved to be highly controversial. For French courts, it was one thing to condemn a German citizen for crimes perpetrated in the name of the ideology preached by Nazi Germany, it was another to prosecute and convict of crimes against humanity a Frenchman who had served in Vichy France's police.

The complexity of the case finds a telling illustration in the judicial saga that ensued – what Conan and Rousso referred to as 'a highly unusual itinerary'.[2] Prior to the proceedings that followed the *Barbie* trial, Paul Touvier had already been tried *in absentia* and twice sentenced to death.[3] The death sentences having been prescribed in 1967, Touvier was subsequently pardoned by President Pompidou in 1971.[4] Henry Rousso gives a detailed account of the proceedings that followed, which is thus reproduced below:

> Following the pardon, however, various groups of former résistants and deportees, acting at the behest of attorneys Serge Klarsfeld and Joe Nordmann . . . filed several complaints of crimes against humanity against Touvier (on 9 November 1973 in Lyons and 27 March 1974 in Chambéry). On 12 February 1974 and 6 June 1974 respectively, the investigating magistrates [*juges d'instruction*] in the two jurisdictions ruled that they

[1] See Wieviorka, 'La France et le Procès de Nuremberg' (n 46) 69, 82–83.

[2] E Conan and H Rousso, *Vichy – An Ever-Present Past* (Hanover, University Press of New England, 1998) 85.

[3] Touvier had indeed been found guilty by the Cour de justice of Lyon on 10 September 1946 and by the Cour de justice of Chambéry on 4 March 1947.

[4] See Décret de grâce, 23 November 1971; S Chalandon, 'Le procès de Paul Touvier' in S Chalandon and P Nivelle, *Crimes contre l'Humanité – Barbie, Touvier, Bousquet, Papon* (Paris, Plon/Libération, 1998) 165–227.

had no authority to pursue the charges, and these decisions were upheld on 30 May and 11 July 1974 by courts of appeal in Lyons and Chambéry on the grounds that the charges alleged concerned only war crimes, not crimes against humanity.[5] The statute of limitations had taken effect in 1967, and the last time Touvier had been convicted (*in absentia*) was 1947. On 6 February 1975, however, the criminal division of the Cour de cassation (supreme appellate court) overturned both decisions on the grounds that the investigating magistrates had not looked into the charges closely enough to determine whether crimes against humanity were involved . . . But then, on 27 October 1975, a criminal court in Paris ruled that it was competent to hear the charges but that the complaints were inadmissible because the statute of limitations had taken effect. On 30 June 1976 the criminal division of the Cour de cassation once again overturned this ruling.[6]

Interestingly, the 1975 ruling of the Cour de cassation – thus issued 10 years before the *Barbie* decision – gave a first definition of crimes against humanity. Establishing a very clear distinction between war crimes and crimes against humanity, the Cour de cassation found that crimes against humanity were 'common crimes perpetrated in certain circumstances and according to certain motives, as specified in the text that defines them', namely, article 6(c) of the Nuremberg Charter ('des crimes contre l'humanité qui sont des crimes de droit commun commis dans certaines circonstances et pour certains motifs précisés dans le texte qui les définit').[7]

If this fairly swift definition of crimes against humanity is at first appealing for its brevity and apparent simplicity, it could also generate fundamental misunderstandings and legal mistakes. As Delmas Saint-Hilaire pointed out, not only could this definition lead to a trivialisation of crimes against humanity as merely aggravated common crimes, it could also make their qualification dependent upon the existence of common crimes, a reading which would be in direct contradiction with the law of Nuremberg which clearly specified that crimes against humanity could be constituted 'whether or not in violation of the domestic law of the country where perpetrated'.[8] These risks were however not to be over-estimated

[5] See Lyon-Caen, 'De Nuremberg au Procès Barbie' 49. The courts of appeal had indeed held that: 'on se trouve en présence du crimes du guerre ou de crimes d'intelligence avec l'ennemi qui sont justiciables de la compétence non pas de juge d'instruction ou de la Chambre d'accusation, mais du Tribunal militaire ou de la Cour de sûreté de l'Etat où l'on ne peut pas se constituer partie civile.'

[6] Rousso, *The Vichy Syndrome* 148.

[7] Cass crim (6 February 1975) Bull crim, n°42; D 1975, Jur 386. For an analysis, see Lyon-Caen, 'De Nuremberg au Procès Barbie' 47–59. See also JP Delmas Saint-Hilaire, 'La définition juridique de la complicité de crime contre l'humanité au lendemain de l'arrêt de la Chambre criminelle du 23 janvier 1997 (affaire *Maurice Papon*)', (1997) *Recueil Dalloz* 249–54.

[8] Art 6(c) of the Nuremberg Charter. See Delmas Saint-Hilaire, 'La définition juridique de la complicité de crime contre l'humanité' 250: 'Cette formule très synthétique séduit par sa simplicité. Mais une mise en garde s'impose à son sujet car elle peut induire en erreur. En donnant en effet, dans la définition qu'elle propose des crimes contre l'humanité, une place de premier plan aux *crimes de droit commun* (arrestation, séquestration, assassinat. . .), elle pèche doublement: et par défaut, et par excès. Elle pèche *par défaut* car, entendue littéralement, elle risque de conduire à banaliser les crimes contre l'humanité, ces derniers pouvant passer pour n'être, en définitive, que des crimes ordinaires plus ou moins «aggravés» par leurs circonstances de commission, des infractions qui perdraient toute spécificité. [Elle pèche aussi par excès]: elle présente en effet les *crimes de droit commun* comme étant le support obligé des crimes contre l'humanité. Or il n'en est rien: ces derniers peuvent en effet exister

insofar as the reference to 'common crimes' ('crimes de droit commun') was only meant as a justification by the Cour de cassation of the jurisdiction of French courts (known as 'juridictions de droit commun'), over crimes which had previously only been dealt with by international instances.[9] This admittedly broad conception of crimes against humanity however stopped there and the judicial specification that, to qualify as crimes against humanity, acts had to be committed in certain circumstances and according to certain motives, laid the grounds for the subsequent *Barbie* requirement that the crimes be perpetrated 'in the name of a state practising a policy of ideological supremacy', a finding that, although arguably unproblematic in the *Barbie* case, inevitably limited the scope of crimes against humanity to crimes perpetrated in the course of the Second World War by the Axis Powers.

Due to the length of the proceedings against Touvier, the *Barbie* definition had occurred in the meantime and was therefore found to apply in his case, thereby revealing its inherent flaws. It was indeed on the basis of the 1985 definition that, on 13 April 1992 in the *Touvier* case, the Court of Appeal in Paris issued a *non lieu* and dismissed the charges, finding that the expression 'state practising a policy of ideological supremacy' could only apply to the Hitlerian Reich and not to Vichy France, and reaching the conclusion that no precise ideology reigned in Vichy, Vichy being 'a constellation of "good intentions and political animosities"'.[10] This infamous finding – in which, incidentally, judges did not hesitate to enter into the expert domain of historians – was fiercely criticised. As Conan and Rousso observed:

> While this ruling is enough to make one shudder with its pseudo-historical reasoning, which would have caused any university student to fail on a history exam, it nevertheless came off as highly clever on a legal level, in that it slipped through the loopholes that had been left open by the contradictions, incertitudes, and variations of the jurisprudence on crimes against humanity.[11]

On 27 November 1992, the Cour de cassation partially overturned the ruling of the lower court, confirming the dismissal of all the crimes but for the murders of the seven Jewish men in Rillieux. In doing so however, the court gave a new – and

même en l'absence des premiers. L'art. 6 du Statut de Nuremberg ne précise-t-il pas qu'il peut y avoir crime contre l'humanité même si ne se rencontrent pas d'actes constituant «une violation du droit interne du pays où ils ont été perpétrés»?' (Emphasis in original.)

[9] See Delmas Saint-Hilaire, 'La définition juridique de la complicité de crime contre l'humanité' 250: 'La formule utilisée par la Chambre criminelle ne doit donc pas être prise au pied de la lettre: la référence à la notion de *crime de droit commun* dans la définition qu'elle propose du crime contre l'humanité n'est en réalité qu'un artifice. En présentant ce dernier comme une sorte de crime de droit commun, se trouve justifiée en la matière la compétence de nos juridictions «de droit commun» d'instruction et de jugement; est assurée ainsi la répression de ce type d'infraction malgré la disparition du Tribunal d'exception mis en place à l'origine pour en connaître.' (Emphasis in original, footnotes omitted.)

[10] Translation by the author. The original reads as follows: 'à Vichy ne régnait pas une idéologie précise', Vichy was 'une constellation de "bonnes intentions" et d'animosités politiques'. See Klarsfeld, *Touvier, Un crime français* 31.

[11] Conan and Rousso, *Vichy – An Ever-Present Past* 91.

artificial – reading of the law of Nuremberg, which only added further confusion and complexity to the case. The court was indeed able to find that, according to article 6 of the Nuremberg Charter,

> the authors or accomplices of crimes against humanity are punished only if they acted for the sake of a European country of the Axis, the Court of Appeals could not without contradicting itself, declare that the murders being prosecuted did not constitute crimes against humanity while at the same time pointing out that they had been perpetrated at the instigation of an official of the Gestapo, an organization that has been declared to be criminal in that it belonged to a country which had practised a policy of ideological hegemony.[12]

If this finding clearly established that the crimes for which Touvier stood accused qualified as crimes against humanity, however, it interpreted article 6 of the Nuremberg Charter[13] problematically by insisting once again on the necessary links between the individual criminal responsibility of both authors and accomplices of crimes against humanity and a state practising a policy of ideological supremacy or, put differently, with one of the Axis Powers, namely Germany or Italy.[14] Vichy France's own ideology was thus safe from scrutiny: to convict him of crimes against humanity, it had to be proven that Touvier – a member of the Milice, Vichy's own police – had acted pursuant to the orders of the German occupier.[15]

When the case was referred back to the criminal court in Versailles, the court unequivocally excluded Vichy France from any possible judicial enquiry:

> [The] responsibility [of Paul Touvier] is engaged by the simple fact of his personal dealings, even though he was not himself a national of a European Axis country. It is therefore not necessary to follow the private parties in their argumentation, which attempts to prove that the Milice and the government of the French State, which Touvier served, had themselves been accomplices of the Nazi state in its policies of ideological hegemony.[16]

[12] Cass crim, 27 November 1992. Translated in Conan and Rousso, *Vichy – An Ever-Present Past* 92. The original version read as follows: 'les auteurs ou complices de crimes contre l'humanité ne sont punis que s'ils ont agi pour le compte d'un pays européen de l'Axe, la chambre d'accusation ne pouvait, sans se contredire, déclarer que les assassinats poursuivis ne constituaient pas des crimes contre l'humanité tout en relevant qu'ils avaient été perpétrés à l'instigation d'un responsable de la Gestapo, organisation déclarée criminelle comme appartenant à un pays ayant pratiqué une politique d'hégémonie idéologique.' See also Wieviorka, 'La France et le Procès de Nuremberg' 83.

[13] Art 6 reads: 'Leaders, organizers, instigators and *accomplices* participating in the formulation or execution of a common plan or conspiracy to commit any of the foregoing crimes are responsible for all acts performed by any persons in execution of a plan.'

[14] See Klarsfeld, *La Cour, Les Nains et Le Bouffon* 32: 'L'arrêt modifiait encore une fois le crime contre l'humanité tel que défini à Nüremberg. Il exigeait que la personne poursuivie eût agi pour le compte d'une puissance européenne de l'Axe, c'est-à-dire l'Allemagne ou l'Italie. Aboutissement cocasse d'un point de vue historique, quand on sait que les Italiens arrêtaient parfois les fonctionnaires de Vichy qui tentaient de procéder à des rafles de Juifs! Mais résultat tout aussi cocasse au niveau du droit, quand l'on se donnait la peine d'étudier les textes sur lesquels se basait la décision de la Chambre d'Accusation.'

[15] See ibid, 33.

[16] Arrêt de la chambre d'accusation de Versailles, 2 June 1993. Translated in E Conan et H Rousso, *Vichy, un passé qui ne passe pas* (Paris, Librairie Arthème Fayard, Collection Folio Histoire, 1996) 93. The original version reads: 'La responsabilité [de Paul Touvier] est engagée du seul fait de ses agissements personnels, bien qu'il n'ait pas été lui-même ressortissant d'un pays européen de l'Axe. Il n'est

In a similar vein, in its ruling of 21 October 1993, the Cour de cassation further considered that:

> it makes no difference whether or not the deeds prosecuted may have been committed following the assassination of a member of the Vichy government who also belonged to the Milice, as long as these deeds were carried out at the instigation of an official of a Nazi criminal organization and involved victims chosen exclusively because they belonged to the Jewish community, the deeds were therefore an integral part of a concerted plan of extermination and systematic persecution of this community that was put into action by the German National-Socialist government.[17]

In a rather clever twist, the Cour de cassation managed to shield Vichy France and its anti-Semitic policy from judicial scrutiny[18] while still finding Touvier guilty of complicity of crimes against humanity for having murdered the seven Jewish men pursuant to the orders of the Gestapo, an organisation belonging to a state practising a policy of ideological hegemony, namely, Nazi Germany. In defiance of the historical truth and of the findings of the investigation in this case, Paul Touvier, the main author of the French crime, and a member of a French organisation whose allegiance was to the Vichy government, was judicially found to be an agent of the German Nazi policy of extermination of Jews, and was sentenced to life imprisonment for having been the accomplice of the Gestapo. Eventually convicted of complicity of crimes against humanity by the Cour d'Assises des Yvelines on 20 April 1994, Touvier died while in prison in 1996.

While the *Touvier* case is remembered as one of extremely lengthy proceedings – with the exception of Maurice Papon, 'Paul Touvier came to trial longer after the crimes took place than any other accused criminal'[19] – it is also remembered for being a rather disturbing event, not only because of the personality of the accused, who was a man of no stature, fanatical and pathetic,[20] but also because of the confusions stemming from the judicial findings in this particular case. As observed by Conan and Rousso, 'Paul Touvier saw the legal definition of the crimes he was accused of modified several times',[21] a singularity which the two authors described as 'one of the most disturbing characteristics of this trial and the defence's strongest argument'.[22] And indeed, the vicissitudes of the case law

donc pas nécessaire de suivre les parties civiles dans leur argumentation tendant à établir que la Milice et le gouvernement de l'État français, dont Touvier était le serviteur, auraient été eux-mêmes complices de l'État nazi dans sa politique d'hégémonie idéologique.'

[17] Cass crim, 21 October 1993. Translated in Conan and Rousso, *Vichy, un passé qui ne passe pas* 93. The original version reads as follows: 'Attendu . . . qu'il n'importe que les faits poursuivis aient pu être commis à l'occasion de l'assassinat d'un membre du gouvernement de Vichy appartenant à la Milice, dès lors qu'exécutés à l'instigation d'un responsable d'une organisation criminelle nazie et concernant des victimes exclusivement choisies en raison de leur appartenance à la communauté juive, ils s'intégraient au plan concerté d'extermination et de persécution systématiques de cette communauté, mis en œuvre par le gouvernement national-socialiste allemand.'

[18] See Conan and Rousso, *Vichy – An Ever-Present Past* 93–95.

[19] See ibid, 85–86.

[20] See ibid, 99.

[21] ibid, 86.

[22] ibid.

were undoubtedly driven by political, rather than by legal, considerations. First, French courts here confirmed the *Barbie* precedent, which had restricted the scope of application of crimes against humanity to the Third Reich, thereby impeding all possibility of ever seeing crimes committed by Frenchmen outside the context of the Second World War, in particular those crimes that occurred during the decolonisation process, punished. Second, with the *Touvier* precedent, the French courts manifested their extreme reluctance to rule on the Vichy regime and its role in the perpetration of crimes against humanity, let alone genocide.[23]

These major flaws notwithstanding, the *Touvier* case still had some impact at the international criminal law level, even if far less than the *Barbie* decision and, in its analysis of crimes against humanity, the *Akayesu* Trial Chamber did explicitly refer to the findings of the *Touvier* case.[24]

When the trial of Maurice Papon started on 14 October 1997, after an initial indictment dating back to 19 January 1983 and after an incredible 14 years of procedure and investigation,[25] what was at stake was completely different – not only because of the personality of the accused, but also because of the role he had played both in the Vichy government and subsequently as a senior civil servant and government minister. During the war, Papon had been general secretary of Gironde (secrétaire général de la préfecture de la Gironde) from May 1942, and had notably been in charge of the 'Jewish section' of the prefecture.

In a rather astonishing fashion, the *Papon* case gave yet another opportunity to French courts to alter and modify their appreciation of crimes against humanity. In its decision of 23 January 1997, the Cour de cassation directly contradicted the *Touvier* precedent and held, without any further explanation or reasoning, that article 6 of the Nuremberg Charter did not require an accomplice in crimes against humanity to have adhered to the policy of ideological supremacy of the main authors of the crime.[26]

If this finding was sharply criticised as a distortion of the truth and a legal mistake, it is however fair to assert that, insofar as the court here dealt with crimes against humanity, it does not seem to have erred in law. While it is probably true that this twist in the case law was – yet again – more driven by political motives and by a judicial willingness to keep a distance between the Vichy regime and the Nazi occupier than by purely legal considerations, it is nonetheless worth noting that the French case law here appears to have pre-empted the understanding of the *mens rea* of crimes against humanity under international criminal law.

And indeed, by affirming that the accomplice of crimes against humanity need not have shared the policy of ideological supremacy of the principal perpetrators,

[23] See A Wieviorka, 'La France et le crime contre l'humanité' in F Brayard, (ed), *Le Génocide des Juifs entre procès et histoire 1943-2000* (Paris, Editions Complexe, Collection 'Histoire du Temps Présent', 2000) 113, 124–25.

[24] See *Akayesu* Trial Judgment paras 571–74.

[25] See 'Le Procès de Maurice Papon. La chronique de Jean-Michel Dumay' *Le Monde* (Paris, 1998) 15. Cited in Wieviorka, 'La France et le crime contre l'humanité' 126.

[26] See Delmas Saint-Hilaire, 'La définition juridique de la complicité de crime contre l'humanité' 251–52.

the finding of the Cour de cassation is in line with the subsequent rulings of the ad hoc international criminal tribunals, which all concur in their findings that the *mens rea* of accomplices is established if they 'knew that [their] own acts assisted in the commission of the specific crime in question by the principal offender',[27] without any further requirement to demonstrate that they knew of the exact crime the principal offender intended to commit[28] or that they shared this intent.[29] In the specific case of crimes against humanity, the principal perpetrator himself need not have adhered to the attack on the civilian population. As held in *Blaškić*,

> It follows that the *mens rea* specific to a crime against humanity does not require that the agent be identified with the ideology, policy or plan in whose name mass crimes were perpetrated nor even that he supported it. It suffices that he knowingly took the risk of participating in the implementation of the ideology, policy or plan.[30]

On 2 April 1998, the longest trial in French judicial history came to an end and, as a result of what was therefore a correct judicial understanding of complicity in crimes against humanity, Maurice Papon was convicted and sentenced to 10 years' imprisonment for the illegal arrest (*arrestations illégales*) of 37 persons and the arbitrary confinements (*séquestrations arbitraires*) of Léon Librach and of 53 persons which led to their deportation in July 1942, August 1942, October 1942 and January 1944. Freed on 18 September 2002 on medical grounds, Papon died at his home in February 2007.

But if French courts here did not err in their legal appreciation of crimes against humanity, the final judgment in the *Papon* case still stands on fairly weak grounds: the consideration of complicity in crimes against humanity and the non-necessity for the accomplice to have shared the criminal intent or to have even known the exact crime the principal offender intended to commit allowed the courts to condemn Maurice Papon, general secretary of Gironde in charge of the 'Jewish section' of the prefecture, while still maintaining that he was unaware of the Nazi extermination plan.

Trials are held to try individuals for their individual criminal responsibility, not to pass judgment on a whole regime. At the time, the *Papon* case received intense media coverage and undoubtedly reopened old French wounds – which had never been healed – and it was in this rather heated atmosphere that the trial hearings

[27] See eg *Tadić* Appeal Judgment para 229; *The Prosecutor v Zlatko Aleksovski* (Appeals Chamber Judgment) IT–95–14/1 (24 March 2000) para 162, *Kunarac* Trial Judgment para 392; *The Prosecutor v Mitar Vasiljević* (Trial Chamber Judgment) IT–98–32 (20 November 2002) para 71; *The Prosecutor v Tihomir Blaškić* (Appeals Chamber Judgment) IT–95–14 (29 July 2004) paras 46 and 49–50.

[28] See eg *The Prosecutor v Miroslav Kvočka* (Trial Chamber Judgment) IT–98–30/1 (2 November 2001) para 255; *Blaškić* Appeal Judgment para 50.

[29] See eg *Aleksovski* Appeal Judgment para 162; *Kunarac* Trial Judgment para 392.

[30] *Blaškić* Trial Judgment para 257. See also *Kordić and Čerkez* Trial Judgment para 185: 'There is no apparent requirement in the jurisprudence . . . that the perpetrator must approve of the context in which his acts occur, as well as have knowledge of it'; *Kunarac* Appeal Judgment para 103: 'The accused need not share the purpose or goal behind the attack'. It also follows that the motives of the perpetrator are irrelevant. See eg *Kordić and Čerkez* Trial Judgment para 187: 'It is . . . settled that the motives of the accused are not relevant in this context.'

took place. In reaching its verdict, the Cour d'assises in Bordeaux resisted – and this is to be welcomed –using this opportunity of trying one man to try, through him, Vichy France.

Where the final judgment is far more questionable however is that it was probably reached so as to ultimately generate the exact contrary: to ensure that, following the trial, Vichy France would remain immune from any further accusation of having played an active role in the genocide of the European Jews. The judicial finding that Papon, responsible for the 'Jewish section' of the Gironde prefecture, did not know of the Nazi extermination plan amounts to affirming that Vichy high civil servants were not aware of the Nazi genocidal enterprise; an assertion that shines by its historical incoherence, if not obvious bad faith; but an affirmation that also enabled French courts to, once again, preserve Vichy France from any accusation of active participation in the Nazi 'Final Solution'. Following the *Papon* verdict, at the most, Vichy France could only be deemed responsible for complicity in illegal arrests and arbitrary confinements.

On 2 March 2001, when the Cour d'assises of Paris sentenced Austrian-born Aloïs Brunner to life imprisonment following a trial *in absentia*,[31] there was no legal – or for that matter political – impediment to finding the accused guilty of crimes against humanity for the following acts committed between 21 July and 4 August 1944: illegal arrests and confinements of 352 children, 345 of whom were deported; complicity in murders and/or attempted murders of 284 children, all of whom – including 15-days-old Alain Blumberg – were murdered in Auschwitz-Birkenau and Bergen-Belsen. Just one question remains: why was Brunner, Eichmann's assistant in the orchestration of the Final Solution and responsible for deporting tens of thousands of Jews throughout Europe (Germany, Austria, Greece, France, Slovakia), charged with, and convicted of, crimes against humanity, and not genocide?

As these developments have demonstrated, the trials which occurred in France and which addressed the destruction of the European Jews were all trials for crimes against humanity. In all these instances, and leaving aside for now the motivations behind the verdicts reached and their consequences, French courts showed a clear and correct command of the law of crimes against humanity, even proving rather advanced at a time when guidance at the international level was hardly existent. The expertise of the French judiciary, in spite of the complexity inherent to all these cases, is therefore beyond doubt. In this context, it seems all the more questionable that the courts should have so rigidly constricted crimes against humanity within a specific timeframe, and all the more incomprehensible that the qualification of genocide, rather than crimes against humanity, was not the one applied to the crimes perpetrated. By relying solely on a very restrictive notion of crimes against humanity, the legacy of these French trials remains most problematic.

[31] Brunner had already been tried twice for war crimes and condemned to death *in absentia* by military tribunals in Paris and Marseille, on 30 January 1954 and 3 May 1954 respectively. See S Maupas, 'Perpétuité pour Aloïs Brunner' (2 March 2001) *Diplomatie Judiciaire*, www.diplomatiejudiciare.com.

3

A Problematic Legacy

Before French courts, the individuals who stood accused of perpetrating crimes, either as principal offenders or as accomplices, in the context of the destruction of the European Jews, all faced charged of crimes against humanity, rather than genocide. Further, French courts seized the different opportunities offered by these trials to define crimes against humanity in a very restrictive fashion, thereby considering Nuremberg purely as a law of circumstances and generating extremely serious consequences in practice.

3.1 Equalising Victims, Confusing Crimes

If by qualifying all the crimes perpetrated as crimes against humanity regardless of the identity of the victims – whether *Resistance* fighters or Jews – French courts allowed for all crimes to be tried and punished, not erring in their subsequent appreciation of these crimes, they nonetheless incorrectly proceeded to an equalisation of the crimes, and thus of the victims.

The 1985 decision in *Barbie* to consider the crimes the defendant had committed against *Resistance* fighters as crimes against humanity is to be welcomed, not only because it prevented the application of statutory limitations to such crimes, thereby permitting their prosecution, but also because, as explained above, it was an accurate characterisation of the acts perpetrated. Where this decision is flawed however is in its erroneous qualification of the crimes perpetrated against the Jews as crimes against humanity rather than as genocide. In this sense, the initial attempts of the lower courts at distinguishing between crimes perpetrated against *Resistance* fighters and crimes perpetrated against Jews were far from ill founded; where these courts were wrong was in the qualification of these crimes as either war crimes or crimes against humanity.

The critical aspect in *Barbie* is thus not that crimes against *Resistance* fighters were ultimately qualified as crimes against humanity: they should have been so qualified from the very beginning, by direct application of article 6(c) of the Nuremberg Charter. The real problem with the *Barbie* decision is that crimes against Jews were also qualified as crimes against humanity and not as genocide.

The *Barbie* case, which received intense media coverage, could have been a major opportunity for the Cour de cassation to ascertain the specificity of the crime of genocide, and most particularly of the Shoah. By failing to adequately qualify the acts, by proceeding to a merging of all the different victims of Nazism and by ignoring the specificity of each crime and of each victim, the trial of Klaus Barbie was ultimately counter-productive,[1] generating a form of concurrence between the different victims[2] and establishing an 'implicit hierarchy in horror',[3] precisely where victims should have been equally treated through the adequate qualification of their particular sufferings.

3.2 Making Nuremberg a Law of Circumstances

As previously analysed, article 6(c) of the Nuremberg Charter defined crimes against humanity as a series of acts committed 'in execution of or in connection with any crime within the jurisdiction of the Tribunal'.[4] This jurisdictional limitation enshrined in the Nuremberg Charter was interpreted by the Cour de cassation, in its decision of 20 December 1985 in the *Barbie* case, and subsequently confirmed in both the *Touvier* and the *Papon* cases, as requiring, for a crime against humanity to be qualified as such, that the crime be committed 'in the name of a state practising a policy of ideological supremacy'.[5] In other words, what was merely a statutory jurisdictional limitation was erroneously interpreted by the French court as a definitional requirement of crimes against humanity, which thus found themselves unduly linked to a particular state policy, namely, Nazism. Practically speaking, this means that there could be no crimes against humanity outside the very specific context of the Second World War.

Is this an incorrect reading of the Nuremberg Charter, or very clever interpretation? One can of course not answer this question with absolute certainty. What is however certain is that French courts, which on other aspects of the law of crimes against humanity have shown expert accuracy, here made a mistake which – conveniently? – impeded both the consideration of Vichy France as 'a state practising a policy of ideological supremacy' but also the possible qualification as crimes against humanity of acts perpetrated after the end of the Second World War, and in particular during the decolonisation process. This major shortcoming of the French definition was in fact upheld by the Cour de cassation in the

[1] In this sense, see A Wieviorka, *Le Procès Eichmann* (Paris, Editions Complexe, 1989) 148. See also C Coquio, 'Du Malentendu' in C Coquio (ed), *Parler des Camps, Penser les Génocides* (Paris, Albin Michel, Bibliothèque Albin Michel Idées, 1999) 17, 47.

[2] See JM Chaumont,*La concurrence des victimes – Génocide, identité, reconnaissance* (Paris, La Découverte & Syros, 2002).

[3] A Finkielkraut, *La mémoire vaine – du crime contre l'humanité* (Paris, Gallimard, 1989) 38. Translated by the author. The original version reads: '[u]ne implicite hiérarchie de l'horreur'.

[4] Art 6(c) of the Nuremberg Charter.

[5] *Fédération Nationale des Déportés et Internés Résistants et Patriotes et Autres c Barbie.*

Boudarel case, in which Georges Boudarel faced charges of crimes against humanity for acts perpetrated during the Vietnam War,[6] and in which the Court unequivocally held that crimes against humanity

> concern exclusively acts committed on behalf of the European Axis Powers . . . the qualification of crimes against humanity can therefore not apply to the acts alleged by the civil parties, which occurred after the Second World War.[7]

Such 'lamentable' judgment[8] should however not happen again. Already in 1994, French legislation had been enriched with a more general definition of crimes against humanity, deprived of any nexus requirement to the European Axis Powers or to the Second World War, with the entry into force of the New Penal Code, article 212-1 of which read as follows:

> Deportation, enslavement or the massive and systematic practice of summary executions, abduction of persons followed by their disappearance, of torture or inhuman acts, inspired by political, philosophical, racial or religious motives, and organised in pursuit of a concerted plan against a section of a civil population are punished by criminal imprisonment for life.[9]

With the entry into force of the Rome Statute of the International Criminal Court, the French legislator further modified the definition of crimes against humanity so that it now encompasses a much wider range of criminal acts, still without any linkage to the Second World War:

> Also constitutes a crime against humanity punished by criminal imprisonment for life any of the following acts perpetrated in pursuit of a concerted plan against a section of a civil population within the context of a widespread or systematic attack:

[6] Georges Boudarel had allegedly deserted the French army to serve the Viet-Minh and act, from 1952 to 1954, as assistant supervisor in a prisoners of war camp where he was accused of having committed atrocities against his fellow countrymen. Even though France had issued a general amnesty concerning crimes committed in connection with the Vietnamese war of independence in 1966, the investigating judge had nonetheless brought charges against Boudarel, on the grounds that crimes against humanity, not being subject to statutory limitations, were not covered by amnesties. Although the court of first instance upheld the qualification of crimes against humanity, it however found that they did benefit from the general amnesty. The qualification of crimes against humanity was to be quashed by the Cour de cassation.

[7] *Affaire Georges Boudarel*, cass crim (1 April 1993) Bull Crim N° 143 and also reprinted in D Alland, 'Jurisprudence Française en Matière de Droit International public' (1994) 98 RGDIP 471, 474. Translation by the author. The original version reads as follows: 'ne concernent que les faits commis pour le compte des pays européens de l'Axe . . . ainsi, les faits dénoncés par les parties civiles, postérieurs à la seconde guerre mondiale, n'étaient pas susceptibles de recevoir la qualification de crimes contre l'humanité aux sens des textes précités.'

[8] The expression is of Axel Marschik. See A Marschik, 'The Politics of Prosecution: European National Approaches to War Crimes' in McCormack and Simpson, *The Law of War Crimes* 65, 86.

[9] Art 212-1 of the New Penal Code (France). Translation available at: legislationline.org/documents/section/criminal-codes. The original version reads as follows: 'La déportation, la réduction en esclavage ou la pratique massive et systématique d'exécutions sommaires, d'enlèvements de personnes suivis de leur disparition, de la torture ou d'actes inhumains, inspirées par des motifs politiques, philosophiques, raciaux ou religieux et organisées en exécution d'un plan concerté à l'encontre d'un groupe de population civile sont punies de la réclusion criminelle à perpétuité.'

1° Murder;

2° Extermination;

3° Enslavement;

4° Deportation or forcible transfer of population;

5° Imprisonment or other severe deprivation of physical liberty in violation of fundamental rules of international law;

6° Torture;

7° Rape, sexual slavery, enforced prostitution, forced pregnancy, enforced sterilization, or any other form of sexual violence of comparable gravity;

8° Persecution against any identifiable group or collectivity on political, racial, national, ethnic, cultural, religious, gender, or other grounds that are universally recognized as impermissible under international law;

9° Arrest, detention or abduction of persons, followed by their disappearance and the refusal to acknowledge that deprivation of freedom or to give information on the fate or whereabouts of those persons, with the intention of removing them from the protection of the law for a prolonged period of time;

10° Acts of segregation committed in the context of an institutionalized regime of systematic oppression and domination by one racial group over any other racial group or groups and committed with the intention of maintaining that regime;

11° Other inhumane acts of a similar character intentionally causing great suffering, or serious injury to body or to mental or physical health.[10]

[10] Art 212-1 of the New Penal Code (France) modifié par la loi n° 2010-930 du 9 août 2010 portant adaptation du droit pénal à l'institution de la Cour pénale internationale. Translation by the author. The original version reads: 'Constitue également un crime contre l'humanité et est puni de la réclusion criminelle à perpétuité l'un des actes ci-après commis en exécution d'un plan concerté à l'encontre d'un groupe de population civile dans le cadre d'une attaque généralisée ou systématique:

1° L'atteinte volontaire à la vie;

2° L'extermination;

3° La réduction en esclavage;

4° La déportation ou le transfert forcé de population;

5° L'emprisonnement ou toute autre forme de privation grave de liberté physique en violation des dispositions fondamentales du droit international;

6° La torture;

7° Le viol, la prostitution forcée, la grossesse forcée, la stérilisation forcée ou toute autre forme de violence sexuelle de gravité comparable;

8° La persécution de tout groupe ou de toute collectivité identifiable pour des motifs d'ordre politique, racial, national, ethnique, culturel, religieux ou sexiste ou en fonction d'autres critères universellement reconnus comme inadmissibles en droit international;

9° L'arrestation, la détention ou l'enlèvement de personnes, suivis de leur disparition et accompagnés du déni de la reconnaissance de la privation de liberté ou de la dissimulation du sort qui leur est réservé ou de l'endroit où elles se trouvent dans l'intention de les soustraire à la protection de la loi pendant une période prolongée;

10° Les actes de ségrégation commis dans le cadre d'un régime institutionnalisé d'oppression systématique et de domination d'un groupe racial sur tout autre groupe racial ou tous autres groupes raciaux et dans l'intention de maintenir ce régime;

The New Penal Code further specifies:

> Where they are committed during wartime in execution of a concerted plan against persons fighting the ideological system in the name of which are perpetrated crimes against humanity, the actions referred to under article 212-1 are punishable by criminal imprisonment for life.[11]
>
> Participation in a group formed or in an agreement established with a view to the preparation, as demonstrated by one or more material actions, of any of the felonies defined by articles 211-1, 212-1 and 212-2 is punishable by criminal imprisonment for life.[12]

This contemporary definition notwithstanding, it still remains the case that the qualification of crimes against humanity is inapplicable under French law to acts perpetrated in the period between 1945 – the end of the Second World War – and 1994 – the date of entry into force of the New Penal Code, a legal loophole which obviously leaves a lot to be desired.

Not only does the New Penal Code provide for a definition of crimes against humanity, it also includes, for the first time, a definition of the crime of genocide,[13] which could thus potentially be applied in the future, thereby avoiding the equalisation of crimes and confusion between the victims generated by the trials of the Second World War; yet, unlike crimes against humanity which are not defined by a specific international convention to which France could have been a party, the crime of genocide had been the object of such a convention which France had ratified long before the trials analysed previously were held. Why therefore wasn't the qualification of genocide used by French courts in instances where the crime the accused stood trial for was nothing else than their participation in the destruction of European Jews?

11° Les autres actes inhumains de caractère analogue causant intentionnellement de grandes souffrances ou des atteintes graves à l'intégrité physique ou psychique.'

[11] Art 212-2 of the New Penal Code (France). Translation available at: legislationline.org/documents/section/criminal-codes. The original version reads as follows: 'Lorsqu'ils sont commis en temps de guerre en exécution d'un plan concerté contre ceux qui combattent le système idéologique au nom duquel sont perpétrés des crimes contre l'humanité, les actes visés à l'article 212-1 sont punis de la réclusion criminelle à perpétuité'.

[12] Art 212-3 of the New Penal Code (France). Translation available at: legislationline.org/documents/section/criminal-codes. The original version reads as follows: 'La participation à un groupement formé ou à une entente établie en vue de la préparation, caractérisée par un ou plusieurs faits matériels, de l'un des crimes définis par les articles 211-1, 212-1 et 212-2 est punie de la réclusion criminelle à perpétuité'.

[13] Art 211-1 of the New Penal Code (France).

Part 2

Punishing Genocide: Too Much To Ask?

> The record on which we judge these defendants today is the record on which history will judge us tomorrow.
>
> Justice Robert Jackson[1]

France was one of the first signatories to the 1948 United Nations Convention on the Prevention and Punishment of the Crime of Genocide,[2] signing it on 11 December 1948, only two days after its adoption by the General Assembly of the United Nations. France subsequently ratified the Genocide Convention on 14 October 1950, thus showing its concern for the prevention and punishment of the crime of genocide, without making any declaration, reservation or objection. As recalled by Karen Smith, France 'signed and ratified the Convention quite quickly and without controversy. The French National Assembly adopted the Convention on 28 April 1950, with no debate considered necessary.'[3] The overwhelming importance of the Genocide Convention was thus duly acknowledged by France and, as Smith further reports, 'Lemkin [who had initially coined the word "genocide"] was quite active in writing to various French parliamentarians to press for early ratification, and was apparently told by Pierre Montel, the chair of the commission on military affairs in the National Assembly, that it was a "matter of national honour" that the Convention would be "ratified without one word of discussion".'[4]

If France only incorporated the crime of genocide in its domestic legislation on 1 March 1994 with the entry into force of the New Penal Code, the Convention had entered into force on 12 January 1951. The question thus arises as to why the

[1] Justice Robert Jackson, 'Opening statement' (1947) 2 *Trial of the Major War Criminals Before the International Military Tribunal* 101. Quoted in M Osiel, *Mass Atrocity, Collective Memory, and the Law* (London, Transaction Publishers, 2000) 82.

[2] Convention for the Prevention and Punishment of the Crime of Genocide, United Nations, 1948. Approved and proposed for signature, ratification or accession by the General Assembly of the United Nations, Resolution 260A(III) of 9 December 1948. Entry into force: 12 January 1951. Herein referred to as the Genocide Convention.

[3] Smith, *Genocide and the Europeans* 44.

[4] ibid, n 37.

qualification of genocide was not used in the French trials dealing with the crimes perpetrated in the course of the Second World War; the following analysis thus proposes to review all the possible legal impediments to this use.

4

The Direct Applicability of the Genocide Convention under French Law

As explained by Nehemiah Robinson in his *Commentary* of the Genocide Convention,

> One of the problems which have arisen in connection with the Convention is whether it creates directly applicable norms or not. In other words, whether the responsible individual will be subject to international or domestic law. Under existing international law, a convention not ratified by a State imposes on its organs, citizens, or residents no obligations. Consequently, the problem is to what extent the Convention possesses direct or indirect validity in the contracting State.[5]

Indeed, the first legal and practical obstacle which could be invoked regarding the application of the Genocide Convention by domestic courts relates to its direct or indirect applicability. In the French context, the question is thus whether the Convention could have applied to acts perpetrated before the entry into force of the French New Penal Code, and the explicit definition of the crime therein. Insofar as the qualification of genocide was only integrated within French domestic legislation in 1994, it could indeed be argued that until then the Convention was de facto inapplicable before French courts. Yet, the French legal principles governing the application of international treaties say otherwise and, considering that France had ratified the Convention in 1950, the Convention should have been of immediate application as soon as it had entered into force in January 1951. France is a country of monist tradition, where treaties once duly ratified have a force superior to that of national laws.

At the time of ratification of the Convention, this principle was stated unequivocally in article 26 of the 1946 French Constitution. It was subsequently reiterated in article 55 of the 1958 Constitution, which is still in force today.[6] The Genocide Convention was thus directly applicable under French law and it is interesting to note that Robinson expressly cited France as one of the states where 'an

[5] N Robinson, *The Genocide Convention – A Commentary* (New York, Institute of Jewish Affairs – World Jewish Congress, 1960) 34–35.

[6] 'Les traités ou accords régulièrement ratifiés ou approuvés ont, dès leur publication, une autorité supérieure à celle des lois, sous réserve, pour chaque accord ou traité, de son application par l'autre partie'. Constitution du 4 octobre 1958.

international agreement becomes domestic law by ratification',[7] without any further need for legislative action:

> The action required to transform an international Convention into municipal law depends on the specific law of the given State (i.e., the law governing the transformation of international agreements into domestic law). In some States, an international agreement becomes domestic law by ratification, as in the United States (at least to the extent that the treaty is self-executing), *in France*, and in some other States; in other States, ratification only imposes on the State an obligation to enact, in the ordinary constitutional processes, the necessary legislation.[8]

In this respect, article V of the Genocide Convention provides that:

> The Contracting Parties undertake to enact, in accordance with their respective Constitutions, the necessary legislation to give effect to the provisions of the present Convention, and, in particular, to provide effective penalties for persons guilty of genocide or any of the other acts enumerated in article III.

Insofar as the Genocide Convention itself does not provide for any penalties, it was for the ratifying states to do so, in accordance with their own domestic legislation. As John Quigley explained,

> The expectation was that states would insert provisions on genocide into their penal codes, legislate a penalty, and use that provision to prosecute. Not all ratifying states have done so. Australia, after ratifying, did not enact a penal provision, and the courts there have said that as a result there can be no prosecution in Australia for genocide.[9] New Zealand took the view that it need not enact a genocide crime, because prosecution could be brought under existing statutes on crimes against the person.[10]

Quigley further observed that

> The states that have conducted genocide prosecutions without an applicable genocide provision in their domestic penal law have all recognized the problem. The Genocide Convention does not leave it clear how a state might deal with this problem. Article V might mean that a state may punish for genocide only after it has enacted a domestic definition of genocide including a penalty, and that prosecution may relate only to acts committed after the enactment. If a state can punish for genocide without a domestic provision, it would be punishing for an act for which no penalty were prescribed at the time the act was committed.[11]

If Article V indeed means that genocide can only be domestically prosecuted once domestic legislation has been enacted, it seems clear that the Genocide Convention was not directly applicable in France or anywhere else for that matter. An analysis of this disposition, including its direct reference – and deference – to the Constitutions

[7] Robinson, *The Genocide Convention – A Commentary* 34–35.
[8] ibid (emphasis added).
[9] *Re Thompson ex parte Nulyarimma and Others*, Supreme Court of the Australian Capital Territory, (1998) 136 Australian Capital Territory Reports 9 (footnote in original).
[10] J Quigley, *The Genocide Convention – An International Law Analysis*, International and Comparative Criminal Justice (Aldershot, Ashgate, 2006) 64–65.
[11] ibid, 65.

of the Contracting Parties as well as of states' practice and understanding of the law show however that this was not the case and that, in countries of monist tradition such as France, the Convention was of direct application.

The trials held in France against Klaus Barbie, Paul Touvier, Maurice Papon and Aloïs Brunner – who all participated in the destruction of the European Jews and thus in genocide –can only show one of two things: either the principles enshrined in the French Constitution regulating the applicability of international treaties were set aside, by omission, ignorance or legal incompetence; or the self-executing characteristic of the Genocide Convention was not recognised by French courts, for reasons which go beyond the law. As previously mentioned, France had shown its attachment to the Genocide Convention early on in the ratification process, making it a 'matter of national honour' – if further legislative action had been required to implement the conventional text at the domestic level, it seems that the French legislator, at the time, would have been inclined to proceed promptly once the Convention had entered into force. And even if this remains mere speculation, the French courts could have – at the very minimum – acknowledged the qualification of genocide, if only to justify why it was not applicable to the instances pending before them.

5

The Non-Applicability of Statutory Limitations to the Crime of Genocide

The second obstacle to the qualification of genocide for the crimes perpetrated against the Jews by Klaus Barbie, Paul Touvier, Maurice Papon and Aloïs Brunner could have been the application of statutory limitations. Although both international law and French domestic law are admittedly rather confusing with respect to this particular issue, the following development will aim at demonstrating that, whether on the international or the French level, the prosecution of the crime of genocide was not – and is not – subject to any time constraints.

Under international law, the legacy of the Genocide Convention on the issue of statutory limitations was undoubtedly one of uncertainty, due simply to the fact that the Convention is totally silent on this particular matter. The first international instrument to explicitly prohibit the application of statutory limitations to the crime of genocide was the 1968 UN Convention on the Non-Applicability of Statutory Limitations to War Crimes and Crimes Against Humanity,[1] which entered into force in 1970, in spite of a notably high incidence of non- ratification, including France. Hardly constitutive of customary international law, considering its failure to attract a substantial number of States Parties, this instrument cannot convincingly be relied on. However, with the entry into force of the Rome Statute of the International Criminal Court, all doubts as to the non-applicability of statutory limitations to acts of genocide perpetrated after the entry into force of the Statute were dispelled. Article 29 of the Statute indeed affirms unequivocally that 'the crimes within the jurisdiction of the Court shall not be subject to any statute of limitations'. Until the Rome Statute therefore, the international law of statutory limitations was thus rather uncertain and failed therefore to constitute an authoritative guide for states to follow.

French domestic law was arguably much clearer. As mentioned previously, faced with the possibility that the most serious crimes perpetrated in the course of the Second World War would soon be beyond the reach of law,[2] France enacted a law on 26 December 1964 on the non-applicability of statutory limitations to

[1] Convention on the Non-Applicability of Statutory Limitations to War Crimes and Crimes Against Humanity New York, 26 November 1968. Entry into force 11 November 1970. Art I(b).

[2] At the time, art 763 of the French Code of Criminal Procedure provided for a 20-year period of limitation.

crimes against humanity. The *travaux préparatoires* and debates which preceded the adoption of this law shed an interesting light on the understanding of the crime of genocide under French law.

Initially, a law proposal was presented on 25 June 1964 to the French National Assembly by Members of Parliament M Coste-Floret and M Schmittlein.[3] While this proposal aimed at prohibiting the application of statutory limitations to both genocide and crimes against humanity,[4] the French legislator ultimately chose to only keep in the final text the qualification of crimes against humanity, considering that genocide was a form of crime against humanity.[5] As a result, the 1964 law integrates the Nuremberg definition of crimes against humanity and only contains a single article:

> Crimes against humanity, as defined by the United Nations resolution of 13 February 1946, recognising the definition of crimes against humanity as enshrined in the Charter of the International Tribunal of 8 August 1945, are by nature imprescriptible.[6]

Why France subsequently did not ratify the 1968 United Nations Convention on the Non-Applicability of Statutory Limitations to War Crimes and Crimes Against Humanity seems fairly straightforward. If the *travaux préparatoires* of the 1964 law do demonstrate that genocide was, in the mind of the French legislator, comprised under the qualification of crimes against humanity, they also reveal that the non-applicability of statutory limitations was to attach to these crimes only, thereby excluding war crimes from its ambit – an interpretation later confirmed in the *Barbie* case in which, as we have seen, it was clear that the prosecution of war crimes was subjected to a time limitation. The French reason for not ratifying the UN Convention therefore was the conventional recognition of the non-applicability of statutory limitations to war crimes which stood in contradiction to domestic law.

[3] It may be noted here that another proposal – with the exact same object – was also presented by the communist group on 18 December 1964 and was later deemed unnecessary due to the enactment of the December 1964 law. See P Mertens, *L'imprescriptibilité des crimes de guerre et contre l'humanité* (Brussels, Editions de l'Université de Bruxelles, 1974) 54, n 159.

[4] See Rapport fait au nom de la Commission des lois constitutionnelles, de la législation et de l'administration générale de la République sur la proposition de loi n°1026 de MM. Coste-Floret et Schmittlein, *Journal officiel*, Documents de l'Assemblée Nationale, annexes aux procès-verbaux des séances, première session ordinaire de 1964–1965, n°13, 27 juillet 1965, Annexe n°1.194, 239. See also Proposition de loi tendant à rendre non prescriptibles le génocide et les crimes contre l'humanité, *Journal officiel*, Document de l'Assemblée Nationale, annexes aux procès-verbaux des séances, 2e session ordinaire de 1963–1964, n°46, 11 mai 1965, Annexe n°1026, 807. See generally P Mertens, *L'imprescriptibilité des crimes de guerre et contre l'humanité* 51.

[5] This was indeed the explanation given by M. Edouard Le Bellegon, then rapporteur au Sénat de la Commission de législation: genocide is 'qu'une forme de crime contre l'humanité', *Journal officiel*, Débats parlementaires, Sénat, première session ordinaire de 1954–1965, compte rendu intégral de la séance du 17 décembre 1964, 18 décembre 1964, 2429. See Mertens, *L'imprescriptibilité des crimes de guerre et contre l'humanité* 53.

[6] Loi n° 64-1326 tendant à constater l'imprescriptibilité des crimes contre l'humanité (26 December 1964). Translation by the author. The original version reads as follows: 'Les crimes contre l'Humanité, tels qu'ils sont définis par la résolution des Nations Unies du 13 février 1946, prenant acte de la définition des crimes contre l'Humanité telle qu'elle figure dans la Charte du tribunal international du 8 août 1945, sont imprescriptibles par nature.'

Interestingly, some 15 years later, the French Foreign Affairs Ministry, addressing the question of whether international treaties established statutory limitations, unequivocally held that: 'international law generally ignores extinctive prescription. According to international law, extinctive prescription cannot be presumed and therefore applies only if expressly mentioned'.[7] In other words, the silence of international treaties on statutory limitations amounts to the non-applicability of such limitations. By direct application of this interpretation – and regardless of its accuracy, as what matters here is the French understanding of international law – the silence of the Genocide Convention on statutory limitations is to be interpreted by French courts as a confirmation that the prosecution of the crime of genocide is not subjected to the passage of time. If the question has now definitively been solved with the adoption of the New Penal Code and its article 213-5, which states unequivocally that '[t]he public action relating to the crimes envisaged by this title [genocide and crimes against humanity], as well as the sentences passed, are imprescriptible', it still remains that, from a practical standpoint, there was – even at the time – no obstacle stemming from a possible application of statutory limitations impeding Klaus Barbie, Paul Touvier, Maurice Papon and Aloïs Brunner from being charged with, and tried for, genocide.

[7] 15 June 1979. Cited in B de Bigault du Granrut, B. 'Le Crime Contre l'Humanité' in Ecole Cathédrale – Institut de Formation Continue du Barreau de Paris *Le Crime Contre l'Humanité, mesure de la responsabilité? Actes du cycle des conférences «Droit, Liberté et Foi», Juin 1997* (Paris, CERP, 1998) 97. Translation by the author. The original version reads as follows: 'le droit international ignore en général la prescription extinctive. Pour lui, celle-ci ne se présume pas, et à défaut d'une mention explicite, elle ne s'applique pas'.

6

The Applicability of Retroactive Criminal Norms

The third and final potential obstacle to the application of the Genocide Convention to acts committed prior to the entry into force of the New Criminal Code relates to the issue of retroactivity.[1] As a matter of principle, both international treaties and, in democratic states observing the rule of law, criminal norms have no retroactive force. As William Schabas however recalled:

> Although as a general rule international treaties do not operate retroactively (or retrospectively), there are exceptions. Indeed, most of the treaties dealing with international criminal prosecution have been given a retroactive effect. Examples include the war crimes provisions of the Treaty of Versailles, the Charter of the International Military Tribunal, and the instruments establishing the Special Court for Sierra Leone and the Special Tribunal for Lebanon.[2]

Examples would also include the Genocide Convention, and Schabas further observed that '[t]he International Court of Justice has made a couple of tantalizing comments to the effect that there is no express temporal limitation in the Genocide Convention to prevent it from having retroactive effect.' And indeed, in the *Application of the Convention on the Prevention and Punishment of the Crime of Genocide* case, the World Court responded to the Yugoslav contention that the Court 'could only deal with events subsequent to the different dates on which the Convention might have become applicable as between the Parties'[3] in the following unequivocal terms:

> In this regard, the Court will confine itself to the observation that the Genocide Convention – and in particular Article IX – does not contain any clause the object or effect of which is to limit in such manner the scope *ratione temporis*, and nor did the Parties themselves make any reservation to that end, either to the Convention or on the occasion of the signature of the Dayton-Paris Agreement.[4]

[1] See generally B Juratowitch, 'Retroactive Criminal Liability and International Human Rights Law', [2004] LXXV BYBIL 337–62.

[2] Schabas, *Unimaginable Atrocities* 63.

[3] *Application of the Convention on the Prevention and Punishment of the Crime of Genocide (Bosnia and Herzegovina v Serbia and Montenegro),* Preliminary Objections, Judgment, ICJ Reports 1996, 595, 617 para 34.

[4] ibid.

In 2008, the ICJ reiterated its finding that 'there is no express provision in the Genocide Convention limiting its jurisdiction *ratione temporis*.'[5]

Both the principled prohibition of retroactive criminal laws and its exception are enshrined in human rights law instruments. Article 15 of the International Covenant on Civil and Political Rights,[6] to which France is a party,[7] indeed reads:

> No one shall be held guilty of any criminal offence on account of any act or omission which did not constitute a criminal offence, under national or international law, at the time when it was committed. Nor shall a heavier penalty be imposed than the one that was applicable at the time when the criminal offence was committed. If, subsequent to the commission of the offence, provision is made by law for the imposition of a lighter penalty, the offender shall benefit thereby.
>
> Nothing in this article shall prejudice the trial and punishment of any person for any act or omission which, at the time when it was committed, was criminal according to the general principles of law recognized by the community of nations.

This disposition calls for two remarks with respect to the crime of genocide. First, the reference to offences under 'international law' in article 15(1) surely encompasses the crime of genocide.[8] The express reference to international law therein interestingly is attributable to proposals made by both Uruguay and France, on the basis that its inclusion would prevent individuals responsible for the commission of international crimes from arguing that these offences were not punishable under the domestic law of their countries and thereby evading punishment.[9] Second, it seems to make little doubt that the 'general principles of law recognized by the community of nations' defined in article 15(2) as exceptions to the principle of non-retroactivity of criminal norms encompass the prohibition of genocide.[10]

[5] *Application of the Convention on the Prevention and Punishment of the Crime of Genocide (Croatia v Serbia)*, Preliminary Objections, Judgment, ICJ Reports 2008, 412, 458 para 123.

[6] International Covenant on Civil and Political Rights, United Nations, 1966. Adopted and opened for signature, ratification and accession by the General Assembly of the United Nations, Resolution 2200 A (XXI) of 16 December 1966. Entry into force: 23 March 1976. Hereafter referred to as the ICCPR.

[7] France ratified the ICCPR on 4 November 1980.

[8] See A Cassese, 'Balancing the Prosecution of Crimes against Humanity and Non-Retroactivity of Criminal Law' (2006) JICJ 414–15.

[9] As explained by Manfred Nowak, 'The reference to international law ("droit international") in Art. 15(1) is attributable to proposals by Uruguay and France in the HRComm in 1949. According to the proponents of these proposals, this was to prevent a person from escaping punishment for an international crime by pleading that his offence was not punishable under the national law of his State [See E/CN 4/SR 112, 5 ff; A/2929, 45 (§94); note in the original]. It can furthermore be seen from the discussions in the 3d Committee of the GA that the term "international" law was to mean both international treaty law and customary international law [See, eg, A/C 3/SR 1008, §§2-3; A/4625, §14; note in the original].' Among examples of such criminal offences under international treaty law, Nowak expressly includes art I of the Genocide Convention. M Nowak, *U.N. Covenant on Civil and Political Rights: CCPR Commentary* (Kehl am Rhein, NP Engel Publishers, 1993) 276.

[10] See ibid.

Adopting a very similar language, article 7 of the European Convention on Human Rights[11] – to which France is a party[12] – also makes an explicit exception to the right to freedom from retroactive criminal legislation:

> No one shall be held guilty of any criminal offence on account of any act or omission which did not constitute a criminal offence under national or international law at the time when it was committed. Nor shall a heavier penalty be imposed than the one that was applicable at the time the criminal offence was committed.
>
> This Article shall not prejudice the trial and punishment of any person for any act or omission which, at the time when it was committed, was criminal according to the general principles of law recognised by civilised nations.

The *travaux préparatoires* of the ECHR reveal that it was the purpose of article 7(2) to ensure that the prohibition of retroactive criminal norms did not 'affect laws which, under very exceptional circumstances at the end of the Second World War, were passed in order to suppress war crimes, treason and collaboration with the enemy.'[13] As a matter of fact, the French Cour de cassation, in the *Barbie* case, expressly recognised the applicability of both article 15(2) of the ICCPR and article 7(2) of the ECHR to crimes perpetrated during the Second World War.[14] The application of the law of crimes against humanity to the French context was further upheld by the Strasbourg Court itself on two occasions, with respect to the *Touvier* case and the *Papon* case respectively.[15]

Insofar as, as demonstrated earlier, the French understanding of crimes against humanity encompasses the crime of genocide, there thus seems to be no reason to exclude the crime of genocide from the exceptions to the principle of non-retroactivity of criminal norms. Had French courts specifically chosen to charge and try Klaus Barbie, Paul Touvier, Maurice Papon and Aloïs Brunner for genocide, they would in fact not have been the first domestic courts to retroactively apply the Genocide Convention. As Quigley recalls,

> the Latvian prosecutions [of former officials for atrocities committed in the 1940s] related to acts committed before the adoption of the applicable genocide statute, and before the drafting of the Genocide Convention. The Supreme Court of Latvia applied

[11] European Convention for the Protection of Human Rights and Fundamental Freedoms, Council of Europe, 1950. Adopted by the Council of Europe on 4 November 1950. Entry into force: 3 September 1953. Hereafter referred to as the ECHR.

[12] France signed the ECHR on 4 November 1950 and subsequently ratified it on 3 May 1974.

[13] See *X v Belgium* (European Commission of Human Rights Decision) Application 1038/61 (18 September 1961) [1961] 4 *Yearbook* 324, 336.

[14] *Fédération Nationale des Déportés et Internés Résistants et Patriotes et Autres c Klaus Barbie*, cass-crim (6 October 1983). Reprinted in (1984) RGDIP 88, 509.

[15] See *Touvier v France* (European Commission of Human Rights Decision) Application 29420/95 (13 January 1997), Decisions and Reports 88-B, 161 and *Papon v France (No 2)* (European Court of Human Rights Judgment) Application 54210/00 (25 July 2002) ECHR 2002-VII. Confirmed in *Kolk and Kislyiy v Estonia* European Court of Human Rights Decision on the admissibility of Application No 23052/04 by August Kolk and Application No 24018/04 by Petr Kislyiy against Estonia) Applications 23052/04 and 24018/04 (17 January 2006), available at www.echr.coe.int. See generally A Cassese, 'Balancing the Prosecution of Crimes against Humanity and Non- Retroactivity of Criminal Law – The *Kolk and Kislyiy v. Estonia* Case before the ECHR' (2006) 4 JICJ 410–18.

> the Latvian code provision on genocide to such acts, on the rationale that the Latvian provision was comparable to the definition of genocide in Article II of the Genocide Convention. The Supreme Court presumed, without specific discussion, that genocide was punishable even if committed prior to the adoption of the Genocide Convention.[16]

Where an issue could admittedly have arisen before French courts is with respect to the principle of legality regarding penalties. As previously mentioned, the Genocide Convention does not provide for any penalties and its article V thus left it to the ratifying states to legislate to this end. It has been suggested that the fact that a given state has not enacted penalties does not bar it from exercising jurisdiction over a conduct qualified as criminal under its legislation:

> If genocide were charged in a state that, at the time of the act, had not enacted a penalty for genocide, the offence would still have been in existence, under international law, at least if the act occurred after genocide came to be considered an international offence. While Article 15 [of the ICCPR] prohibits sentencing a person to a penalty higher than that in effect at the time of the act, it does not require that there be a penalty in effect at the time of the act. The prohibition against imposing a penalty higher than one that was in effect at the time of the act does not, writes Alicia Gil Gil, require that a particular penalty be previously set. All that is required, she writes, is 'the recognition of the criminality of the conduct, even if the penalty to be imposed has not been set.'[17]

This interpretation appears to be in line with international law principles, the International Law Commission having recognised that with respect to international crimes, including genocide, it is 'not necessary for an individual to know in advance the precise punishment so long as the actions constitute a crime of extreme gravity for which there will be severe punishment.'[18] If international law thus does not require penalties to be specifically enacted to prosecute offences legally qualified as crimes, it still remains that some states, such as Spain, 'take the principle of legality further, to require that a specific penalty have been in effect at the time of the act, even for an internationally defined crime':[19]

> Even though under Spanish law a treaty, like the Genocide Convention, is automatically incorporated into domestic law when it enters into force for Spain, it would not have the effect of creating a penal prohibition that the Spanish courts could apply. A conviction would be proper under Spanish law only after the parliament enacts a penalty for genocide, and only for acts after that date.[20]

Whether this could be the reason why French courts did not try Klaus Barbie, Paul Touvier, Maurice Papon and Aloïs Brunner is plausible yet unsustainable. Plausible because, as the following developments will highlight, this was precisely

[16] Quigley, *The Genocide Convention* 45 (footnotes omitted).

[17] ibid 70, citing A Gil Gil, *Derecho Penal Internacional: Especial Consideración del Delito de Genocidio* (Madrid, Editorial Tecnos, 1999) 92.

[18] Draft Code of Crimes against the Peace and Security of Mankind (commentary), *Report of the International Law Commission on the work of its forty-eighth session 6 May – 26 July 1996*, UN GAOR, 51st sess, Supp (No. 10) 29–30, UN Doc A/51/10 (1996). See Quigley, *The Genocide Convention* 71.

[19] Quigley, *The Genocide Convention* 71. Here referring to Gil Gil, *Derecho Penal Internacional*.

[20] ibid.

the line of argument used by French courts to declare themselves incompetent in genocide cases involving the crimes perpetrated in the former Yugoslavia and in Rwanda. Unsustainable because the qualification of crimes against humanity equally postdated the commission of the criminal acts and was therefore applied by French courts retrospectively. Further, at the time of the trials of Klaus Barbie and Paul Touvier, no penalty had been enacted either with respect to crimes against humanity, which were nonetheless prosecuted and punished, while at the time of the trials of Maurice Papon and Aloïs Brunner, the New Penal Code had already entered into force, making the debate on the direct applicability of the Convention obsolete and any arguments based on non-retroactivity unconvincing: once it had been duly defined under French law, there was no reason why the qualification of genocide could not benefit from the same applicability.

Here again therefore, the only conclusion that can be drawn from the exclusion of the qualification of genocide in the respective trials of Klaus Barbie, Paul Touvier, Maurice Papon and Aloïs Brunner is this: either it reflects a clear misunderstanding of the law of genocide on the part of French courts, thereby simultaneously revealing a certain degree of incompetence, or it represents an obvious reluctance to apply the law of genocide, for reasons of politics which should have no place at all in legal proceedings.

7

The Contemporary Understanding of the Law of Genocide by the French Judiciary: Dualism in Disguise?

If the foregoing has demonstrated that there should have been no legal impediments justifying the non-qualification of the acts perpetrated by Klaus Barbie and Paul Touvier as genocide, the enactment of the 1994 New Penal Code – which specifically includes the crime of genocide – should in any event have allowed this qualification to be used in the respective cases of Maurice Papon and Aloïs Brunner, whose trials occurred after it had entered into force. Since 1994, article 211-1 of the French Penal Code has provided that:

> A genocide is the fact, in the execution of a *concerted plan* aiming at the destruction, in whole or in part, of a national, ethnical, racial or religious group, or of *a group determined by reference to any other arbitrary criterion*, of committing or causing to be committed, against members of this group, one of the following acts:
>
> – wilful attack on life;
> – causing serious bodily or mental harm;
> – deliberately inflicting on the group conditions of life calculated to bring about its physical destruction in whole or in part;
> – imposing measures intended to prevent births;
> – forced transfer of children.
>
> Genocide is punished by life imprisonment.[1]

[1] Art 211-1 of the New Penal Code (France) (emphasis added). Translation available at: www.preventgenocide.org/fr/droit/codes/france.html. The original version reads as follows: 'Constitue un génocide le fait, en exécution d'un plan concerté tendant à la destruction totale ou partielle d'un groupe national, ethnique, racial ou religieux, ou d'un groupe déterminé à partir de tout autre critère arbitraire, de commettre ou de faire commettre, à l'encontre de membres de ce groupe, l'un des actes suivants:

– atteinte volontaire à la vie;
– atteinte grave à l'intégrité physique ou psychique;
– soumission à des conditions d'existence de nature à entraîner la destruction totale ou partielle du groupe;
– mesures visant à entraver les naissances;
– transfert forcé d'enfants.

Le génocide est puni de la réclusion criminelle à perpétuité.'

Although the French definition draws upon the definition enshrined in article II of the Genocide Convention, it also departs significantly from it in two important – and arguably positive – aspects. Article II of the Genocide Convention defines the crime as:

> In the present Convention, genocide means any of the following acts committed with intent to destroy, in whole or in part, a national, ethnical, racial or religious group, as such:
>
> (a) Killing members of the group;
> (b) Causing serious bodily or mental harm to members of the group;
> (c) Deliberately inflicting on the group conditions of life calculated to bring about its physical destruction in whole or in part;
> (d) Imposing measures intended to prevent births within the group;
> (e) Forcibly transferring children of the group to another group.

First, while the 1948 Genocide Convention affords protection exclusively to 'national, ethnic, racial or religious' groups as such, the French disposition not only grants protection to these groups but also to 'group[s] established by reference to any other arbitrary criterion', thereby extending the conventional scope of application. Yet, the use of the word 'arbitrary' could lead to misinterpretation and to the exclusion from the definitional scope of application of groups whose members share an objectively recognised feature. Even in light of unhelpful *travaux préparatoires*, the term 'arbitrary' is to be understood as referring to the subjective definition of the groups by the genociders (*libre arbitre*).[2] Still, the Genocide Convention has been criticised by several authors regarding its narrow sphere of application and its selective protection of groups, and it thus seems that the French legislator here adopted a more progressive approach, recognising that genocide could be committed against other groups than the ones expressly listed in the Convention.

Second, while the Genocide Convention defines the crime of genocide by the *intent* to destroy a group, the French definition adopts an arguably more objective criterion, that of the existence of a concerted plan,[3] thereby putting the emphasis on the planned and systematic feature of the crime – a definition which incidentally should bring to mind the definition initially proposed by Polish lawyer Raphaël Lemkin, who coined the word 'genocide' through the combination of the ancient Greek word *genos* (race, tribe) and the Latin *cide* (killing), defining it as 'a co-ordinated plan of different actions aiming at the destruction of essential foundations of the life of national groups', and adding that '[t]he objectives of such a plan would be disintegration of the political and social institutions, of culture, language, national feelings, religion, and the economic existence of national groups'.[4]

[2] Débat, Assemblée Nationale, *Journal Officiel* (décembre 1991) 6897.

[3] Art 211-1 of the New Penal Code (France). Translation by the author. The original version uses the terns 'plan concerté'.

[4] R Lemkin, *Axis Rule in Occupied Europe – Laws of Occupation, Analysis of Government, Proposals for Redress* (Washington, Carnegie Endowment for International Peace, Division of International Law, 1944) 79.

The French legislator has thus opted for a fairly progressive definition of the crime of genocide, which should therefore have facilitated its use by French courts. This however has proved far from being the case and, if anything, French courts have proved very reluctant in using the qualification of genocide, even after the entry into force of the New Penal Code and even in instances not directly linked to the Second World War and Vichy France.

So as to declare themselves incompetent in such cases of genocide, French courts have invoked the non-applicability of the principle of universal jurisdiction to the crime of genocide and, to this end, have relied on article 689 of the Code of Penal Procedure, which defines the universal jurisdiction's mechanism in the following terms:

> Perpetrators of or accomplices to offences committed outside the territory of the Republic may be prosecuted and tried by French courts either when French law is applicable under the provisions of Book I of the Criminal Code or any other statute, or when an international Convention gives jurisdiction to French courts to deal with the offence.[5]

Further, article 689-1 provides that:

> In accordance with the international Conventions quoted in the following articles, a person guilty of committing any of the offences listed by these provisions outside the territory of the Republic and who happens to be in France may be prosecuted and tried by French courts. The provisions of the present article apply to attempts to commit these offences, in every case where attempt is punishable.[6]

The Genocide Convention fails to explicitly provide for universal jurisdiction and does not impose an express duty to prosecute or extradite: it therefore cannot qualify under article 689 as 'an international Convention [giving] jurisdiction to French courts to deal with the offence'. This was unfortunately not remedied at the domestic level, insofar as the Genocide Convention is not included within the list of 'international Conventions quoted in the following articles' expressly referred to in article 689-1 and which grants French courts jurisdiction to try and prosecute certain offences, even if perpetrated outside the French territory. Yet, nothing in the French Criminal Code provides that this list contained in articles 689-2 to 689-9 is exhaustive.[7]

[5] Art 689 of the Code of Penal Procedure (France). Translation available at: www.legifrance.gouv.fr. The original version reads as follows: 'Les auteurs ou complices d'infractions commises hors du territoire de la République peuvent être poursuivis et jugés par les juridictions françaises soit lorsque conformément aux dispositions du livre Ier du Code pénal ou d'un autre texte législatif, la loi française est applicable, soit lorsqu'une convention internationale donne compétence aux juridictions françaises pour connaître de l'infraction.'

[6] Art 689-1 of the Code of Penal Procedure (France). Translation available at: www.legifrance.gouv.fr. The original version reads as follows: 'En application des conventions internationales visées aux articles suivants, peut être poursuivie et jugée par les juridictions françaises, si elle se trouve en France, toute personne qui s'est rendue coupable hors du territoire de la République de l'une des infractions énumérées par ces articles. Les dispositions du présent article sont applicables à la tentative de ces infractions, chaque fois que celle-ci est punissable.'

[7] See C Lombois, 'De la compassion territoriale' (1995) *Revue de science criminelle et de droit pénal comparé* 397, 401. Cited in M-A Swartenbroekx, 'Vers un ordre répressif international intégré' in

Although the Genocide Convention does not provide for universal jurisdiction, the Advisory Opinion on the *Reservations to the Genocide Convention* case is here worth recalling insofar as the International Court of Justice had unequivocally emphasised the universal character of the Genocide Convention, as intended by the UN General Assembly and the States Parties:

> The origins of the Convention show that it was the intention of the United Nations to condemn and punish genocide as 'a crime under international law' involving a denial of the right of existence of entire human groups, a denial which shocks the conscience of mankind and results in great losses to humanity, and which is contrary to moral law and to the spirit and aims of the United Nations. The first consequence arising from this conception is that the principles underlying the Convention are principles which are recognized by civilized nations as binding on States, even without any conventional obligation. A second consequence is the *universal character both of the condemnation of genocide and of the co-operation required* 'in order to liberate mankind from such an odious scourge' (Preamble to the Convention). The Genocide Convention was therefore intended by the General Assembly and by the contracting parties to be definitely *universal in scope.*[8]

Still, in the *Javor* case, involving the policy of ethnic cleansing in Bosnia and Herzegovina, both the Court of Appeals[9] and the Cour de cassation,[10] thereby confirming the position of the investigating judge not to rely on the Genocide Convention,[11] asserted that they had no jurisdiction with respect to the crime of genocide. The failure of the Genocide Convention to expressly provide for universal jurisdiction here was interpreted by French courts as impeding their jurisdiction over the crimes perpetrated in Bosnia and Herzegovina. It is absolutely true that, the above opinion of the World Court notwithstanding, the Genocide Convention only provides for territorial jurisdiction or for an international tribunal, but not for universal jurisdiction:

> Persons charged with genocide or any of the other acts enumerated in article III shall be tried by a *competent tribunal of the State in the territory of which the act was committed,* or by such international penal tribunal as may have jurisdiction with respect to those Contracting Parties which shall have accepted its jurisdiction.[12]

Interestingly, the *travaux préparatoires* of the Genocide Convention reveal that France strongly supported the express reference in the Convention to an international penal tribunal, ironically on the grounds that, genocide being primarily a

JF Dupaquier (ed), *La justice internationale face au drame rwandais* (Paris, Editions Karthala, 1996) 221, 224.

[8] *Reservations to the Convention on the Prevention and Punishment of the Crime of Genocide,* Advisory Opinion, [1951] ICJ Reports 15, 23 (28 May) (emphasis added).

[9] Cour d'appel de Paris (24 October 1994). See B Stern, 'Universal jurisdiction over crimes against humanity under French law' (1999) 93 AJIL 525, 527.

[10] *Javor,* cass crim (26 March 1996), (1996) Bull crim 132, 379.

[11] See Tribunal de grande instance de Paris, Order (ordonnance) (6 May 1994). The investigating judge – Juge Jean-Pierre Getty – indeed chose to rely on the 1984 Torture Convention and the 1949 Geneva Conventions, which explicitly provide for universal jurisdiction, to establish the jurisdiction of French courts. See Stern, 'Universal jurisdiction over crimes against humanity under French law' 526.

[12] Art VI of the Genocide Convention (emphasis added).

state crime, its prosecution before domestic courts would be purely illusory. As Karen Smith recalled,

> France was also firmly in favour of the setting up of an international criminal court . . . France's insistence on including a reference to an international criminal tribunal stemmed from its belief that genocide was a crime perpetrated by states or government officials, and therefore prosecution by national courts would be inconceivable.[13]

Notwithstanding their interpretation of the Genocide Convention – strict, yet admittedly correct in law – the reluctance of the French courts to know of the crimes perpetrated in Bosnia and Herzegovina became all the more obvious when they refused to exercise jurisdiction over violations of international humanitarian law and over crimes of torture, whose respective governing instruments nonetheless expressly provide for universal jurisdiction.[14] As Brigitte Stern observed,

> there is a certain imperfection in the incorporation of international instruments in the French domestic order just as there is a certain imperfection, to say the least, in the judicial interpretation of existing instruments.[15]

As she further argued,

> The imperfection of incorporation in French law of conventions establishing universal jurisdiction is first reflected in the fact that certain conventions, although ratified by France, have not been incorporated in the dispositions following article 689-1, while they should have been: this is for instance the case of the Apartheid Convention and of the Convention against the Illicit Traffic in Narcotic Drugs and Psychotropic Substances. The result is that this universal jurisdiction, provided for by conventions duly ratified by France, has no legal value in France insofar as it is not used by our courts, which somehow empties of their substance our international engagements.[16]

[13] Smith, *Genocide and the Europeans* 40–41 (footnote omitted).

[14] See art 49, Geneva Convention (I) for the Amelioration of the Condition of the Wounded and Sick in Armed Forces in the Field, 12 August 1949; art 50, Geneva Convention (II) for the Amelioration of the Condition of Wounded, Sick and Shipwrecked Members of Armed Forces at Sea, 12 August 1949; art 129, Geneva Convention (III) Relative to the Treatment of Prisoners of War, 12 August 1949; art 146, Geneva Convention (IV) Relative to the Protection of Civilian Persons in Time of War, 12 August 1949. All available on the website of the International Committee of the Red Cross: www.icrc.org. See also art 5, Convention against Torture and Other Cruel, Inhuman or Degrading Treatment or Punishment. Adopted and opened for signature, ratification and accession by the General Assembly of the United Nations, Resolution 39/46 of 10 December 1984. Entry into force: 26 June 1987.

[15] B Stern, 'Le génocide rwandais face aux autorités françaises' in L Burgorgue-Larsen (ed), *La répression internationale du génocide rwandais* (Brussels, Bruylant, Collection du CREDHO, 2003) 137, 142. Translation by the author. The original version reads as follows: 'Il y a une certaine imperfection de l'incorporation des textes internationaux dans l'ordre français comme il existe une certaine imperfection, pour ne pas dire plus, de l'interprétation donnée par les juges, des textes existants.'

[16] ibid, 142–43. Translation by the author. The original version reads as follows: 'L'imperfection de l'incorporation en France des conventions de compétence universelle se traduit d'abord dans le fait que certaines conventions pourtant ratifiées par la France n'ont pas été incorporées à la suite de l'article 689-1, alors qu'elles auraient dû l'être: c'est, par exemple, le cas de la convention contre l'apartheid, c'est également le cas de la convention contre le trafic illicite de stupéfiants. Il en résulte donc que cette compétence universelle prévue par des conventions, conventions dûment ratifiées par la France, n'a aucune valeur en France, c'est-à-dire n'est pas utilisée par nos tribunaux, ce qui vide quelque peu de leur contenu nos engagements internationaux.'

With respect to the 1949 Geneva Conventions, duly ratified by France, French courts considered that the Conventions did not create a basis for their exercise of universal jurisdiction. The French Cour de cassation indeed held that the Geneva Conventions were not self-executing and that, in the absence of any specific domestic legislation incorporating the Conventions' universal jurisdiction provisions into the French legal system, these instruments could have no direct effect in France.[17] As Brigitte Stern pointed out, these arguments put forward by the Cour de cassation fail to convince: first, the language of the 1949 Geneva Conventions is clear and specific enough to qualify as self-executing, and second, the fact that these Conventions are not listed among these instruments addressing offences over which French courts can exercise their jurisdiction does not mean that they fail to create universal jurisdiction for French courts: quite to the contrary, it simply indicates that, being self-executing, the Geneva Conventions had no place in this list. [18] According to Stern,

> the highest Court could have relied on Article 689, and considered that the Geneva Conventions are precisely the type of convention referred to by this article, as they provide directly for universal jurisdiction. But the Cour de cassation preferred to state that no universal jurisdiction was directly created by the Geneva Conventions and that Article 689 could therefore not be a basis of universal jurisdiction in the French legal order. Moreover, this decision implies that the French courts are not ready to accept that universal jurisdiction can be based on customary international law.[19]

With respect to the 1984 Torture Convention, the situation was slightly different, as not only has France duly ratified it but it has also incorporated it into its domestic law. The Torture Convention is accordingly referred to in Article 689-2 of the French Code of Criminal Procedure, thereby providing a basis for universal jurisdiction, on the condition that the accused be found on French territory as further upheld by both the Court of Appeals and the Cour de cassation in the *Javor* case. French courts here again 'adopted a narrow interpretation of the scope of judicial powers implied by universal jurisdiction; they declared that no universal jurisdiction exists as long as the perpetrator is not on French territory, not even the jurisdiction to try to ascertain his whereabouts.'[20] This 'vicious circle' was convincingly denounced by Claude Lombois who pointed out that 'to know whether X is hiding on [French] territory, one must look for him there; but to look for him, one should already have ascertained (by illumination or intuition) his presence there'.[21]

[17] See M Massé, 'Ex-Yougoslavie, Rwanda: une compétence "virtuelle" des juridictions françaises?' (1997) *Revue de science criminelle et de droit pénal comparé* 895. Cited in cass crim (6 January 1998). Reprinted in D Alland and F Ferrand, 'Jurisprudence Française en matière de Droit International Public' [1998] RGDIP 825, 829.

[18] *Javor* 381. See Stern, 'Le génocide rwandais face aux autorités françaises' 143. See also Lombois, 'De la compassion territoriale' 397–403.

[19] Stern, 'Universal jurisdiction over crimes against humanity under French law' 529.

[20] ibid, 527.

[21] Lombois, 'De la compassion territoriale' 401. Translated by the author. The official version reads as follows: 'exprimée ou non, la condition de présence doit être supposée pour les besoins de la

The first cases regarding the Rwanda genocide were no more successful than the Bosnian complaints.[22] When M. Munyeshyaka, a Hutu priest suspected of having actively participated in the Rwanda genocide, was found to be in France, a joint complaint was filed for acts of genocide and of torture and led to the suspect's arrest. While the court of first instance found that it had jurisdiction only over the acts of torture and cruel and inhuman treatment as defined by the Torture Convention,[23] the Court of Appeal of Nîmes subsequently reversed that decision on the grounds that jurisdiction could only be established on the basis of the 'highest criminal qualification namely, genocide'.[24] Insofar as, as explained earlier, the Genocide Convention fails to provide for universal jurisdiction, the finding of the Court of Appeals amounted to dismissing the case by excluding any possible exercise of jurisdiction by French courts. Where the court of appeals found this principle of the 'highest criminal qualification' remains a mystery. Its judgment was reversed by a subsequent decision of the Cour de cassation, which emphasised that it was sufficient for the acts to qualify as offences over which French courts could have jurisdiction for them to be able to exercise it.[25] The Court however recalled that the enforcement of the prohibition of genocide before French courts requires an express domestic statute of implementation.[26]

The reluctance of French courts to exercise their jurisdiction in the abovementioned cases is all the more surprising insofar as, in other instances, they have proved rather progressive in their understanding of universal jurisdiction. In the *Ely Ould Dah* case, the Cour d'assises de Nîmes convicted a Mauritian defendant for crimes of torture perpetrated in 1990 and 1991.[27] Not only did the French court see no obstacle in applying the New Penal Code retroactively but, even further, it established its jurisdiction regardless of the Mauritanian law of amnesty, thereby concurring with the previous judgment of the Cour de cassation in the same case:

> With respect to the application of domestic law, only the amnesty promulgated by the French authorities can be taken into account: the contrary would amount to depriving the principle of universal jurisdiction of all effect . . . the exercise by a French court of

"recherche", qui la vérifiera au cours de sa progression. Sans quoi, c'est le cercle vicieux: pour savoir si X se cache sur notre territoire, il faut l'y chercher; mais pour le chercher, il faudrait déjà avoir découvert (par illumination ou par intuition) qu'il s'y trouve.'

[22] See *Kalinda et al*, Tribunal de grande instance de Paris, complaint filed on 4 July 1994; *Dupaquier et al*, Tribunal de grande instance de Paris, complaint filed on 19 July 1994; Ordonnance, Tribunal de grande instance de Paris (23 February 1995). See Stern, 'Universal jurisdiction over crimes against humanity under French law' 527, n 15.

[23] *Dupaquier, Kalinda et al*, Ordonnance, Tribunal de grande instance de Privas (9 January 1996). See Stern, 'Universal jurisdiction over crimes against humanity under French law' 528.

[24] Cour d'appel de Nîmes (20 March 1996). See Stern, 'Universal jurisdiction over crimes against humanity under French law' 528. Translation by the author. The original version reads as follows: 'la compétence du juge doit s'apprécier uniquement au regard de la plus haute acception pénale qui est le génocide'.

[25] Cass crim (6 January 1998). Reprinted in Alland et Ferrand, 'Jurisprudence Française en matière de Droit International Public' [1998] 825–32.

[26] See ibid, 829–30.

[27] *Ely Ould Dah* case, Cour d'assises de Nîmes Arrêt (1 July 2005).

universal jurisdiction implies the jurisdiction of French law, even where a foreign amnesty law has been enacted.[28]

Could the reluctance of French courts to exercise universal jurisdiction be due to the fact that these cases ultimately dealt with the crime of genocide? It is indeed unsettling that, in cases related to the former Yugoslavia and to Rwanda, the courts consistently refused the application of universal jurisdiction, even putting forward arguments which fail to convince in law, while proving progressive in a case unrelated to a genocidal occurrence.

Further legislative steps were however taken to adapt French domestic legislation to international criminal law and, in particular, to enhance the universal jurisdiction principle. On 2 January 1995, a law adapting French legislation to Security Council resolution 827 creating the ICTY was adopted.[29] On 22 May 1996, a similar law was enacted, adapting French legislation to Security Council Resolution 955 creating the ICTR.[30] Although limited *ratione temporis* and *ratione loci* to crimes perpetrated in the former Yugoslavia since 1991 and in Rwanda or neighbouring countries in 1994 respectively, these laws provide for universal jurisdiction over the crimes falling under the jurisdiction of the ad hoc international criminal tribunals namely, war crimes, crimes against humanity and genocide. These two laws had immediate consequences in practice,[31] as exemplified by the above-mentioned *Munyeshyaka* case, in which the Cour de cassation was thus able to rule that French courts could have jurisdiction not only over acts of torture or inhuman treatment as defined in the Torture Convention, but also over acts falling within the jurisdiction of the International Criminal Tribunal for Rwanda, and therefore over the crime of genocide.[32] Insofar as these laws still require the presence of the accused on the French territory, the outcome of the above-mentioned *Javor* case was not altered by their adoption.

[28] Cass crim (23 October 2002). Translation by the author. The original reads as follows: 'au regard du principe de l'application de la loi nationale, seule peut être prise en considération l'amnistie décidée par les autorités françaises sauf à priver de toute portée le principe de la compétence universelle . . . l'exercice par une juridiction française de la compétence universelle emporte la compétence de la loi française, même en présence d'une loi étrangère portant amnistie.'

[29] Loi n° 95-1 portant adaptation de la législation française aux dispositions du Statut du Tribunal pénal international pour l'ex-Yougoslavie (TPIY) No. 95-1 (2 January 1995) *Journal officiel*, 3 January 1995, 71.

[30] Loi n° 96-432 portant adaptation de la législation française aux dispositions du Statut du Tribunal pénal international pour le Rwanda (TPIR) (22 May 1996) *Journal officiel*, 23 May 1996, 7695.

[31] These new laws being procedural, they could be retroactively applied to pending cases.

[32] Following an arrest warrant issued by the ICTR on 21 June 2007, the *Munyeshyaka* case underwent a series of judicial events. See S Maupas, 'Le TPIR demande à la France d'arrêter et de juger deux Rwandais, un prêtre et un ex-préfet, accusés de génocide', *Le Monde* (4 July 2007); S Maupas, 'Deux Rwandais accusés de génocide ont été arrêtés en France', *Le Monde* (21 July 2007); Le Monde, 'La justice française libère deux Rwandais accusés de génocide', *Le Monde* (1 August 2007); Le Monde, 'Deux Rwandais inculpés pour génocide ont été à nouveau interpellés en France', *Le Monde* (8 September 2007); Le Monde, 'La cour d'appel reporte sa décision sur les deux Rwandais réclamés par le TPIR', *Le Monde* (26 September 2007); Le Monde, 'Le TPIR se dessaisit au profit de la France pour juger deux Rwandais', *Le Monde* (21 November 2007). In November 2007, the ICTR ultimately decided to defer the case to French courts. See *Munyeshyaka*, Décision relative à la requête du procureur aux fins de renvoi de l'acte d'accusation contre Wenceslas Munyeshyaka aux autorités françaises, Chambre de première instance (20 November 2007).

The incoherence and inconsistency of the French application of universal jurisdiction did not go unnoticed, and was heavily criticised. According to Professor Géraud de la Pradelle,

> such disparity is not reasonable: the system which recognises universal jurisdiction over acts of torture, but not over genocides; which acknowledges this same jurisdiction over crimes perpetrated in the former Yugoslavia and in Rwanda over a certain period of time, but not in other places or in other times, is an incoherent system. Under these conditions, reasons of coherence would call for the adoption by France of universal jurisdiction over all the offences defined in articles 5 and following of the Rome Statute.[33]

Just as it had enacted laws adapting French legislation to the respective Statutes of the ad hoc international criminal tribunals, the French legislator more recently adopted a law adapting domestic legislation to the Rome Statute of the International Criminal Court,[34] which added an article 689-11 to the Code of Criminal Procedure labeled in the following terms:

> May be prosecuted and tried before French courts any individual, usually residing on the territory of the Republic, guilty of committing outside the territory of the Republic any of the offences falling under the jurisdiction of the International Criminal Court by application of the Statute of the International Criminal Court signed in Rome on 18 July 1998, if the acts are punished by the legislation of the State where they were committed or if this State or the national State of the offender is a party to the above mentioned statute.
>
> The prosecution of these crimes can only be engaged on the initiative of the public prosecutor if no international or national court has requested the transfer or the extradition of the individual. To this end, the public prosecutor must ensure that the International Criminal Court has expressly declined its jurisdiction, that no other competent international court has requested the individual's transfer and that no other state has requested his extradition.[35]

[33] Translation by the author. The original version reads as follows: 'Selon le professeur de droit Géraud de la Pradelle, "une telle disparité n'est pas raisonnable: le système qui reconnaît la compétence universelle pour des actes de torture, mais non pour des génocides; qui comporte cette même compétence pour des crimes commis en ex-Yougoslavie et au Rwanda pendant une certaine période, mais non ailleurs ou en d'autres temps, est un système incohérent. Dans ces conditions, la cohérence voudrait que la France adopte la compétence universelle pour toutes les infractions définies à partir de son article 5 par la Convention de Rome".' Cited in Fédération Internationale des ligues des Droits de l'Homme, *France- Compétence universelle: État des lieux de la mise en œuvre du principe de compétence universelle* (October 2005) 11. Available at: www.fidh.org.

[34] See Loi n° 2010-930, portant adaptation du droit pénal à l'institution de la Cour pénale internationale (9 August 2010) *Journal officiel*, 10 August 2010, 14678.

[35] Art 689-11 to the Code of Criminal Procedure (France). Translation by the author. The original version reads as follows: 'Peut être poursuivie et jugée par les juridictions françaises toute personne qui réside habituellement sur le territoire de la République et qui s'est rendue coupable à l'étranger de l'un des crimes relevant de la compétence de la Cour pénale internationale en application de la convention portant statut de la Cour pénale internationale signée à Rome le 18 juillet 1998, si les faits sont punis par la législation de l'Etat où ils ont été commis ou si cet Etat ou l'Etat dont elle a la nationalité est partie à la convention précitée. La poursuite de ces crimes ne peut être exercée qu'à la requête du ministère public si aucune juridiction internationale ou nationale ne demande la remise ou l'extradition de la personne. A cette fin, le ministère public s'assure auprès de la Cour pénale internationale qu'elle

While this law undoubtedly marks a step forward in the adoption of a more coherent system of universal jurisdiction under French law, such jurisdiction remains problematically subjected to a series of conditions. If the requirement that 'the State [where the acts were committed] or the national State of the offender is a party' to the Rome Statute is in line with international criminal law, the alternative requirement that the acts be 'punished by the legislation of the State where they were committed' is far more questionable and hardly reconcilable with the spirit itself of international crimes which, since their very inception in the Nuremberg Charter, have been conceived as crimes 'whether or not in violation of the domestic law of the country where perpetrated'.[36] Furthermore, the French law conditions the exercise of universal jurisdiction by French courts to the 'usual residence' of the suspect on the territory of the French Republic; a reinforcement of the condition of mere presence provided for by the laws adapting French legislation to the respective statutes of the ad hoc international criminal tribunals which endangers the practical and effective application of universal jurisdiction in France and which could ultimately defeat the whole purpose of the universal jurisdiction principle.

In 1983, responding to Klaus Barbie's contention that his extradition was contrary to international law, the French Cour de cassation had affirmed that

> Crimes against humanity do not solely fall within the competence of French domestic law but also of a repressive international order, legally integrated into French domestic law, which fundamentally ignores notions of frontiers and extradition rules.[37]

It is ironic that this same Cour de cassation failed to subsequently support the 'repressive international order' it had itself referred to.

décline expressément sa compétence et vérifie qu'aucune autre juridiction internationale compétente pour juger la personne n'a demandé sa remise et qu'aucun autre Etat n'a demandé son extradition.'

[36] Art 6(c) of the Nuremberg Charter.

[37] *Fédération Nationale des Déportés et Internés Résistants et Patriotes et Autres c Klaus Barbie.* Translation by the author. The original version reads as follows: 'Les crimes contre l'humanité ne relèvent pas seulement du droit interne français, mais encore d'un ordre répressif international, régulièrement intégré à l'ordre interne français, auquel la notion de frontière et les règles extraditionnelles qui en découlent sont fondamentalement étrangères.'

8

Concluding Observations

Why this judicial reluctance to implement the law of genocide? None of the potential counter-arguments – be they the applicability of the Convention under French law, statutory limitations, the prohibition of retroactive criminal norms, or principles regulating the exercise of universal jurisdiction – are convincing.

One – perhaps more sustainable – explanation lies in the French traditional understanding of genocide as a crime against humanity. If France was ultimately among the states supporting the adoption of the Genocide Convention, it is worth recalling that this had not always been the case. As Karen Smith explained, France

> had initially described the term 'genocide' as a 'useless and even dangerous neologism'. Instead, it persistently argued that the issue of genocide should be considered as one aspect of crimes against humanity, and therefore initially rejected the idea that genocide was a crime of war and of peacetime. For example, it wanted the preamble to describe genocide as a crime against humanity. But other states successfully argued that the two concepts were distinct and separate.[1]

Indeed, in preparation for the debate on the Secretariat's draft of a convention on the crime of genocide, France had circulated a memorandum 'on the subject of genocide and crimes against humanity' which challenged the use of the term 'genocide'. France preferred to approach the problem of extermination of racial, social, political, or religious groups from the standpoint of crimes against humanity.[2] During the second session of the General Assembly, the heart of the issue was whether to consider genocide as a variety of crime against humanity, or to treat it as a distinct form of criminal behaviour. During the debates in the ad hoc Committee, France was the most insistent about the linkage between genocide and crimes against humanity, while others firmly believed that the concepts had to be made distinct and separate. France had urged that the preamble described genocide as 'a crime against humanity',[3] but this was rejected by the ad hoc Committee, which chose instead to characterise it as 'a crime against mankind'.[4] According to the final report of the Committee, its members 'categorically opposed the expression "crimes against humanity" because, in their opinion, it had acquired a well-defined legal meaning in the Charter of the Nuremberg Tribunal'.[5]

[1] Smith, *Genocide and the Europeans* 40 (footnote omitted).
[2] UN Doc A/AC.20/29.
[3] UN Doc E/AC 25/SR 20, 7.
[4] UN Doc E/794/, 2.
[5] ibid, 3.

As further noted by William Schabas,

> France, on the other hand, regarded the draft [of the Genocide Convention] as too preoccupied with domestic prosecution for genocide: 'The utility of such provisions would appear to be relative since the crime can only take place with the complicity of the government.'[6] According to France, the convention should affirm its relationship with the principles of the Nuremberg Tribunal, and explained that genocide was merely one aspect of crimes against humanity. It believed that genocide ought to relate directly to State action and punishment, on an international basis, and should be restricted to rulers who would otherwise enjoy impunity within their own States.[7]

Equally revealing was the report drafted by French jurist and Nuremberg prosecutor Henri Monneray on the notion of 'genocide' at the time when the Genocide Convention was being debated. If it might be too much to read into this report a full reflection of the French position on the matter, the overlap – if not interchangeability – between the notions of persecutions, thus crimes against humanity, and genocide therein is still worth noting. As the report explained,

> Two conceptions are being confronted with one another: the West wants to include political groups within the groups protected and to repress all *persecutions* for 'political motives'. The East, on the contrary, opposes this position and wants *to limit the definition of genocide to the persecution* of national, religious, racial and linguistic groups.[8]

As mentioned earlier, the indictment against Klaus Barbie of 23 February 1983 explicitly included acts of genocide within the definitional ambit of crimes against humanity;[9] an inclusion which probably found its origins in the law of Nuremberg, the Charter of the International Military Tribunal having not expressly given jurisdiction to the Tribunal over genocide, which was admittedly included within the broader category of crimes against humanity.[10] As a matter of fact, the International Law Commission expressly recognised the Nuremberg understanding of the crime against humanity of persecutions as equivalent to the modern concept of genocide in its unequivocal affirmation that '[s]hortly after the Judgment of the Nürnberg Tribunal, the General Assembly affirmed that the *persecution type of crimes against humanity or "genocide"* constituted a crime under international law for which individuals were subject to punishment.'[11]

[6] UN Doc A/401 (footnote in the original).

[7] WA Schabas, *Genocide in International Law – The Crime of Crimes*, 2nd edn (Cambridge, Cambridge University Press, 2009) 65.

[8] H Monneray, *Rapport*, Session du Conseil Economique et Social (Genève, août 1948) (Microfiches, Centre de Documentation Juive Contemporaine, Ref. CCCLXVI-34), 3. Translation by the author. The original version reads as follows: 'Deux conceptions s'affrontent: l'Ouest désire comprendre parmi les groupes protégés, les groupes politiques et réprimer toutes *persécutions* pour «motif politique». L'Est, au contraire, s'y oppose et désire *limiter la définition du génocide à la persécution* des groupes d'ordre national, religieux, racial, linguistique.' Emphasis added.

[9] Translation available in Rousso, *The Vichy Syndrome* 203–04 (emphasis added).

[10] See art 6 of the Nuremberg Charter.

[11] ILC, 'Draft Code of Crimes against the Peace and Security of Mankind', *Report of the International Law Commission, on the work of its Forty-Eight Session* [1996] II(2) *ILC Yearbook* 44 (emphasis added).

The close relationship between the two offences is further reflected in contemporary international criminal justice which, while firmly affirming that '[g]enocide . . . is different from other crimes against humanity',[12] also acknowledges that the 'crime of genocide is a type of crime against humanity'[13] – 'the most abhorrent'[14] – and that its definition 'was based upon that of crimes against humanity, that is, a combination of "extermination and persecutions on political, racial or religious grounds"'.[15] Judicial findings are therefore indicative of the inescapable links between genocide and the crime against humanity of persecutions, the latter having been defined as 'one of the most vicious of all crimes against humanity . . . *only one step away from genocide*'[16] and as

> an offence belonging to the same *genus* as genocide. Both persecution and genocide are crimes perpetrated against persons that belong to a particular group and who are targeted because of such belonging. . .Thus, it can be said that, from the viewpoint of *mens rea, genocide is an extreme and most inhuman form of persecution*. To put it differently, when persecution escalates to the extreme form of wilful and deliberate acts designed to destroy a group or part of a group, it can be held that such persecution amounts to genocide.[17]

Ultimately, the explanation of the French judicial attitude towards the crime of genocide based on a domestic conception of the crime as one against humanity finds its most compelling illustration in the French New Penal Code itself, which expressly includes a section entitled 'Crimes against humanity and against persons' ('des crimes contre l'humanité et contre l'espèce humaine'),[18] which first article interestingly defines genocide[19] while 'other crimes against humanity' ('des autres crimes contre l'humanité') are defined in the following disposition.

Even if it can find an explanation, the French persistence in considering genocide as a crime against humanity, and in trying genociders for crimes against humanity, is to be regretted, not only because it is deprived of any solid legal grounds but also because the qualification of acts of genocide as genocide would have brought the trials of the Second World War in line with international criminal law and with the reality of the facts.

[12] *Kayishema and Ruzindana* Trial Judgment para 89.
[13] ibid.
[14] *Kupreškić* Trial Judgment para 751 (emphasis added). See also *Nikolić* Initial Indictment para 24; *Krstić* Trial Judgment para 684.
[15] ibid.
[16] ibid.
[17] *Kupreškić* Trial Judgment para 636 (emphasis added).
[18] Arts 211-1 to 215-4 of the New Penal Code (France).
[19] Art 211-1 of the New Penal Code (France).

Part 3

Why Genocide?

While the temptation of trying History via the judicial route is to be resisted, and while the trials of Klaus Barbie, Aloïs Brunner, Paul Touvier and Maurice Papon should not be seen as the collective trials of Nazi Germany and of Vichy France respectively, the fact remains that these individuals have participated to the extermination of the Jews, the qualification of which is undoubtedly genocide. Some states – including France – have even adopted legislation prohibiting its denial as genocide.[1] Yet, by misinterpretation of the law or conscious choice, these individuals have been tried as criminals against humanity or as accomplices to crimes against humanity. As the previous developments have shown, there was no compelling legal impediment under French law not to use the qualification of genocide and, as the following analysis will now demonstrate, this qualification would have been much better suited to the atrocities perpetrated by those who stood trial before French courts.

[1] See Loi n° 90-615 tendant à réprimer tout acte raciste, antisémite ou xénophobe (13 July 1990). See also Loi n° 2001-70 relative à la reconnaissance du génocide arménien (29 January 2001) *Journal officiel*, 30 January 2001. See also Austrian Law no 148: Federal Law – Amendment of the Prohibition Law (1992); Belgian Law for the Repression of the denial of the genocide committed by the German National-Socialist regime during the Second World War (23 March 1995); Arts 130 (incitement to hatred), 131 (instigation of race hatred) and 185 (insult) of the West German Criminal Code; Israeli Denial of Holocaust (Prohibition) Law 5746-1986; Art 261bis of the Swiss Penal Code.

9

Responding to the Incorrect Ill-Qualification of Vichy France in the *Touvier* and *Papon* Cases

The fact that Klaus Barbie and Aloïs Brunner were tried and found guilty of crimes against humanity, rather than of genocide, if incomprehensible from a legal perspective, did thankfully not put into question the qualification of the destruction of the European Jews perpetrated by Nazi Germany as genocide. The same however cannot be said with respect to the trials of Paul Touvier and Maurice Papon, which by ending with verdicts of complicity of crimes against humanity, contributed to minimising Vichy France's role in the extermination of the Jews.

As previously explained, Paul Touvier was an agent of the French Milice, Vichy's own police force, who was tried and convicted for the murders of seven Jewish men as crimes against humanity.[2] Throughout the proceedings, and thereby resisting and dismissing arguments to the contrary raised by some lawyers,[3] French courts did their best to twist the definition of crimes against humanity so as show that Touvier the *milicien* had acted under the orders of the Gestapo.

The *Barbie* precedent having set the condition that crimes against humanity could only be acts committed 'in the name of a state practising a policy of ideological supremacy',[4] French courts could have ruled that Vichy was such a state, thereby recognising the autonomy of the Vichy regime and anti-Semitic ideology. In their persistent refusal to do so, the French courts – which ultimately could not reasonably acquit the defendant – were thus left with no other choice than to consider, in defiance of all historical truth and in contradiction to the conclusions of the investigation in the case, that Paul Touvier had acted pursuant to the orders of the Gestapo, an organisation of the state practising a policy of ideological hegemony that was Nazi Germany. Touvier was eventually convicted of complicity in crimes against humanity.

It is this complicity in crimes against humanity which also constituted the verdict in the trial of Maurice Papon. As mentioned earlier, Papon, a high-ranking civil servant in the Vichy administration, in charge of the 'Jewish section' of the

[2] cass crim (20 April 1994).
[3] See Klarsfeld, *La Cour, les Nains et le Bouffon.*
[4] *Fédération Nationale des Déportés et Internés Résistants et Patriotes et Autres c Klaus Barbie.*

Gironde prefecture , was judicially found to have been unaware of the Nazi extermination plan[5] – a finding which implies that, according to French courts, Vichy's administration did not know a genocide was occurring during the Second World War.

9.1 The Laws of Vichy France: 'An Impeccable Style for an Infinite Horror'[6]

Born of the defeat by Nazi Germany's army in 1940, the Vichy government ruled over France for four years, which were to become the darkest pages in the history of the country.

As soon as it was established, the Vichy regime adopted a series of anti-Semitic measures, thereby operating 'a legislative assault upon Jews living in France',[7] which the Vichy government was swift to implement. The legislation of a country is highly reflective of its political inclinations and the enactment of the infamous Vichy laws is therefore symptomatic of the ideology of this regime; whether this ideology was self-standing and independent from Nazi ideology is a fundamental question to address and answer so as to establish the responsibility of the Vichy regime in the genocide and assess the legacy of the trials of Paul Touvier and Maurice Papon.

'Did Vichy, *acting on its own initiative*, indeed commit such crimes?'[8] asked Éric Conan and Henry Rousso while simultaneously recognising that '[t]he answer is hardly simple'[9] and explaining that

> when one of the most subtle legal minds in the field, Attorney General Pierre Truche, was asked whether Vichy's anti-Semitic laws of 1940 and 1941, laws that were genuinely French, made as they were prior to Vichy's participation in the 'Final Solution', which began in the summer of 1942 (and even before the Germans put the machinery of the 'Final Solution' into operation), were crimes against humanity, he answered in the negative, while specifying that they could rather be considered as 'apartheid' crimes. In this case, the historian agrees with the legal scholar: the French anti-Semitic laws did not originally fit into the framework of a process of physical elimination, but reflected the desire to exclude Jews from society. On the other hand, however, the active participation into the massive roundups and deportations from 1942 to 1944 clearly fits into the framework of complicity in crimes against humanity. Pierre Laval's spontaneous delivery of Jewish children less than sixteen years old (whatever his real motivations may have been) during the summer of 1942 might even be a case not of complicity (since the

[5] cass crim (23 January 1997).

[6] D Rémy, 'Introduction' in D Rémy, *Les lois de Vichy – Actes dits 'lois' de l'autorité de fait se prétendant 'gouvernement de l'État français'* (Paris, Éditions romillat, 1992) 16. Translated by the author. The original version reads as follows: 'Une forme irréprochable pour une horreur sans fond.'

[7] MR Marrus and RO Paxton, *Vichy France and the Jews* (Stanford, Stanford University Press, 1995) 3.

[8] Conan and Rousso, *Vichy – An Ever-Present Past* 94 (emphasis in original).

[9] ibid.

Germans were not requesting the children at that time), but of a direct crime, on the condition that one could solve the knowledge he had – or wanted to have – at that time about the destination of trains of deportees.[10]

If 'the French anti-Semitic laws did not originally fit into the framework of a process of physical elimination, but reflected the desire to exclude Jews from society',[11] if the initial decision taken by the dignitaries of the Vichy regime to collaborate with the Nazis was not purely ideological, if collaboration was at first a means to maintain France outside of the armed conflict and to restore national sovereignty,[12] Rousso nonetheless observed that this political choice remains rather peculiar:

> After 1944, the proponents of the [Vichy] regime have argued that the word 'collaboration' appeared in the armistice convention and that this policy had therefore been imposed on the French government. And yet it is this government which made offers to the occupier who, for various tactical or political reasons, accepted while imposing his own conditions. If collaboration is a phenomenon common to all the countries occupied by the Nazis, the case of France is unusual insofar as it was established through the demand of an autochthonous government of a defeated country, which can facilitate the control of the occupied zone of this country. [13]

If the restoration and containment of national sovereignty were overriding objectives of the Vichy regime, 'the blackest mark on the whole Vichy experience [is] anti-Semitism'.[14] Not content with collaborating with the Nazi occupier, Vichy initiated and developed its own anti-Semitic ideology. In his seminal *Vichy France – Old Guard and New Order 1940–1944*, Robert Paxton indeed acknowledged that he had 'been unable to turn up any direct German order for French anti-Masonic, anti-Semitic, or other legislation during the most active period of Vichy legislation in 1940.'[15] In other words, the Vichy government acted on its own initiative to promulgate its own anti-Semitic legislation and '[i]n 1940, therefore, an indigenous French anti-Semitism was free to express its own venom.'[16]

Mirroring the legislative process in Nazi Germany which had channelled anti-Semitism into law,[17] Vichy France used the legislative apparatus to implement its own racist and xenophobic ideology; and this without any constraint from Nazi

[10] ibid (emphasis in original, footnote omitted).

[11] ibid.

[12] See H Rousso, *Le régime de Vichy* (Paris, Presses Universitaires de France, Collection Que sais-je?, 2007) 31–32.

[13] ibid, 32. Translation by the author. The original version reads as follows: 'Les partisans du régime ont argué après 1944 que le mot «collaboration» figurait dans la convention d'armistice, et donc que cette politique avait été imposée au gouvernement français. Or c'est bien ce dernier qui fait des offres à l'occupant, lequel, pour diverses raisons tactiques ou politiques, accepte en imposant ses propres conditions. Si la collaboration est un phénomène touchant l'ensemble des pays occupés par les nazis, la situation de la France est singulière dans la mesure où il s'agit d'une demande venue d'un gouvernement autochtone d'un pays vaincu, qui peut faciliter la gestion de la partie occupée du pays.'

[14] RO Paxton, *Vichy France – Old Guard and New Order 1940–1944* (New York, Columbia University Press, 2001) 173.

[15] ibid, 142–43.

[16] ibid, 173–74.

[17] See Nuremberg Race Laws (1935).

Germany. The research conducted by Robert Paxton showed that '[l]ong before the Germans began to apply any pressure, the Vichy government began setting up a purge and quota system.'[18] Did Vichy France thus plant the seeds for genocide through its own laws? Did it orchestrate the genocide of Jews in France?

The Vichy laws were legislatively very well thought through and indicated a clear command of the law and of legal technicalities. As noted by Dominique Rémy, their reading reveals 'the apex of the normative art, their legibility and clarity are undoubtedly better.'[19] Put differently, the absurdity of these monstrous laws took on a legally correct form; a travesty of the law with the design to serve inhumane purposes. In the words of Dominique Rémy,

> It is distressing to have to note that these texts are often of a remarkable technical quality: these are clear texts, without embellishment, without this verbosity, which taints our contemporary texts . . . An impeccable style for an infinite horror.[20]

The Vichy government was swift in enacting such measures, and within two weeks of its establishment, the new regime had amended the legislation concerning naturalisation, soon followed by the repeal of the *décret Marchandeau* punishing anti-Semitism in the media. Worse however was still to come, and Henry Rousso identified as a 'turning point' the 'Statute of Jews' (*Statut des Juifs*) of 3 October 1940, in which, for the first time in French legislative history, 'the State proposes a definition of the "Jew"', [21] determining who was to be legally considered as Jewish, based on ancestry, and attaching to this determination a prohibition to access and exercise public functions. Completely breaking with French tradition, this statute introduced race into French law, 'a concept foreign to its tradition and a violation of the republican principle of equality of all French citizens, by excluding Jews from public state functions.'[22] It provided the following definition:

> Article 1. For the purposes of the present law, a Jew is one who has three grandparents of the Jewish race; or who has two grandparents of that race, if his or her spouse is Jewish.[23]

[18] Paxton, *Vichy France – Old Guard and New Order* 174.

[19] Rémy, 'Introduction' 16. Translation by the author. The original version reads as follows: 'ce qui est le sommet de l'art du normateur, le plan de la lisibilité et de la clarté est incontestablement meilleur.'

[20] ibid. Translation by the author. The original version reads as follows: 'Il est pénible de devoir dire que ces textes sont souvent d'une qualité technique remarquable: ce sont des textes clairs, sans fioritures, sans cette logomachie législative qui pollue nos textes contemporains.'

[21] Rousso, *Le régime de Vichy* 80–81: 'La première mesure de Vichy contre les juifs date du 22 juillet 1940, *moins de deux semaines* après l'instauration du nouveau régime. Elle concerne la révision des naturalisations. Elle est suivie de l'abrogation du décret Marchandeau (avril 1939) réprimant l'antisémitisme dans la presse (27 août 1940). Le tournant s'opère le 3 octobre 1940 avec le premier «statut des juifs» (publié le 18 octobre). Conçu par Raphaël Alibert (Justice) et Marcel Peyrouton (Intérieur), il constitue une rupture majeure dans les traditions républicaines, même si des discriminations ethniques existent déjà dans le système colonial. Pour la première fois dans l'histoire de France, l'État propose une définition du «juif».'

[22] Y Beigbeder, *Judging War Crimes and Torture – French Justice and International Criminal Tribunals and Commissions (1940-2005)* (Leiden, Martinus Nijhoff Publishers, 2006) 145.

[23] See Loi portant statut des juifs (3 October 1940) *Journal officiel*, 18 October 1940, 5323: 'Art. 1er. Est regardé comme juif, pour l'application de la présente loi, toute personne issue de trois grands-parents de race juive ou de deux grands-parents de la même race, si son conjoint lui-même est juif.' Translation available in Beigbeder, *Judging War Crimes and Torture* (2006) 145.

What is crucial for the purposes of the present analysis is that this law applied to individuals living in the unoccupied zone, which is to say the zone that was not under Nazi Germany's rule and which was governed by the Vichy government. At this stage, the Vichy government was under no pressure from Nazi Germany to take legislative steps against the Jews.[24] The Nazi occupier had adopted its own anti-Semitic regulations applicable in the occupied zone,[25] and left the administration of the unoccupied zone to the Vichy government.

The very next day, on 4 October 1940, the law on foreign nationals of the Jewish race (*ressortissants étrangers de race juive*) completed the previous text by allowing prefects to assign a forced residence to foreign Jews or to intern them in 'special camps' to that effect:

> Foreign nationals of the Jewish race may, from the promulgation date of the present law, be interned in special camps by a decision of the prefect of the department of their residence.[26]

On 2 June 1941, a new – harsher – law repealed the law of 3 October 1940 and provided that:

> A Jew is: He or she, of whatever faith, who is an issue of at least three grandparents of the Jewish race, or simply two if his/her spouse is an issue herself/himself of two grandparents of the Jewish race.
>
> A grandparent having belonged to the Jewish religion is considered to be of the Jewish race.
>
> He or she who belongs to the Jewish religion, or who belonged to it on 25 June 1940, and who is the issue of two grandparents of the Jewish race.[27]

Operating an amalgam between race and religion,[28] the law of 2 June 1941 created a presumption of belonging to the Jewish race based on the individual's

[24] See Rousso, *Le régime de Vichy* 81. See also Rémy, 'Introduction' 90.

[25] See Ordonnance relative aux mesures contre les juifs (27 September 1940), Verordnungsblatt des Militärbefehlshabers in Frankreich, 92–93 in Mission d'étude sur la spoliation des Juifs de France, *La Persécution des Juifs de France 1940–1944 et le Rétablissement de la Légalité Républicaine – Recueil des textes officiels 1940–1999* (Paris: La documentation Française, 2000) 49–51.

[26] Loi sur les ressortissants étrangers de race juive (4 October 1940) *Journal officiel*, 18 October 1940, 5324: 'Art. 1er. Les ressortissants étrangers de race juive pourront, à dater de la promulgation de la présente loi, être internés dans des camps spéciaux par décision du préfet du département de leur résidence.' Translation available in Beigbeder, *Judging War Crimes and Torture* 146. See Rémy, 'Introduction' 92. See also law allowing for the detention of foreign Jews living in the unoccupied zone and abolishing the décret Crémieux which had awarded French nationality to Algerian Jews (7 October 1940) in Rousso, *Le régime de Vichy* 81.

[27] Loi portant second statut des juifs (14 June 1941) *Journal officiel*, 14 June 1941, 2475–476: 'Est regardé comme juif: 1° Celui ou celle, appartenant ou non à une confession quelconque, qui est issu d'au moins trois grands-parents de race juive, ou de deux seulement si son conjoint est lui-même issu de deux grands-parents de race juive. Est regardé comme étant de race juive le grand-parent ayant appartenu à la religion juive.' Translation available in Beigbeder, *Judging War Crimes and Torture* 146–47. See L Joly, *Vichy dans la 'Solution Finale' – Histoire du Commissariat général aux Questions juives (1941–1944)* (Paris, Editions Grasset & Fasquelle, 2006) 185–200. See also Rémy, 'Introduction' 123–24. On the same day, a law providing for a census of the Jews was enacted. See Loi prescrivant le recensement des juifs (14 June 1941) *Journal officiel*, 14 June 1941, 2476 (loi prorogée par une loi du 13 juillet 1941).

[28] Rémy, 'Introduction' 123–24.

religious belief. Its inherent absurdity notwithstanding, this piece of legislation also appears to be ideologically incoherent, as duly noted by Isabelle Lecoq-Caron, who qualified this technique as contradicting 'the anti-Semitic and racist doctrine of the time: according to this law, racial belonging is acquired by religion while the doctrine at the time affirmed that there existed an inherent racial belonging.'[29] Not content with defining who was to be considered as Jewish, this law further attached penal repercussions to this consideration, criminalising the offence of 'non-declaration of Judaism' (*non-déclaration de judéité*).[30] Put differently, the Jew became 'criminally suspect – by atavism – of the mere fact of existing if he did not recognise the "quality of Jew" under which he was now labelled.'[31]

The French anti-Semitic legislative apparatus was soon to be reinforced by the adoption of a series of laws, all aiming at systematically excluding Jews from both economic and social life[32] and from all professional activities.[33] Among these laws, the law of 21 June 1941 was enacted to regulate the admission of Jewish students to higher education,[34] while the law of 22 July 1941[35] initiated the process of 'aryanisation' of Jewish goods and property, thereby marking the start of the gradual

[29] I Lecoq-Caron, 'La preuve de la qualité de Juif' in Le genre humain (collectif), *Juger sous Vichy* (Paris, Éditions du Seuil, 1994) 41. Translation by the author. The original version reads as follows: 'Cette technique paraît contraire à la doctrine antisémite et raciste de l'époque: en effet, selon la loi, l'appartenance raciale s'acquiert par la religion; alors que la doctrine de l'époque affirme qu'il existe une appartenance raciale originaire.' See also L Poliakov, *Sur les traces du crime* (Paris, Berg International Éditeurs, 2003) 111–12.

[30] Art 9, Loi portant second statut des juifs (14 June 1941).

[31] D Gros, 'Le droit antisémite de Vichy contre la tradition républicaine' in Le genre humain (collectif), *Juger sous Vichy* 17, 25 (footnote omitted). Translation by the author. The original version reads as follows: 'Pénalement, il est suspect – par atavisme – du seul fait d'exister, s'il ne reconnaît pas la «qualité de Juif» dont on l'affuble.'

[32] In particular, the law of 9 November 1942 regulated the movement of foreign Jews, see Loi n° 979, *Journal officiel*, 8 December 1942, 4026 while the law of 11 December 1942 required the superimposition of 'Jew' on all identity documents delivered to French and foreign Jews, see Loi n°1077, *Journal officiel*, 12 December 1942, 4058.

[33] See Décret réglementant, en ce qui concerne les Juifs, la profession d'avocat (16 July 1941) *Journal officiel*, 17 July 1941, 2999–3000; Décret réglementant, en ce qui concerne les Juifs, les fonctions d'officier public ou ministériel (16 July 1941) *Journal officiel*, 17 July 1941, 3000–3001; Décret réglementant en ce qui concerne les Juifs la profession de médecin (11 August 1941) *Journal officiel*, 6 September 1941, 3787–88; Décret d'application sur les professions interdites (14 August 1941); Décret réglementant, en ce qui concerne les Juifs, la profession d'architecte (24 September 1941), *Journal officiel*, 25 September 1941, 4113–14; Décret n° 5338 réglementant, en ce qui concerne les Juives, la profession de sage-femme (26 December 1941) *Journal officiel*, 21 January 1942, 296–97); Décret n° 5339 réglementant, en ce qui concerne les Juifs, la profession de pharmacien (26 December 1941) *Journal officiel*, 21 January 1942, 297–98); Décret n° 1631 réglementant, en ce qui concerne les Juifs, la profession dentaire (5 June 1942) *Journal officiel*, 11 June 1942, 2037–38; Décret n° 1301 réglementant, en ce qui concerne les Juifs, les professions d'artiste dramatique, cinématographique ou lyrique (6 June 1942) *Journal officiel*, 11 June 1942, 2038 and Rectificatif *Journal officiel*, 13 June 1942, 2060. For an analysis of these measures, see Joly, *Vichy dans la 'Solution Finale'* 201–208.

[34] See Loi réglant les conditions d'admission des étudiants juifs dans les établissements d'enseignement supérieur (21 June 1941) *Journal officiel*, 24 June 1941, 2628 (modified by a law of 19 December 1941). See Joly, *Vichy dans la 'Solution Finale'* 200–201.

[35] See Loi relative aux entreprises, biens et valeurs appartenant aux juifs (22 July 1941) *Journal officiel*, 26 August 1941, 3594–95 (modified by a law of 17 November 1941). See Mission d'étude sur la spoliation des Juifs de France, *Rapport Général* (Paris: La documentation Française, 2000) 42. See also Joly, *Vichy dans la 'Solution Finale'* 208–27 and Rémy, 'Introduction' 157.

affirmation of the legal incapacity of Jewish citizens [36] and their simultaneous 'progressive de-integration', 'step-by-step eradication'.[37] Over a very short period of time, these meticulously drafted and abject laws methodically orchestrated the systematic exclusion of Jews from the rest of society, paving the way for their systematic annihilation. [38] And if Vichy does not symbolise 'the fanatical Nazi hatred of Jews', [39] if Vichy did not conceive the project of exterminating the Jewish population, if Vichy did not want – at least at first – to target French Jews, if 'French cultural anti-Semitism, with its acceptance of assimilated Jews, was built upon bases entirely foreign to Nazi racial anti-Semitism',[40] its 'State anti-Semitism, within the context of collaboration, brought the regime to actively participate to the Final Solution'. [41] As Robert Paxton further explained:

> the French laws of 1940 and 1941 made the Final Solution much easier. By the summer of 1942, some 20,000 Jews had already been interned in French concentration camps in the unoccupied zone under the law of 4 October 1940. The census of all Jewish persons and property ordered under the law of 2 June 1941 made escape harder. The creation of the Union Générale des Israélites Français on 29 November 1941, the obligatory welfare and representation organization of all French Jews, helped set them apart even more clearly. Expulsion from jobs and 'Aryanization' of businesses reduced more to destitution. Finally, the official government attitude and the gutter press lent an air of respectability to Vichy anti-Semitism from which Nazi anti-Semitism profited.[42]

[36] The law of 2 November 1941 further subjected the acquisition of businesses by Jewish citizens to special authorisation. See *Journal officiel*, 6 November 1941, 4806. The law of 17 November 1941 regulated the access of Jewish citizens to property. See *Journal officiel*, 5 December 1941, 5179.

[37] The expressions are from Alfred Grosser and here translated by the author. The original versions read as follows: 'désinsertion progressive', 'arrachement par étapes'. A Grosser, *Le crime et la mémoire* (Paris, Flammarion, Collection Champs, 1989) 68.

[38] See Antoine Prost, cited in X Ternisien, 'Les 62 000 dossiers de la honte', *Le Monde*, 17 April 2000. See also Gros, 'Le droit antisémite de Vichy contre la tradition républicaine' (1994) 26: 'Est-il besoin de dire que le pas à franchir entre l'effacement – par des moyens de droit – de toute personnalité et la Solution finale n'est pas immense? *L'élimination des Juifs en surnombre*, selon l'expression de certains textes relatifs aux interdictions professionnelles, trouva son sens littéral dans un programme militaire décidé ailleurs, par l'état-major allemand . . . Une appréciation synthétique du droit antisémite de Vichy soulève cette question: dès que l'on touche à la capacité des personnes, n'est-ce pas tout le droit qui est contaminé par cette atteinte? N'est-ce pas, sous l'effet de ce qui peut sembler d'abord n'être qu'un simple accroc, tout l'édifice juridique qui est menacé? On pourrait également prendre la métaphore de la gangrène. Si tel est le cas, nous savons désormais comment le génocide peut s'articuler, dans le respect des lois, avec des mesures dont les auteurs ne perçoivent pas forcément, *ab initio*, la portée désastreuse. Et cette connaissance, celle des conséquences ultimes d'un droit d'exclusion qui fait de l'étranger un bouc émissaire et du citoyen un apatride, est très précieuse sur le plan prospectif: elle nous avertit du fait que l'*identification* des exclus est l'amorce nécessaire du processus qui peut conduire au génocide. La création de *catégories d'incapables* fondées sur la race, également sur l'opinion religieuse ou philosophique, contient en germe la possibilité du génocide.' (Emphasis in original.)

[39] Rousso, *Le régime de Vichy* 79. Translation by the author. The original version reads as follows: '[l]a haine fanatique des nazis envers les juifs'.

[40] Paxton, *Vichy France – Old Guard and New Order*183.

[41] Rousso, *Vichy – L'événement, la mémoire, l'histoire* 63. Translation by the author. The original version reads as follows: 'l'antisémitisme d'État de Vichy, associé à l'engrenage de la collaboration, amènera le régime à participer activement à la Solution finale, bien qu'il n'ait pas conçu le projet d'exterminer, ni même chasser du territoire les juifs français.'

[42] Paxton, *Vichy France – Old Guard and New Order* 184. He also explained: 'In view of what was to come, it may seem casuistical to observe that Vichy anti-Semitism rested upon different bases from Nazi

The first train for Auschwitz left France on 27 March 1942, marking a change in the Nazis' policy in France. Upon the instigation of Adolf Eichmann, the Nazis required contingents and quotas, which could only be reached with the help and support of the French government and police forces.[43] In exchange for its full collaboration, the Vichy government first succeeded in obtaining from the German Nazis the concession that only foreign Jews would be arrested[44] yet, in so doing, showing one of its darkest features. While, at this stage, the Nazis had not yet requested the arrest of children, Vichy took the initiative of arresting and deporting them. As SS Hauptsturmführer Theodor Dannecker reported to Adolf Eichmann:

> President Laval [Head of the Vichy government] asks that, in the course of the evacuation of Jewish families in the unoccupied zone, children under 16 years of age be taken with them. As for the children who would stay in the occupied zone, the matter does not interest him.[45]

Laval subsequently justified his decision by 'a consideration of humanity' and 'by a willingness to authorise the children, including those under 16 years of age, to accompany their parents'.[46] As Serge Klarsfeld wrote:

> We are alas obliged to question this humanitarian consideration: it would be absurd to imagine that Laval really believes the intention of the Nazis to prepare in Eastern Europe conditions of living which would be acceptable for the Jewish people massively transported there from all the territories now under the influence of the Reich.
>
> . . . Laval had at his disposal many more elements than public opinion to understand that . . . deportation had for the Jews a meaning at least as tragic as the detention in the French camps in the unoccupied zone where approximately 3,000 Jews had already perished, notably in the course of the two preceding winters. How could the high-ranking political, administrative and police figures conceive that the Jews deported to the East

anti-Semitism. Left to itself, Vichy would probably have stopped short of job discrimination and measures calculated to hasten the further emigration of foreign Jews. Vichy xenophobia was more cultural and national than racial, in a French assimilationist tradition . . . Traditional conservative French xenophobia demanded cultural conformity (which any individual may acquire) more insistently than physical resemblance . . . There were racist anti-Semites in France, and with Darquier de Pellepoix in 1942 they even entered the government. But, as long as Vichy had a free hand in Jewish matters, a Catholic and national anti-Semitism rather than a racial anti-Semitism lay at the base of French policy.' Ibid, 174–76 (footnote omitted).

[43] See Rousso, *Le régime de Vichy* 89–90.

[44] ibid, 90.

[45] 6 July 1942. See Rousso, *Le régime de Vichy* 91. See also S Klarsfeld, *La Shoah en France – Vichy-Auschwitz, La «solution finale» de la question juive en France* (Paris, Librairie Arthème Fayard, 1983–1985, reprint 2001) 116. Translation by the author. The French version reads as follows: 'Le Président Laval a proposé que, lors de l'évacuation de familles juives de la zone non occupée, les enfants de moins de 16 ans soient emmenés eux aussi. Quant aux enfants juifs qui resteraient en zone occupée, la question ne l'intéresse pas.'

[46] Klarsfeld, *La Shoah en France* 116. Translation by the author. The original version reads as follows: 'Dans une intention d'humanité, le Chef du Gouvernement a obtenu – contrairement aux premières propositions allemandes – que les enfants, y compris ceux de moins de 16 ans, soient autorisés à accompagner leurs parents'.

would have an acceptable fate when the only means employed by Vichy to treat the 'refuse' had already led thousands to their death?[47]

In spite of Nazi administration, Vichy government retained some authority over the occupied zone and it was French police – acting pursuant to Nazi orders directly relayed by French officials René Bousquet and Jean Leguay – who, on 16 and 17 July 1942, orchestrated the first massive round-up in Paris, proceeding to the arrest of 12,800 foreign Jews – 3,000 men, 5,800 women and 4,000 children of all ages – who were then brought to the Vélodrome d'hiver before being deported and sent to their death. A letter of instruction dated 13 July 1942 and signed by Hennequin, then director of the French municipal police, constitutes excruciating proof of the involvement of the French police in these arrests. It was indeed addressed to all chiefs of police in Paris and its region and contained very precise orders the police teams in charge of the arrests were to follow:

> The Occupying Authorities have decided on the arrest and gathering of a certain number of foreign Jews . . . The measure . . . concerns all the Jews of the above-mentioned nationalities [German, Austrian, Polish, Czechoslovakian, Russian, stateless], regardless of their gender, as long as they are aged from 16 to 60 years old (women from 16 to 55 years old). Children under 16 years of age will be taken with the parents.[48]

Further round-ups occurred in Bordeaux, Rennes, Le Mans and Angers. Henry Rousso reported that, from August to October 1942, 10,500 foreign Jews were transferred from camps located in the unoccupied zone to the transit camp of Drancy and that, by the end of 1942, thus over just a few months, close to 42,000 people were deported to be exterminated.[49] More specifically, Serge Klarsfeld explained that

> Between 27 March and 11 November 1942, 43 deportation convoys took to Auschwitz 41,951 deported, including 6,000 children under 17 years of age. It must however be

[47] S Klarsfeld, *Vichy-Auschwitz, Le Rôle de Vichy dans la Solution Finale de la Question Juive en France – 1942* (Paris, Librairie Arthème Fayard, 1983) 107–09. Translation by the author. The original version reads as follows: 'On est obligé, hélas, de douter de cette volonté humanitaire: il serait absurde d'imaginer que Laval croie réellement en l'intention des Nazis de préparer dans l'Est européen des conditions d'existence acceptables pour les masses juives qui y seront transportées de tous les territoires tombés sous la dépendance ou sous l'influence du Reich . . . Laval disposait de beaucoup plus d'éléments que l'opinion publique pour se représenter que la déportation avait . . . une signification au moins aussi tragique pour les Juifs que l'internement dans les grands camps français de la zone libre, où déjà 3 000 Juifs environ avaient péri, surtout pendant les deux hivers précédents. Comment le haut personnel politique, administratif et policier de Vichy pouvait-il concevoir, pour les Juifs déportés à l'Est, un destin convenable, alors que la seule façon vichyssoise de traiter les «déchets» avait jusque-là conduit des milliers d'entre eux dans la tombe?'

[48] Circulaire n° 173-42, Préfecture de Police, Paris (13 July 1942). Available at the Mémorial de la Shoah. Also reproduced in K Taieb (ed), *Je vous écris du Vel d'Hiv – Les lettres retrouvées* (Paris, Editions Robert Laffont, 2011) 175–83. Translation by the author. The original version reads as follows: 'Les Autorités Occupantes ont décidé l'arrestation et le rassemblement d'un certain nombre de juifs étrangers . . . La mesure . . . concerne tous les juifs des nationalités ci-dessus [Allemands, Autrichiens, Polonais, Tchécoslovaques, Russes, Apatrides], quel que soit leur sexe, pourvu qu'ils soient âgés de 16 à 60 ans (les femmes de 16 à 55 ans). Les enfants de moins de 16 ans seront emmenés en même temps que les parents.'

[49] See Rousso, *Le régime de Vichy* 92.

noted that, between 17 July and 30 September, 34 convoys amounting to 33,057 Jews left. During these 11 weeks of massive help from the Vichy government, the French administration and the French police, 3,000 Jews were deported each week from France.[50]

It was the same French police force which was described by Generalfeldmarshall von Rundstedt as 'cooperative' (*entgegenkommend*) and 'willing' (*bereitwillig*),[51] and whose zealous attitude, in the South of France, was reined in by the Italian authorities, who very efficiently contributed to the round-ups ordered by the Nazi occupier. It was with the active participation of the French police that nearly 80,000 Jews of France were murdered – 3,000 died in French camps, 1,000 were executed as hostages or *Resistants,* and close to 76,000 were deported. Only 2,600 survived.[52] In the words of Henry Rousso, 'without the collaboration of the French government, the Nazis would probably not have been able to deport as many Jews from France'.[53]

Robert Paxton concurred, with this damning conclusion:

> It is true that the Vichy government had not planned to turn discrimination into genocide . . . The fact remains that the Vichy government had tried to single out a group for special contempt and for measures of discrimination. Those measures were a great help to the Germans when the more bestial program of the Final Solution began.[54]

In reaching their verdicts in the respective trials of Paul Touvier and Maurice Papon, the French courts ignored the charge of genocide and found both accused guilty of complicity of crimes against humanity, one for having murdered Jewish men and the other for having supervised the deportation of Jews from France. In doing so, the courts simultaneously qualified the Vichy regime as an accomplice of crimes against humanity; a qualification which does not correspond to the reality of the facts. Paul Touvier the *milicien,* and Maurice Papon, high civil servant in charge of the Jewish affairs in Gironde, were active agents of Vichy's policy. Vichy

[50] Klarsfeld, *Le Rôle de Vichy dans la Solution Finale de la Question Juive en France* 192. Translation by the author. The original version reads as follows: 'Nous sommes en mesure de faire de même pour le bilan des déportations de 1942: on dénombre 43 convois de déportation qui ont emporté vers Auschwitz 41 951 déportés entre le 27 mars et le 11 novembre, dont 6 000 enfants de moins de 17 ans. Mais il faut souligner que 34 convois totalisant 33 057 Juifs sont partis entre le 17 juillet et le 30 septembre. Pendant ces onze semaines de concours massif du gouvernement de Vichy, de l'administration et de la police françaises, 3 000 Juifs par semaine ont été déportés de France.'

[51] See Grosser, *Le crime et la mémoire* 158–59.

[52] See Rousso, *Le régime de Vichy* 93. See also Paxton, *Vichy France – Old Guard and New Order* 183: 'In the end, about 76,000 Jews were deported from France, mostly foreigners who had relied upon traditional French hospitality. About one quarter of them were French citizens. Some 2,600 of the deportees got back' (footnote omitted). See also S Klarsfled, *Le Calendrier de la persécution des Juifs de France* (Paris, 1993), 1125: Serge Klarsfeld, also including the Jews assassinated by the Milice or the SS, and those who died in the French transit camps, reaches an approximate figure of 80,000 victims.

[53] Rousso, *Le régime de Vichy* 95. Translation by the author. The original version reads as follows: 'Sans la collaboration du gouvernement français, les nazis n'auraient sans doute pas pu déporter autant de juifs en France'.

[54] Paxton, *Vichy France – Old Guard and New Order* 184–85.

France contributed heavily to the genocide, and the acts of its agents were crucial in its orchestration.

Such acts would undoubtedly fall within the categories of acts prohibited by the Genocide Convention, which covers killing members of the group, causing serious bodily or mental harm to members of the group, deliberately inflicting on the group conditions of life calculated to bring about its physical destruction in whole or in part, imposing measures intended to prevent births within the group, and forcibly transferring children of the group to another group. Yet, according to the law of genocide, the *actus reus* is not enough and criminal acts may only be characterised as genocidal if perpetrated with the very specific '*intent* to destroy in whole or in part, a national, ethnical, racial, or religious groups, as such'.[55] Not only must the offender have meant to engage in the conduct or to cause the consequences of his or her conduct, he or she must also have had a 'specific intent' or *dolus specialis.* Indeed, it appears from the debates during the drafting of the text that the drafters chose the intent to destroy the group as the distinctive element in genocide,[56] so as to clearly distinguish 'the international crime of genocide from the municipal crime of homicide'.[57]

This is probably where the biggest impediment to the qualification of Vichy's acts as genocide lies, namely in the intent to destroy the group as such. As demonstrated above, historical research has shown that if Vichy undoubtedly facilitated the genocide, it may not have had the intention to destroy the group as such. Yet, and as also demonstrated above, 'Vichy's share of responsibility for the bestial deportations of 1942-44 was probably greater than the German documents themselves would suggest.'[58] Through the enactment and active implementation of anti-Semitic legislation, Vichy France excluded Jews from society, through the active contribution of the French police to the round-ups and arrests of Jews, Vichy France allowed for their brutal murder in death camps, through a willingness to please the occupier and to get rid of all foreign Jews, Vichy France requested the deportation of children. If these acts do not constitute genocide, one can legitimately wonder what types of acts would qualify as genocidal.

Furthermore, the possible doubt regarding genocidal intent cannot reasonably be raised with respect to the cases of Klaus Barbie and Aloïs Brunner, who were also charged with crimes against humanity and not with genocide. Coming to a contrary conclusion would amount at no less than denying the Holocaust the qualification of genocide.

[55] Art II of the Genocide Convention (emphasis added).

[56] 3 UN GAOR, Sixth Committee, 89–87 (1948). Cited in B Bryant 'Comment: The United States and the 1948 Genocide Convention, Part I' (1975) 16 HILJ 692.

[57] ibid. In this respect, Robinson also pointed out that 'from the viewpoint of the minority groups, which are or may be exposed to acts described in the Convention, it makes a great difference whether those who commit these acts against them are prosecuted on that basis or only on the basis of ordinary violations of the criminal code'. See Robinson, *The Genocide Convention – A Commentary* 33–34.

[58] Paxton, *Vichy France – Old Guard and New Order* 183.

9.2 The Criminal Acts of Vichy France: The Question of Genocidal Intent

As mentioned above, the definition of the crime of genocide requires an extremely high standard of proof regarding the mental element in the sense that a very specific 'intent to destroy in whole or in part, a national, ethnical, racial, or religious groups, as such'[59] must exist in order to qualify the act as genocide. The inescapable combination between intent and acts is clearly established by Article II of the Genocide Convention itself, which provides that

> In the present Convention, genocide means any of the following acts committed with intent to destroy, in whole or in part, a national, ethnical, racial or religious group, as such:
>
> (a) Killing members of the group;
> (b) Causing serious bodily or mental harm to members of the group;
> (c) Deliberately inflicting on the group conditions of life calculated to bring about its physical destruction in whole or in part;
> (e) Imposing measures intended to prevent births within the group;
> (f) Forcibly transferring children of the group to another group.[60]

The case law of the international criminal tribunals has strengthened further the interdependence between the genocidal *actus reus* and the genocidal intent. The definition of the crime of genocide indeed falls short of specifying the scope of the different genocidal acts and the tribunals, faced with the brevity of the conventional text, were left with no other choice than to themselves define the meaning of these criminal acts. In so doing, it is striking that they have consistently considered the intent of the perpetrator(s) as the qualifying factor rather than the nature of the acts themselves. Put differently, the acts listed in the conventional definition, while inherently criminal, are only potentially genocidal: they can only be considered as such if, and only if, perpetrated with the very specific intent to destroy the group as such.

9.2.1 Killing Members of the Group

While 'killing members of the group' may seem a fairly straightforward description, it is noticeable nevertheless that '[t]he term "killing" reads oddly in this context. "Killing" is not a term ordinarily used to define crime in English-speaking countries, since it implies no culpability. A killing can be accidental, or in self-defence.'[61] Far from purely theoretical, this choice of terminology raised serious

[59] Art II of the Genocide Convention.
[60] This definition was reproduced verbatim in art 4 of the ICTY Statute; art 2 of the ICTR Statute and art 6 of the ICC Statute.
[61] Quigley, *The Genocide Convention* 94.

questions of interpretation in practice, notably due to the fact that the French version of the Genocide Convention refers to '*meurtre*', a penal qualification requiring culpability, which does not apply to non-culpable homicide. In its groundbreaking *Akayesu* decision, Trial Chamber I of the ICTR addressed the matter by concurring with the French version of the text:

> With regard to Article 2(2)(a) of the Statute, like in the Genocide Convention, the Chamber notes that the said paragraph states '*meurtre*' in the French version while the English version states 'killing'. The Trial Chamber is of the opinion that the term 'killing' used in the English version is too general, since it could very well include both intentional and unintentional homicides, whereas the term '*meurtre*', used in the French version, is more precise. It is accepted that there is murder when death has been caused with the intention to do so, as provided for, incidentally, in the Penal Code of Rwanda which stipulates in its Article 311 that 'Homicide committed with intent to cause death shall be treated as murder'.[62]

This jurisprudential choice in favour of the French terminology was subsequently confirmed by the *Kayishema and Ruzindana* Trial Chamber, which, after noting that the 'French language version refers to *meurtre,* a term that requires the additional mental element of intent',[63] observed that

> the *Akayesu* Judgement does not fully define the term 'killing.' It is the opinion of the Trial Chamber that there is virtually no difference between the term 'killing' in the English version and '*meurtre*' in the French version of Article 2 (2)(a) of the Statute within the context of genocidal intent. Hence 'killing' or 'meurtre' should be considered along with the specific intent of genocide, that is, the intent to destroy in whole or in part, a national, ethnical, racial or religious group as such.[64]

This equivalence between the two versions of the text – and thus the welcomed harmonisation of the law – since became the constant jurisprudential understanding of the term 'killing' as embodied in the Genocide Convention.[65] Having overcome the linguistic issue, it was left for the tribunals to clearly delineate the scope of the act of 'killing members of the group'. The *Musema* Trial Chamber defined 'killing' as 'homicide committed with intent to cause death',[66] Trial Chamber II of the ICTY was itself satisfied that '"[k]illing" in sub-paragraph (a) needs no further explanation. As regards the underlying acts, the word "killing" is understood to refer to intentional but not necessarily premeditated acts.'[67] In other words,

[62] *Akayesu* Trial Judgment para 500. See also *Rutaganda* Trial Judgment para 50; *Musema* Trial Judgment para 155; *Bagilishema* Trial Judgment para 57.

[63] *Kayishema and Ruzindana* Trial Judgment para 101.

[64] ibid, para 104 (footnote omitted).

[65] See eg *Bagilishema* Trial Judgment para 58.

[66] *Musema* Trial Judgment para 155. See also *The Prosecutor v Athanase Seromba* (Trial Chamber) ICTR–2001–66–I (13 December 2006) para 317.

[67] See *The Prosecutor v Milomir Stakić* (Trial Chamber Judgment) IT–97–24–T (31 July 2003) para 515. See also *The Prosecutor v Jean de Dieu Kamuhanda* (Trial Chamber Judgment) ICTR–95–54A–T (22 January 2004) para 632; *The Prosecutor v Emmanuel Bagambiki* (Trial Chamber Judgment) ICTR–97–36 (25 February 2004) para 664.

> In order to be held criminally liable for genocide by killing members of a group, in addition to showing that an accused possessed an intent to destroy the group as such, in whole or in part, the Prosecutor must show the following elements: (1) the perpetrator intentionally killed one or more members of the group, without the necessity of premeditation; and (2) such victim or victims belonged to the targeted ethnical, racial, national, or religious group.[68]

In light of the above, it seems fair to assert that, refraining from any abusive interpretation, the international criminal tribunals linked the qualification of the act of 'killing' as genocidal to the intent to destroy of the perpetrator(s).

9.2.2 Causing Serious Bodily or Mental Harm to Members of the Group

On first reading, the act of 'causing serious bodily or mental harm to members of the group' appears to be a vaguer category than 'killing members of the group', insofar as it seems to cover a whole series of non-fatal acts.[69] Yet this has not discouraged the ICTR's various Trial Chambers from the view that

> to a large extent, 'causing serious bodily harm' is self-explanatory. This phrase could be construed to mean harm that seriously injures the health, causes disfigurement or causes any serious injury to the external, internal organs or senses.[70]

Failing to clearly define the act, the *Krstić* Trial Chamber nonetheless specified that

> The serious bodily or mental harm, included within Article 4 of the Statute, can be informed by the Tribunal's interpretation of the offence of wilfully causing great suffering or serious injury to body or health under Article 2 of the Statute. The latter offence was defined in the *Celebici* Judgement as 'an act or omission that is intentional, being an act which, judged objectively, is deliberate and not accidental, which causes serious mental or physical suffering or injury'.[71]

And that

> serious harm need not cause permanent and irremediable harm, but it must involve harm that goes beyond temporary unhappiness, embarrassment or humiliation. It must be harm that results in a grave and long-term disadvantage to a person's ability to lead a normal and constructive life. In subscribing to the above case-law, the Chamber holds that inhuman treatment, torture, rape, sexual abuse and deportation are among the acts which may cause serious bodily or mental injury.[72]

[68] *The Prosecutor v Laurent Semanza*, (Trial Chamber Judgment) ICTR–97–20–T (15 May 2003) para 319 (footnotes omitted). See also *The Prosecutor v Juvénal Kajelijeli* (Trial Chamber Judgment) ICTR–98–44A–T (1 December 2003) para 813.

[69] See eg *Semanza* Trial Judgment para 320; *Bagambiki* Trial Judgment para 664.

[70] *Kayishema and Ruzindana* Trial Judgment para 109. See also *Semanza* Trial Judgment para 320; *Bagambiki* Trial Judgment para 664; *Seromba* Trial Judgment para 317.

[71] *Krstić,* Trial Judgment para 484 (footnote omitted).

[72] ibid, para 486 (footnote omitted).

Based on the double predicament that both 'serious bodily harm' and 'serious mental harm' are 'not defined in the Statute'[73] and that the act of '[c]ausing serious bodily or mental harm to members of the group does not necessarily mean that the harm is permanent and irremediable',[74] it has been recognised that it includes acts of bodily or mental torture,[75] inhumane or degrading treatment, cruel treatment,[76] persecution,[77] deportation,[78] rape[79] and sexual violence,[80] mutilations and interrogations combined with beatings, and/or threats of death.[81] With respect specifically to serious mental harm, and while expressly acknowledging that '[r]eference to serious mental harm, in the context of the Genocide Convention, appears to have been restricted originally to the injection of pharmacological substances occasioning the serious impairment of mental faculties',[82] the ICTR ultimately opted for a case-by-case determination,[83] finding that 'serious mental harm can be construed as some type of impairment of mental faculties, or harm that causes serious injury to the mental state of the victim'[84] and that it would include such acts as the infliction of strong fear or terror, intimidation or threat[85] while the Appeals Chamber further noted that 'nearly all convictions for the causing of serious bodily or mental harm involve rapes or killings'.[86] Not only does such a list of acts fall outside the express enumeration provided by the Genocide Convention but, even further, the international criminal tribunals have also specified that this list remains illustrative and does not constitute an exhaustive enumeration.[87]

[73] *Semanza* Trial Judgment paras 320–21. In this respect, the ICTR Appeals Chamber expressly referred to the '*quintessential examples* of serious bodily harm [which] are torture, rape, and non-fatal physical violence that causes disfigurement or serious injury to the external or internal organs. *The Prosecutor v Athanase Seromba* (Appeals Chamber Judgment) ICTR–2001–66–A (12 March 2008) para 46 (emphasis added).

[74] *Akayesu* Trial Judgment para 502; *Kayishema and Ruzindana* Trial Judgment para 110; *Rutaganda* Trial Judgment para 51; *Musema* Trial Judgment para 156; *Bagilishema* Trial Judgment para 59; *Semanza* Trial Judgment paras 320–22; *Stakić* Trial Judgment para 516; *Kajelijeli* Trial Judgment para 815.

[75] *The Prosecutor v Mikaeli Muhimana* (Trial Chamber Judgment) ICTR–95–1B–T (28 April 2005) para 502.

[76] *The Prosecutor v Radovan Karadzić and Ratko Mladić* (Review of the Indictments pursuant to Rule 61 of the Rules of Procedure and Evidence) IT–95–5–R61 and IT–95–18–R61 (11 July 1996) para 93.

[77] *Akayesu* Trial Judgment para 504. See also *Rutaganda* Trial Judgment para 51.

[78] *Karadzić and Mladić* Review of the Indictment para 93.

[79] ibid.

[80] *Muhimana* Trial Judgment para 502.

[81] See notably *Akayesu* Trial Judgment paras 706–707 and 711–12. See also *Kayishema and Ruzindana* Trial Judgment para 108; *Stakić* Trial Judgment para 516; *Kajelijeli* Trial Judgment para 815.

[82] *Akayesu* Trial Judgment para 502.

[83] *Kayishema and Ruzindana* Trial Judgment paras 110 and 113.

[84] *The Prosecutor v Sylvestre Gacumbtsi* (Trial Chamber Judgment) ICTR–2001–64–T (17 June 2004) para 291 (footnote omitted). See also *Muhimana* Trial Judgment para 502.

[85] *Kayishema and Ruzindana* Trial Judgment para 110; *Semanza*, Trial Judgment para 321; *Seromba* Appeal Judgment para 46.

[86] *Seromba* Appeal Judgment para 46.

[87] *Akayesu* Trial Judgment para 502; *Kayishema and Ruzindana* Trial Judgment para 110; *Rutaganda* Trial Judgment para 51; *Musema* Trial Judgment para 156; *Semanza* Trial Judgment paras 320–21; *Seromba* Trial Judgment para 317.

At first glance, such findings could be criticised as illustrative of judicial activism which dangerously grazes legislative action. The international criminal tribunals indeed seem to adopt such a wide understanding of the act of 'causing serious bodily or mental harm' that it now covers a whole series of acts which were not initially covered by the conventional scope of application. Yet, an analysis of these findings shows that, here also, the tribunals have put the emphasis on the intent of the perpetrator(s) to qualify the act as genocidal. As they have constantly recalled, '[t]he phrase serious bodily harm should be determined on a case-by-case basis, using a common sense approach'.[88] Using this approach, the international criminal tribunals have consistently considered the intent behind the act to qualify it as genocidal or not, thereby refraining from unduly stretching, and trivialising, the definitional scope of the crime of genocide. As expressly specified by the ICTR Appeals Chamber, the given acts need to be serious enough to trigger their characterisation as genocidal:

> To support a conviction for genocide, the bodily harm or the mental harm inflicted on members of a group must be of such a serious nature as to threaten its destruction in whole or in part.[89]

9.2.3 Deliberately Inflicting on the Group Conditions of Life Calculated to Bring about its Physical Destruction in Whole or in Part

During the drafting of the Convention, the United Nations Secretariat included within the concept of 'physical destruction' of the group 'deprivation of all means of livelihood, by confiscation of property, looting, curtailment of work, denial of housing and of supplies otherwise available to the other inhabitants of the territory concerned'.[90] Due to its alleged lack of clarity, this disposition raised a series of concerns and it was ultimately agreed that:

> If a state systematically denies to members of a certain group its *elementary means of existence* enjoyed by other sections of the population, it condemns such persons to a wretched existence maintained by illicit or clandestine activities and public charity, and in fact condemns them to death at the end of a medium period instead of a quick death in concentration camps; there is only a difference of degree.[91]

Admittedly embodying within the law the Nazi policies carried out in the different ghettos and camps, the above statement probably constitutes more an *ex-post facto* consideration of the crimes perpetrated by the Nazis, than a workable guide for the future. As explained by Nehemiah Robinson,

[88] See eg *Kayishema and Ruzindana* Trial Judgment para 108; *Kajelijeli* Trial Judgment para 815.
[89] ibid (footnote omitted).
[90] Art I(II)(1)(d) of the first draft of the Genocide Convention prepared by the UN Secretariat in 1947.
[91] UN Doc E/447, 25. Emphasis added.

> it is impossible to enumerate in advance the 'conditions of life' that would come within the prohibition of Article II . . . Instances of genocide that could come under subparagraph (c) are such as placing a group of people on a subsistence diet, reducing medical services below a minimum, withholding sufficient living accommodations, etc., provided that these restrictions are imposed with intent to destroy the group in whole or in part.[92]

When, in the first international trial for genocide, the ICTR had to address the notion of 'deliberately inflicting on the group conditions of life calculated to bring about its physical destruction in whole or in part', the Trial Chamber found that this expression 'should be construed as the methods of destruction by which the perpetrator does not immediately kill the members of the group, but which, ultimately, seek their physical destruction'[93] before specifying the material scope of such methods which would 'include, *inter alia*, subjecting a group of people to a subsistence diet, systematic expulsion from homes and the reduction of essential medical services below minimum requirement.'[94]

Interestingly, subsequent case law has taken this opportunity to create the concept of 'slow death genocide', which, although absent from the Genocide Convention, still arguably sits well with the definition it gives of the crime. The *Kayishema and Ruzindana* Trial Chamber indeed expressly concurred

> with the explanation within the Draft Convention, prepared by the UN Secretariat which interpreted this concept to include circumstances which will lead to a slow death, for example, lack of proper housing, clothing, hygiene and medical care or excessive work or physical exertion.[95]

The Trial Chamber was thus able to find that

> 'deliberately inflicting on the group conditions of life calculated to bring about its physical destruction in whole or in part,' includes methods of destruction which do not immediately lead to the death of members of the group. The Chamber adopts the above interpretation. Therefore the conditions of life envisaged include rape, the starving of a group of people, reducing required medical services below a minimum, and withholding sufficient living accommodation for a reasonable period, provided the above would lead to the destruction of the group in whole or in part.[96]

In the *Rutaganda* case, the scope of the act of 'deliberately inflicting on the group conditions of life calculated to bring about its physical destruction in whole or in part' was further seen to include 'subjecting a group of people to a subsistence diet, systematic expulsion from their homes and deprivation of essential medical supplies below a minimum vital standard.'[97]

[92] Robinson, *The Genocide Convention – A Commentary* 64.
[93] *Akayesu* Trial Judgment para 505.
[94] ibid, para 506.
[95] *Kayishema and Ruzindana* Trial Judgment para 115 (footnote omitted). See also *Stakić*, Trial Judgment para 517.
[96] *Kayishema and Ruzindana* Trial Judgment para 116 (footnote omitted).
[97] *Rutaganda* Trial Judgment para 52. See also *Musema* Trial Judgment para 157.

Rather interestingly, it was also found that "[d]eliberately inflicting on the group conditions of life calculated to bring about its physical destruction in whole or in part' under sub-paragraph (c) does not require proof of a result.'[98] In other words, the emphasis is here also put on the genocidal intent with which the act is perpetrated and not on whether the act actually brings about the destruction of the group. The infliction of conditions of life calculated to bring about the physical destruction of the group must be intentional and it is this intent to destroy which will then, and only then, characterise the act as genocidal.

9.2.4 Imposing Measures Intended to Prevent Births within the Group

In his *Commentary of the Genocide Convention*, Nehemiah Robinson had explained that the act of 'imposing measures intended to prevent births within the group' 'need not be the classic action of sterilization; separation of the sexes, prohibition of marriages and of the like are measures equally restrictive and produce the results.'[99] Admittedly following this line of reasoning, the *Akayesu* Trial Chamber specified that:

> For purposes of interpreting Article 2(2)(d) of the Statute, the Chamber holds that the measures intended to prevent births within the group, should be construed as sexual mutilation, the practice of sterilization, forced birth control, separation of the sexes and prohibition of marriages. In patriarchal societies, where membership of a group is determined by the identity of the father, an example of a measure intended to prevent births within a group is the case where, during rape, a woman of the said group is deliberately impregnated by a man of another group, with the intent to have her give birth to a child who will consequently not belong to its mother's group.[100]

The Trial Chamber further observed that such measures intended to prevent births within the group could be both physical and mental:

> measures intended to prevent births within the group may be physical, but can also be mental. For instance, rape can be a measure intended to prevent births when the person raped refuses subsequently to procreate, in the same way that members of a group can be led, through threats or trauma, not to procreate.[101]

[98] *Stakić* Trial Judgment para 517.

[99] Robinson, *The Genocide Convention – A Commentary* 64.

[100] *Akayesu* Trial Judgment para 507. It is worth noting here that this finding did raise some criticism based on its confusion between the crime of genocide and crimes against humanity. See notably the analysis made by Payam Akhavan: 'This appears to confuse biological destruction with the new crime against humanity of "forced pregnancy", which is defined under Art 7(2)(f) of the ICC Statute in relevant part as "the unlawful confinement of a woman forcibly made pregnant, with the intent of affecting the ethnic composition of any population". Preventing births as a form of genocide is conceptually different from forced impregnation intended to affect the ethnic composition of a group.' P Akhavan, 'The Crime of Genocide in the ICTR Jurisprudence' (2005) 3 JICJ, 989, 1005.

[101] *Akayesu* Trial Judgment para 508. See also *Kayishema and Ruzindana* Trial Judgment para 117; *Rutaganda* Trial Judgment para 53; *Musema* Trial Judgment para 158.

If the ICTR here also proceeded to an extensive reading of the definition of the crime of genocide, it here again did so while emphasising the determining aspect of the intent of the perpetrator(s).

9.2.5 Forcibly Transferring Children of the Group to another Group

The Tribunals have unsurprisingly applied the same line of reasoning to the act of 'forcibly transferring children of the group to another group'. As expressly recognised by the *Akayesu* Trial Chamber:

> With respect to forcibly transferring children of the group to another group, the Chamber is of the opinion that, as in the case of measures intended to prevent births, the objective is not only to sanction a direct act of forcible physical transfer, but also to sanction acts of threats or trauma which would lead to the forcible transfer of children from one group to another.[102]

Providing a wide understanding of the act of 'forcibly transferring children of the group to another group', the Trial Chamber nonetheless remained within the ambit of the spirit of the conventional text. Payam Akhavan explains that

> [a]lthough the International Law Commission has considered forcible transfer of children as 'biological' destruction, the *travaux préparatoires* of the Convention indicate that it was conceived as 'cultural destruction', implying destruction of 'the specific characteristics of the group' without its material destruction through physical or biological means.[103]

Here again, it is not solely the nature of the act but also the intent of the perpetrator(s) to destroy one of the conventionally protected groups as such that will trigger the qualification of the act as genocidal. As held by the *Krstić* Trial Chamber, 'any act committed with the intent to destroy a part of a group, as such, constitutes an act of genocide within the meaning of the [Genocide] Convention.'[104]

Where does this preponderance of the intent to destroy in the characterisation of a criminal act as genocidal leave the qualification of the acts perpetrated by Vichy France? As it has been shown earlier, there is no doubt that the Vichy government, through its own anti-Semitic ideology and a politics of shameful obedience, of zealous collaboration and at times of pre-emption of the Nazis' requests, eased and increased the efficiency of the occupier's genocidal enterprise. Yet, as also demonstrated above, the majority of historians tend to agree that 'the Vichy government had not planned to turn discrimination into genocide',[105] that 'it had

[102] *Akayesu* Trial Judgment para 509. See also *Kayishema and Ruzindana* Trial Judgment para 118; *Rutaganda* Trial Judgment para 54; *Musema* Trial Judgment para 159.
[103] Akhavan, 'The Crime of Genocide in the ICTR Jurisprudence' 1005 (footnotes omitted).
[104] *Krstić* Trial Judgment para 584.
[105] Paxton, *Vichy France – Old Guard and New Order* 185.

not, at any point, elaborated a genocidal policy *sui generis*',[106] that '[l]eft to itself, Vichy would probably have stopped short of job discrimination and measures calculated to hasten the further emigration of foreign Jews',[107] while still concurring in the opinion that Vichy still 'actively participated in the "Final Solution"'[108] and 'made the Final Solution much easier'.[109]

Translated in legal terms, Vichy France was thus guilty of complicity in genocide, an act punishable under article III(e) of the Genocide Convention and its agents, including Paul Touvier and Maurice Papon, should thus have been tried for complicity in genocide, rather than for complicity in crimes against humanity. By finding these two individuals guilty of complicity in crimes against humanity, French courts misread the law of genocide – which, as it has been demonstrated, could have been applied in these instances – and simultaneously minimised the responsibility of Vichy France.

9.3 The Criminality of Vichy France: Complicity in Genocide

As previously analysed, French courts did not err in law with respect to the *mens rea* of crimes against humanity. Holding that crimes would only qualify as ones against humanity if the individual was a willing participant in the state's systematic policy of ideological supremacy[110] was indeed arguably compliant with both the law of Nuremberg and contemporary international criminal law. French courts did not misread the law of crimes against humanity with respect to the *mens rea* of accomplices either. Where they erred is in applying the law of crimes against humanity rather than the law of genocide, an error which culminated in the absurd finding in the *Papon* case that one of Vichy's high civil servants could have been unaware of the Nazi extermination plan. That Maurice Papon did not know of the unimaginable horror of the death camps, and that he could not have guessed the extent of the atrocities being perpetrated, is possible. That he however remained ignorant of the fate awaiting those being deported, under his authorisation, is incoherent and impossible to believe.

Applying the law of genocide and finding both Paul Touvier and Maurice Papon guilty of complicity in genocide would thus have been a more adequate qualification of their criminal acts, and a more accurate reflection of their individual criminal responsibility. As previously demonstrated, there was no obstacle for French courts to apply the Genocide Convention, in which article III(e)

[106] Rousso, *Le régime de Vichy* 78. Translation by the author. The original version reads as follows: 'À aucun moment il n'a élaboré de politique génocidaire *sui generis*'.

[107] Paxton, *Vichy France – Old Guard and New Order* 174.

[108] Rousso, *Le régime de Vichy* 78. Translation by the author. The original version reads as follows: 'il a participé activement à la «Solution finale»'.

[109] Paxton, *Vichy France – Old Guard and New Order* 184.

[110] See generally Lyon-Caen, 'De Nuremberg au Procès Barbie' 58–59.

expressly criminalises complicity in genocide. Such a finding would however have implied a recognition by French courts that the crime of genocide had indeed been committed: there can logically be no complicity in a crime if there is no such crime in the first place. As held by the *Akayesu* Trial Chamber,

> complicity can only exist when there is a punishable, principal act, in the commission of which the accomplice has associated himself. Complicity, therefore, implies a predicate offence committed by someone other than the accomplice . . . [F]or an accused to be found guilty of complicity of genocide, it must, first of all, be proven . . . that the crime of genocide has, indeed, been committed.[111]

Considering however that the crimes for which the accused stood trial before French courts were nothing less than committed in the context of the Nazi enterprise of destruction, the qualification of the event as genocide obviously would not have been an issue.

With respect to the *actus reus* of complicity in genocide, insofar as both Paul Touvier and Maurice Papon were agents of the Vichy government which facilitated the genocide through active collaboration, qualifying their criminal acts as forms of accomplice participation in genocide would have been more appropriate. It would also have been later confirmed by international criminal case law, the analysis of which shows that the crimes being tried before French courts in these instances fitted the definition of complicity in genocide. As a matter of fact, the *Semanza* Trial Chamber held that 'complicity to commit genocide in Article 2(3)(e) refers to all acts of assistance or encouragement that have substantially contributed to, or have had a substantial effect on, the completion of the crime of genocide.'[112] As also specified by the *Bagilishema* Trial Chamber, here recalling the findings in *Akayesu*,[113]

> With regard to the *actus reus* of complicity in genocide, the Chamber notes that, under Common Law, the forms of accomplice participation are usually defined as 'aiding and abetting, counselling and procuring'. On the other hand, in most Civil Law systems, three forms of accomplice participation are recognised: complicity by instigation, by aiding and abetting, and by procuring means. The Rwandan Penal Code, in its Article 91, defines, *inter alia*, these three forms of complicity:
>
> '(a) Complicity by procuring means, such as weapons, instruments or any other means, used to commit genocide, with the accomplice knowing that such means would be used for such a purpose;
> (b) Complicity by knowingly aiding or abetting a perpetrator of a genocide in the planning or enabling acts thereof;
> (c) Complicity by instigation, for which a person is liable who, though not directly participating in the crime of genocide, gave instructions to commit genocide, through gifts, promises, threats, abuse of authority or power, machinations or culpable artifice, or who directly incited the commission of genocide.'[114]

[111] *Akayesu* Trial Judgment paras 527–31. See also *Musema* Trial Judgment paras 170–73.
[112] *Semanza* Trial Judgment paras 393, 395
[113] *Akayesu* Trial Judgment paras 533–37. See also *Musema* Trial Judgment para 179; *Bagilishema* Trial Judgment paras 69–70.
[114] *Bagilishema* Trial Judgment para 69 (footnote omitted).

As regards complicity by aiding and abetting genocide more specifically, which should admittedly have been the form of complicity referred to in the cases of Paul Touvier and Maurice Papon, the ICTR Appeals Chamber recalled that

> to establish the *actus reus* of aiding and abetting under Article 6(1) of the Statute, it must be proven that the alleged aider and abettor committed acts specifically aimed at assisting, encouraging, or lending moral support for the perpetration of a specific crime, and that this support had a substantial effect on the perpetration of the crime. [115]

With respect to the *mens rea*, retaining a form of complicity in genocide for both Paul Touvier and Maurice Papon would also have been more satisfactory – even if the question of genocidal intent, central to the qualification of an act as genocidal, might have arguably proven critical insofar as whether such intent is also required in the context of complicity in genocide is unclear.

The *Akayesu* Trial Chamber had unequivocally held that the *mens rea* 'required for complicity in genocide is *knowledge* of the genocidal plan'[116] and that it implies 'that, at the moment he acted, the accomplice *knew* of the assistance he was providing in the commission of the principal offence. In other words, the accomplice must have acted knowingly'.[117] The Trial Chamber had also added that he was not required to 'wish that the principal offence be committed'[118] and that 'anyone who knowing of another's criminal purpose, voluntarily aids him or her in it, can be convicted of complicity even though he regretted the outcome of the offence.'[119]

The Trial Chamber made it very clear that complicity in genocide did not require genocidal intent, ruling that the intent of the accomplice is

> to knowingly aid or abet one or more persons to commit the crime of genocide . . . [A]n accomplice to genocide need not necessarily possess the *dolus specialis* of genocide, namely the specific intent to destroy, in whole or in part, a national, ethnic, racial or religious group, as such . . . [A]n accused is liable as an accomplice to genocide if he knowingly aided or abetted or instigated one or more persons in the commission of genocide, while knowing that such a person or persons were committing genocide, even though the accused himself did not have the specific intent to destroy, in whole or in part, a national, ethnical, racial or religious group, as such.[120]

Taking an opposite stand however, the *Semanza* Trial Chamber subsequently stated that '[t]he accused must have acted intentionally and with the awareness that he was contributing to the crime of genocide, including all its material elements.'[121] This conflicting case law has yet to be settled and, as observed by Elies van Sliedregt,

[115] *Seromba* Appeal Judgment para 44 (footnote omitted).
[116] *Akayesu* Trial Judgment para 544 (emphasis added).
[117] ibid, para 538 (emphass added).
[118] ibid.
[119] ibid, para 539.
[120] ibid, paras 540–45. See also *Musema* Trial Judgment para 183; *Bagilishema* Trial Judgment para 71.
[121] *Semanza* Trial Judgment para 395

> [i]t remains unclear, however, exactly what the appropriate mental standard for other types of complicity in genocide comprises. The rather enigmatic phrase that 'there is authority to suggest that complicity in genocide, where it prohibits conduct broader than aiding and abetting, requires proof that the accomplice had the specific intent to destroy a protected group',[122] stated in a footnote in the *Krstić* appeal judgment and reiterated in the *Milošević* Acquittal Decision,[123] leaves the issues of complicity in genocide unresolved.[124]

Yet, the *mens rea* requirement with regards to aiding and abetting genocide seems less problematic and the different judicial decisions all concur in the finding that it does not require such intent: knowledge of genocidal intent suffices.[125] For instance, in the *Blagojević and Jokić* case, the Trial Chamber held that:

> An individual may be held responsible for aiding and abetting genocide if it is shown that he assisted in the commission of the crime *in the knowledge of the principal perpetrator's specific intent.* Aiding and abetting genocide is therefore defined by the following elements:
>
> – the accused carried out an act which consisted of practical assistance, encouragement or moral support to the principal that had a 'substantial effect' on the commission of the crime;
> – the accused had knowledge that his or her own acts assisted in the commission of the specific crime by the principal offender; and
> – the accused knew that the crime was committed with specific intent.[126]

As further explained by Elies van Sliedregt,

> [t]here has been confusion at both the ICTR and the ICTY on the interpretation of 'aiding and abetting genocide' and 'complicity in genocide'. The former is encapsulated as a mode of non-genocidal liability in Article 6(1)/7(1) of the ICTR/Y Statutes; the latter is penalized as a form of genocide in Article 2/4(3)(e) of the ICTR/Y Statutes.[127]

These doubts regarding the *mens rea* of complicity in genocide notwithstanding, insofar as genocidal intent, that is the very specific intent to destroy the group as such, is not required for aiding and abetting in genocide, both Paul Touvier and Maurice Papon could have been convicted of this form of complicity in genocide rather than of complicity in crimes against humanity. Not only could article III(e) of the Genocide Convention have been applied, but its interpretation as 'aiding

[122] *The Prosecutor v Radislav Krstić* (Appeals Chamber Judgment) IT–98–33–A (19 April 2004) footnote 247 (footnote in original).

[123] *The Prosecutor v Slobodan Milošević* (Decision on Motion for Judgment of Acquittal) IT–02–54 (16 June 2004) para 248 (footnote in original).

[124] E van Sliedregt, 'Joint Criminal Enterprise as a Pathway to Convicting Individuals for Genocide' (2007) 5 JICJ 184, 194–95.

[125] *Krstić* Appeal Judgment para 140. See also *The Prosecutor v Elizaphan Ntakirutimana* (Appeals Chamber Judgment) 1: ICTR–96–10 and 2: ICTR–96–17 (13 December 2004) para 364.

[126] *The Prosecutor v Vidoje Blagojević and Dragan Jokić* (Trial Chamber Judgment) IT–02–60–T (17 January 2005) para 782 (emphasis added).

[127] van Sliedregt, 'Joint Criminal Enterprise as a Pathway to Convicting Individuals for Genocide' 194.

and abetting' would also have been supported by the *travaux préparatoires* of the Convention – available at the time of the *Touvier* and *Papon* trials – which had defined complicity in genocide as 'accessorship before and after the act, and to aiding and abetting in the commission of any of the crimes enumerated in the Convention'.[128] Incidentally, it would also have implied Vichy France's responsibility in the genocide that was taking place on its territory, against the people under its jurisdiction and with the active help of its agents.

As mentioned earlier, the issue of genocidal intent in the respective cases of Klaus Barbie and Aloïs Brunner would not have impeded their conviction for genocide rather than for crimes against humanity. If genocidal intent 'is a mental factor which is difficult, even impossible, to determine', and which, without the confession of the accused, can only be 'inferred from a certain number of presumptions of fact',[129] it seems reasonable to point here that even the strictest understanding of such specific intent to destroy a group as such would not have hampered the qualification of the acts perpetrated by Klaus Barbie and Aloïs Brunner as genocidal. Not only would there have been direct explicit evidence but, even in cases of doubt, facts and circumstances would have been overwhelmingly revealing of their genocidal intent. As held by the ICTY Appeals Chamber in the *Jelisic* case:

> As to proof of specific intent, it may, in the absence of direct explicit evidence, be inferred from a number of facts and circumstances, such as the general context, the perpetration of other culpable acts systematically directed against the same group, the scale of atrocities committed, the systematic targeting of victims on account of their membership of a particular group, or the repetition of destructive and discriminatory acts.[130]

It is now settled case law to consider that the specific genocidal intent to destroy, in whole or in part, a group as such requires an intentional attack against this group combined with the intent to participate in or carry out the attack. As ruled by the *Jelisić* Trial Chamber, there must have been 'both an intentional attack against a group and an intention upon the part of the accused to participate in or

[128] See the draft of the *Ad Hoc* Committee. See Robinson, *The Genocide Convention – A Commentary* 69. It is worth noting here that the very first draft of the Convention, prepared by the United Nations Secretariat in 1947, did not refer to complicity in genocide.

[129] *Akayesu* Trial Judgment para 523. Already in his 1985 Report, Whitaker suggested that 'a court should be able to infer the necessary intent from sufficient evidence'. See *Whitaker Report* 19, para 39. See also *Rutaganda* Trial Judgment paras 61–63: '[I]ntent can be, on a case-by-case basis, inferred from the material evidence submitted to the Chamber, including the evidence which demonstrates a consistent pattern of conduct by the Accused'; *Musema* Trial Judgment para 167; *Semanza* Trial Judgment para 313: 'A perpetrator's *mens rea* may be inferred from his actions'; *Bagilishema* Trial Judgment para 63: '[E]vidence of the context of the alleged culpable acts may help the Chamber to determine the intention of the Accused, especially where the intention is not clear from what that person says or does. The Chamber notes, however, that the use of context to determine the intent of an accused must be counterbalanced with the actual conduct of the Accused. The Chamber is of the opinion that the Accused's intent should be determined, above all, from his words and deeds, and should be evident from patterns of purposeful action.'

[130] *Jelisić* Appeal Judgment para 47. See also *Akayesu* Trial Judgment paras 523–24; *Kayishema and Ruzindana* Trial Judgment para 93; *Musema* Trial Judgment para 166.

carry out this attack',[131] two elements which were undoubtedly met in the cases of Barbie and Brunner, even if they both stood accused before French courts for crimes perpetrated in France.

In this regard, it is worth recalling that the Genocide Convention applies to both genocide 'in whole' and genocide 'in part', meaning that it is not necessary for the crime to be perpetrated against the whole group for the crime of genocide to qualify as such, as subsequently confirmed by international criminal case law. A series of criteria have indeed been judicially elaborated so as to establish genocidal intent and thus the perpetration of genocide when not committed 'in whole'. The international criminal tribunals have notably relied on the geographical criterion to explicitly find that genocide could be committed even on a restricted geographical scale. As held in the *Krstić* case, 'the intent to eradicate a group within a limited geographical area such as the region of a country or even a municipality' could be considered as genocidal,[132] a finding subsequently confirmed by the Appeals Chamber:

> The historical examples of genocide also suggest that the area of the perpetrators' activity and control, as well as the possible extent of their reach, should be considered. Nazi Germany may have intended only to eliminate Jews within Europe alone; that ambition probably did not extend, even at the height of its power, to an undertaking of that enterprise on a global scale. Similarly, the perpetrators of genocide in Rwanda did not seriously contemplate the elimination of the Tutsi population beyond the country's borders. The intent to destroy formed by a perpetrator of genocide will always be limited by the opportunity presented to him. While this factor alone will not indicate whether the targeted group is substantial, it can – in combination with other factors – inform the analysis.[133]

Next to the geographical approach, the international criminal tribunals have also elaborated a quantitative criterion, relying on the number of victims to infer genocidal intent. As already pointed out by Nehemiah Robinson in his early *Commentary* of the Genocide Convention, the characterisation of genocide requires a substantial number of victims, even if it is left to the courts to decide in each case whether 'the number was *sufficiently large*'.[134] Similarly, Special Rapporteur Whitaker believed that the term 'in part' implied 'a *reasonably significant number*, relative to the total of the group as a whole, or else a significant section of a group such as its leadership'.[135] On the judicial front, the ICTR merely found that there must be a *'considerable number'* of victims for the crime to qualify as genocide,[136] while the ICTY admittedly remained equally cryptic, referring to a *'substantial'* part, although not neccessarily a *'very important part'*.[137] Perhaps

[131] *Jelisić* Trial Judgment para 78

[132] *Krstić* Trial Judgment para 589. See also *The Prosecutor v Dusko Sikirica, Damir Dosen and Dragan Kolundžija* (Judgment on Defence Motions to Acquit) IT–95–8 (3 September 2001) para 68.

[133] *Krstić* Appeal Judgment para 13.

[134] Robinson, *The Genocide Convention – A Commentary* 58 (emphasis added).

[135] *Whitaker Report* 16, para 29 (emphasis added).

[136] *Kayishema and Ruzindana* Trial Judgment para 97 (emphasis added).

[137] *Jelisić* Trial Judgment para 82 (emphasis added).

predictably, the conventional uncertainty generated conflicting case law, as tellingly illustrated by the *Krstić* case, when the Trial Chamber had to determine whether genocidal intent existed in an instance where only military-aged men had been targeted:

> The Bosnian Serb forces could not have failed to know, by the time they decided to kill all the men, that this selective destruction of the group would have a lasting impact upon the entire group . . . By killing all the military aged men, the Bosnian Serb forces effectively destroyed the community of the Bosnian Muslims in Srebrenica as such and eliminated all likelihood that it could ever re-establish itself on that territory.[138]

Using the judicially created concept of 'the group as a distinct entity' in order to assess the commission of genocide, the Trial Chamber accordingly found that the killing of all military-aged men amounted to genocide and further explained that:

> The Trial Chamber is therefore of the opinion that the intent to destroy a group, even if only in part, means seeking to destroy a *distinct part of the group* as opposed to an accumulation of isolated individuals within it. Although the perpetrators of genocide need not seek to destroy the entire group protected by the Convention, they must view the part of the group they wish to destroy as a *distinct entity* which must be eliminated as such. A campaign resulting in the killings, in different places spread over a broad geographical area, of a finite number of members of a protected group might not thus qualify as genocide, despite the high total number of casualties, because it would not show an intent by the perpetrators to target the very existence of the group as such. Conversely, the killing of all members of the part of a group located within a small geographical area, although resulting in a lesser number of victims, would qualify as genocide if carried out with the intent to destroy the part of the group as such located in this small geographical area. Indeed, the physical destruction may target only a part of the geographically limited part of the larger group because the perpetrators of the genocide regard the intended destruction as sufficient to annihilate *the group as a distinct entity* in the geographic area at issue. In this regard, it is important to bear in mind the total context in which the physical destruction is carried out.[139]

Only one month after the *Krstić* judgment however, the *Sikirica* Trial Chamber reached an opposite conclusion,[140] and it thus had to be waited for the Appeals Chamber to ultimately concur with the *Krstić* Trial Chamber to see the matter solved.[141]

Finally, the international criminal tribunals have also developed a more qualitative approach to trigger the qualification of genocide 'in part'. Already in his report on the Convention, Benjamin Whitaker had pointed out that the term 'in part' implied 'a reasonably significant number, relative to the total of the group as a whole, or else a *significant section of a group such as its leadership*',[142] an under-

[138] ibid, paras 595–97.
[139] ibid, para 590 (emphasis added).
[140] See *Sikirica* Judgment on Defence Motions to Acquit paras 55–97.
[141] *Krstić* Appeal Judgment para 23.
[142] *Whitaker Report* 16, para 29 (emphasis added).

standing subsequently upheld by the international criminal tribunals[143] which found that a 'targeted part of a group would be classed as substantial either because the intent sought to harm a large majority of the group in question or the most representative members of the targeted community'[144] and that the 'important element here is the targeting of a selective number of persons who, by reason of their special qualities of leadership within the group as a whole, are of such importance that their victimisation within the terms of Article 4(2)(a), (b) and (c) would impact upon the survival of the group, as such.'[145]

It thus seems clear that the qualification of the acts perpetrated by Klaus Barbie and Aloïs Brunner respectively fell within the definitional scope of the crime of genocide. As largely evidenced by the case law, there is no need for the genocider to target the group as a whole for his acts to qualify as genocide: if the acts were perpetrated with the intent to destroy the group as such – and in these two instances they overwhelmingly were – they are constitutive of genocide. By erroneously considering as individuals the Jewish victims of Barbie and Brunner, rather than as members of a group targeted for destruction, the French courts ultimately equated all the crimes perpetrated by these two defendants, thereby failing to grasp the specificity of the crime of genocide.

[143] See eg *Jelisić* Trial Judgment para 82; *Krstić* Trial Judgment paras 585–87; *Sikirica* Judgment on Defence Motions to Acquit para 77.

[144] *Jelisić* Trial Judgment para 82 (emphasis in original).

[145] *Sikirica* Judgment on Defence Motions to Acquit paras 76–77.

10

Responding to the Equalisation of Victims in the *Barbie* Case

As demonstrated in the previous analysis of the *Barbie* case, the French Cour de cassation defined crimes against humanity as committed 'against *individuals* by reason of their belonging to a racial or religious community as well as against the adversaries of this policy, whatever the form of their opposition – whether armed or not'.[1] Unlike the different international definitions of crimes against humanity which have all characterised the crimes as committed 'against any civilian population',[2] the French definition refers to 'individuals' as victims of such crimes.

This definition had been applauded at the time for allowing French courts to bypass the statutory limitations imposed by the qualification of war crimes and to thus try and punish atrocities perpetrated against *Resistance* fighters. The legal technicalities notwithstanding, the finding in *Barbie* also explicitly extended the scope of application of crimes against humanity to combatants, thereby constituting a legitimate and appropriate recognition that the crimes committed against the opponents of the Nazi occupiers and the Vichy government were indeed crimes against humanity rather than war crimes; a finding which was subsequently upheld in international criminal case law.[3]

Yet, in substituting the qualification of war crimes with that of crimes against humanity with respect to *Resistance* fighters, while maintaining the latter characterisation with respect to the crimes perpetrated against Jews, the French court applied the same law to crimes which were inherently different. If the acts committed against *Resistance* fighters were indeed committed against individuals, or in contemporary international criminal law language, against a civilian population, those perpetrated against Jews were directed at a group so as to orchestrate its full annihilation.[4]

[1] *Fédération Nationale des Déportés et Internés Résistants et Patriotes et Autres c Klaus Barbie*, cass crim, 20 December 1985 (emphasis added). See Lyon-Caen, 'De Nuremberg au Procès Barbie' 56.

[2] See art 6(c) of the IMT Charter; art II(c) of CCL N° 10; art 18 of the ILC 1996 Draft Code of Crimes, [1996] II(2) *ILC Yearbook* 47; art 5 of the ICTY Statute; art 3 of the ICTR Statute; art 7(1) of the ICC Statute.

[3] See above. See *Akayesu* Trial Judgment paras 569–76; *The Prosecutor v Mile Mrkšić et al* (Review of the Indictment Pursuant to Rule 61 of the Rules of Procedure and Evidence) IT–95–13–R61 (3 April 1996) para 29; *Tadić* Trial Judgment paras 639, 641 and 643.

[4] It is worth noting here that the 'Elements of Crimes' adopted by the Preparatory Commission specify that '*one or more* persons' may be the victim of the crime of genocide. See Elements of Crimes,

In failing to qualify the crimes perpetrated against Jews as genocide, the French Cour de cassation simultaneously fell short of adequately acknowledging the specificity of the crimes, and of their victims as members of a group which, as such, was destined to destruction. And indeed, as mentioned earlier, the central element of the crime of genocide is a very specific intent to destroy a 'national, ethnical, racial or religious *group* as such'.[5] In fact, the notion of group victim of genocide is so important that any form of identification of the group by deduction, analogy or similar reasoning is excluded. Proving rather proactive, the *Jelisić* Trial Chamber had been tempted to turn to a negative approach to define the victim group,[6] an attitude swiftly refuted by the *Stakić* Trial Chamber which argued that in 'cases where more than one group is targeted, it is not appropriate to define the group in general terms, as, for example, "non-Serbs"'.[7] In its subsequent upholding of the findings of the Trial Chamber, the ICTY Appeals Chamber in *Stakić*[8] unequivocally affirmed that 'genocide was originally conceived of as the destruction of a race, tribe, nation, or other group with a particular positive identity – not as the destruction of various people lacking a distinct identity.'[9]

It is this 'distinct identity' of the members of the group targeted that constitutes the very essence of the crime of genocide. If the selective protection of groups under article II of the Genocide Convention has been heavily criticised, the fact that the crime had to be perpetrated against a group to qualify as genocide, however, remained uncontroversial – what proved problematic is the assessment of the existence of a group as an objective entity targeted for destruction.

Problematically, the Genocide Convention merely refers to 'national, ethnical, racial [and] religious' groups,[10] without providing for any form of indication as to what these categories of groups cover in reality. While it could be argued that such definition was unnecessary, groups being by their very nature objective entities, the reality proved somewhat different. The confusing aspect of this group classification had already emerged during the drafting of the conventional text, when it

art 6(a)(1) (emphasis added). As had already been explained by Pieter Drost, 'both as a question of theory and as a matter of principle nothing in the present [Genocide] Convention prohibits its provisions to be interpreted and applied to *individual cases* of murder by reason of the national, racial, ethnical or religious qualities of the *single victim* if the murderous attack was done with the intent to commit similar acts in the future and in connection with the first crime.' PN Drost, *The Crime of State – Penal Protection for Fundamental Freedoms of Persons and Peoples, Book II: Genocide,* United Nations Legislation on International Criminal Law (Leyden: A.W. Sythoff, 1959) 85. Interestingly, s 6 of the 2002 German Code of Crimes Against International Law explicitly provides that a single act could qualify as genocide if perpetrated with genocidal intent. See S Wirth, 'Germany's New International Crimes Code: Bringing a Case to Court' (2003) JICJ 151, 155.

[5] Art II of the Genocide Convention (emphasis added).

[6] *Jelisić* Trial Judgment para 71.

[7] *Stakić* Trial Judgment para 512.

[8] *The Prosecutor v Milomir Stakić* (Appeals Chamber Judgment) IT–97–24–A (22 March 2006) para 28.

[9] ibid, para 21.

[10] ibid.

had been argued that 'ethnic' was equivalent to both 'racial' and 'national',[11] and when the distinction between religious groups and national groups proved controversial.[12] Notwithstanding the fact that the reference to 'racial' groups is highly questionable, if not altogether literally racist, it also appears that, from its very inception, the categorisation drawn by the conventional text, by ignoring the interweaving of the different groups, proved artificial and hardly a workable tool. In the words of Pieter Drost,

> a convention on genocide cannot effectively contribute to the protection of certain described minorities when it is limited to particular defined groups . . . it serves no purpose to restrict international legal protection to some groups; firstly, because the protected members always belong at the same time to other unprotected groups.[13]

As the first international instances in which the Genocide Convention was applied, the international criminal tribunals had to define the groups protected; a task that proved rather arduous, even in 'obvious' cases of genocide, as illustrated by the improbable and extensive interpretation of the conventional text by the *Akayesu* Trial Chamber. And indeed, as Tutsis did not fit in any of the conventional categories,[14] the Trial Chamber decided to twist the letter of the law, reading into the conventional text that it was meant to cover 'permanent and stable' groups, [15] an argument which however fails to convince.[16]

More specifically, the Trial Chamber also individually defined the different groups conventionally protected, holding that 'a national group is defined as a collection of people *who are perceived* to share a legal bond based on common citizenship, coupled with reciprocity of rights and duties';[17] 'an ethnic group is

[11] See 3 UN GAOR C6 (75th meeting), 115–16, UN Doc A/633 (1948). Cited in LJ LeBlanc, 'The United Nations Genocide Convention and Political Groups: Should the United States Propose an Amendment?' (1988) 13 YJIL 268, 271.

[12] See Report of the *Ad Hoc* Committee on Genocide, 3 UN ESCOR Supp 6, UN Doc E/794 (1948), 6.

[13] Drost, *The Crime of State – Penal Protection for Fundamental Freedoms of Persons and Peoples, Book II: Genocide*, 122–23.

[14] The Tutsis are not really a different ethnic group, compared to the Hutus: they share the same language, and probably the same culture: 'The Hutu and the Tutsi cannot even correctly be described as ethnic groups for they both speak the same language and respect the same traditions and taboos. It would be extremely difficult to find any kind of cultural or folkloric custom that was specifically Hutu or Tutsi... [There] were certainly distinguishable *social categories* in existence before the arrival of the colonisers, but the differences between them were not based on ethnic or racial divisions. [The colonisers reinforced the antagonism between Hutus and Tutsis which] has since become absorbed by the people themselves'. A Destexhe, *Rwanda and Genocide in the Twentieth Century* (London, Pluto Press, 1995) 36 (emphasis added).

[15] *Akayesu* Trial Judgment paras 511–16 and para 701.

[16] Only one day after the adoption of the Genocide Convention, the General Assembly adopted the UDHR, under which Arts 15(2) and 18 expressly recognise the rights to change nationality as well as religion, respectively. Art 15(2) provides that 'No one shall be ... denied the right to change his nationality' and Art 18 that 'Everyone has the right to ... freedom to change his religion'. In the words of the UK representative, the Genocide Convention 'should also provide protection to groups the members of which were as free to leave them as they were to join them. National or religious groups were obvious instances of that kind.' UN GAOR, 6th Committee, 3rd session, 69th Meeting, (1948), para 60 of the official records of the 3rd session of the General Assembly.

[17] *Akayesu* Trial Judgment para 512 (emphasis added).

generally defined as a group whose members share a common language or culture';[18] a 'racial group is based on the hereditary physical traits often identified with a geographical region, irrespective of linguistic, cultural, national or religious factors';[19] and a 'religious group is one whose members share the same religion, denomination or mode of worship'.[20]

If the *Akayesu* Trial Chamber here recognised the intrinsic subjectivity of national groups, subsequent case law extended the defining characteristic of the 'perception by others' to the other groups conventionally protected. For instance, the *Kayishema and Ruzindana* Trial Chamber gave a rather wide definition of 'ethnic group' as a group 'whose members share a common language and culture; or, a group which distinguishes itself as such (self identification); or, a group *identified as such by others*, including perpetrators of the crimes (identification by others)'.[21]

Adopting a more general stance, the ICTY acknowledged the near impossibility of defining the different groups protected based on objective criteria, and opted for an understanding of the notion of group that would integrate both objective and subjective components:

> To attempt to differentiate each of the named groups on the basis of scientifically objective criteria would thus be inconsistent with the object and purpose of the Convention . . . A group's cultural, religious, ethnical or national characteristics must be identified within the socio-historic context which it inhabits. As in the *Nikolic* and *Jelisic* cases, the Chamber identifies the relevant group by using as a criterion the stigmatisation of the group, notably by the perpetrators of the crime, on the basis of its perceived national, ethnical, racial or religious characteristics.[22]

Occurrences of genocide have shown that '[g]enerally, it is the perpetrator of genocide who defines the individual victim's status as a member of a group protected by the Convention'[23] and the judicial acknowledgement of the importance of subjective elements in determining the perpetration of genocide is thus to be welcomed as an accurate reflection of the specificity of the crime. As explained by the *Bagilishema* Trial Chamber, 'the perpetrators of genocide may characterize the targeted group in ways that do not fully correspond to conceptions of the group shared generally, or by other segments of society.'[24] Although expressing the view that 'a subjective definition alone is not enough to determine victim groups',[25] the *Rutaganda* Trial Chamber also recognised that 'for the purposes of applying the Genocide Convention, membership of a group is, in essence, a subjective rather than an objective concept. The victim is perceived by the perpetrator of genocide

[18] ibid, para 513.
[19] ibid, para 514.
[20] ibid, para 515. See also *Kayishema and Ruzindana* Trial Judgment para 98.
[21] ibid (emphasis added).
[22] *Krstić* Trial Judgment paras 556–57 (footnotes omitted).
[23] Schabas, *Genocide in International Law* 125.
[24] *Bagilishema* Trial Judgment para 65.
[25] *Rutaganda* Trial Judgment para 57. See also *Musema* Trial Judgment para 162.

as belonging to a group slated for destruction.'[26] The necessity to adopt a semi-subjective approach also seems to justify judicial recourse to a case-by-case assessment of the facts by the judicial instances:

> The determination of whether a group comes within the sphere of protection created by Article 2 of the Statute ought to be assessed on a case-by-case basis by reference to the *objective* particulars of a given social or historical context, and by the *subjective* perceptions of the perpetrators.[27]

Adopting a similar view, the *Blagojević and Jokić* Trial Chamber found that the qualification of the group could be achieved 'by using as a criterion the stigmatisation of the group, notably by the perpetrators of the crime, on the basis of its perceived national, ethnical, racial or religious characteristics',[28] and further held that 'the correct determination of the relevant protected group has to be made on a case-by-case basis, consulting both objective and subjective criteria.'[29]

Yet, no matter how reasonable and justifiable the judicial comprehension of protected groups might be, the fact remains that subjectivity sits at odds with legal predictability and could ultimately hamper the effective adjudication of the crime. In the words of William Schabas, 'the label "group" is flexible'[30] and the fact is that, just like subjectivity, flexibility does not sit well with legal certainty and could impede effective prosecution.

In a sense, the international criminal tribunals cannot be criticised for having turned to subjectivity to define the victim group, insofar as subjectivity is intrinsic to the concept of genocide itself and as the targeted groups might only exist, as

[26] *Rutaganda* Trial Judgment para 56. See also *Musema* Trial Judgment para 161; *Kajelijeli* Trial Judgment para 811; *Gacumbtsi* Trial Judgment para 254.

[27] *Semanza* Trial Judgment para 317 (emphasis in original). See also *Musema* Trial Judgment para 163; *Kajelijeli* Trial Judgment para 811; *Seromba* Trial Judgment para 318.

[28] *Krstić* Trial Judgment para 557.

[29] *Blagojević and Jokić* Trial Judgment para 667.

[30] Schabas, *Genocide in International Law* 123. In this respect, it is worth noting that an overview of domestic legislation also shows that the lack of detailed definitions in the conventional provisions left States Parties with significant discretion as to the groups which are to be protected. As 'defining the groups more precisely was presumably left to the implementing legislation which parties to the Convention are to adopt in accordance with Article V', 'different states have varying definitions of protected groups and problems could arise in interpreting and applying the Convention'. LeBlanc, 'The United Nations Genocide Convention and Political Groups: Should the United States Propose an Amendment?' 271–72. It is for instance striking that, while the Convention famously excludes political and social groups from its protective ambit, some domestic provisions chose to depart from the conventional sphere, thereby raising questions as to possible interpretations of the Convention in the future. See notably Art 211-1 of the French New Penal Code; Art 281 of the Ethiopian Penal Code (1957); Art 373 of the Costa Rican Penal Code and Art 127 of the Costa Rican Penal Code Project (1998), which offers an extremely wide protection as the definition of genocide covers groups identified by gender, age, political, sexual, social, economic, or civil factors; Art 319 of the Peruvian Penal Code (1998); Art 356 of the Romanian Socialist Republic Penal Code (1976). It may be recalled here that, in its Resolution 96(I) on the crime of genocide, the UN General Assembly expressly included political groups within the definitional scope of the crime of genocide. See GA Resolution 96(I), UNDoc A/231 (11 December 1946). It is also noteworthy that, in his Report, Special Rapporteur Whitaker proposed to include genocide against social and political groups in an additional optional protocol to the Genocide Convention. See *Whitaker Report* 19, para 37.

groups, in the minds of the genociders: the existence of a 'group' as such might not have any basis in reality and it is the genocider's delirium which will create this group as such. In other words, the crime of genocide aims at the destruction of a group *arbitrarily defined by the genociders*, and the perpetration of the crime of genocide therefore does not necessarily mean that the group actually exists. As explained by Jean-Michel Chaumont:

> Last but not least, *victimized 'groups' may only exist in the mind of the perpetrators.* This is the reason why the demarcation of groups to be protected is so delicate and, to tell the truth, impossible to fix *a priori.* This argument in itself suffices to radically contest the validity of the current approach of the concept of genocide. As incongruous as it may seem, *genocide does not presuppose the existence of a constituted* genos, understood as a group conscious of its existence in the eyes of its members. This was the case even during the judeocide as, on one hand, some individuals who did not consider themselves as Jews, or who had ceased to do so, were persecuted as such while, on the other hand, others which were often considered as Jews were spared because they were not Jews according to the Nazi pseudo-racial sense.[31]

The arbitrariness of the definition of the victim group by the genociders themselves finds a telling illustration in the destruction of the European Jews. It is indeed a well-established historical fact that the Nazis arbitrarily and artificially defined the concept of 'Jew' and proceeded to the mythical transposition of a religion – the Jewish religion – into a race. Under the Nazi ideology, individuals could not choose to be Jewish or not, this characteristic was arbitrarily and artificially imposed on them, and no one but the Nazis could actually determine who was a Jew under the Nazi regime. The Nuremberg Race Laws gave a precise – although illogical – definition of who should be considered as Jewish and who should not, depending notably on ancestry and obscure hereditary rules.[32] As previously developed, the Vichy government was swift in following in the occupier's footsteps and in enacting its own legislation aimed at defining who was to be considered a Jew, based on ancestry and on an amalgam of race and religion.[33] It thus did not matter whether individuals had the feeling of being Jewish or not, whether they saw themselves as being Jewish or not, whether they wanted to be considered as Jewish or not. They had no say, no choice, in the definition of their own identity.

[31] Chaumont, *La concurrence des victimes* 211. Translation by the author. Emphasis in original. The original version reads as follows: 'Enfin et surtout, *les «groupes» victimisés peuvent n'exister que dans la tête de leurs bourreaux.* C'est pourquoi la délimitation des groupes à protéger est tellement délicate et, à vrai dire, impossible à fixer *a priori.* Cet argument à lui seul suffit pour contester radicalement la validité de l'approche courante du concept de génocide. Aussi étrange que cela puisse paraître, *le génocide ne présuppose nullement l'existence d'un* genos *constitué* au sens d'un groupe conscient d'exister aux propres yeux de ses membres. Ce fut le cas même durant le judéocide, en ce sens que, d'une part, certains individus qui ne se considéraient pas ou plus comme des Juifs furent persécutés comme tels tandis que, d'autre part, certains autres qui étaient souvent considérés comme tels furent épargnés parce qu'ils n'étaient pas juifs au sens – pseudo-racial – où les nazis l'avaient défini.'

[32] See Law for the Protection of German Blood and German Honour (15 September 1935); Law on Citizenship and Race (15 September 1935); art 5, First Supplementary Decree (14 November 1935).

[33] See Loi portant statut des juifs (3 October 1940) *Journal officiel*, 18 October 1940, 5323; See also Loi du 2 juin 1941portant second statut des juifs (2 June 1941) *Journal officiel*, 14 June 1941, 2475–76.

The recognition by the international criminal tribunals of the subjective and arbitrary aspects in the designation of the group targeted for destruction, coupled with the express protection in the Genocide Convention of both racial (sic) and religious groups makes it undisputable that Jews constituted a 'group' within the meaning of the Convention rather than 'individuals' part of a 'civilian population'. The difference is crucial and its blurring by the French courts is clearly incompatible with the recognition of the specificity of the crime of genocide. As Guénaël Mettraux explained,

> A protected 'group' under the genocide regime differs from a 'population' for the purpose of crimes against humanity. A population may contain several protected groups, and a widespread and systematic attack upon a civilian population may have no discriminatory effect upon any particular protected group that forms part thereof. The attack could, for instance, have been directed against a certain civilian population which is not distinguishable on national, ethnic, racial or religious grounds from the attacking side.[34]

It is in this regard symptomatic that the ICTR Appeals Chamber firmly affirmed the importance of this distinction:

> Genocide requires proof of an intent to destroy, in whole or in part, a national, ethnical, racial or religious group; this is not required by extermination as a crime against humanity. Extermination as a crime against humanity requires proof that the crime was committed as a part of a widespread or systematic attack against a civilian population, which proof is not required in the case of genocide.[35]

By including all the crimes perpetrated during the Second World War within the ambit of crimes against humanity, French courts missed an opportunity to distinguish between these two inherently different crimes. By failing to consider the Jews victims of the Nazi extermination enterprise, facilitated by the Vichy regime, as targeted because of their belonging to a group predefined by the genociders, French courts made a mistake of law and of fact.[36] A mistake of law, because the law of genocide could and should have been applied. A mistake of fact, because it is simply not the same crime to arrest, torture and murder a *Resistant* fighter because of his political inclinations and actions, and to arrest, torture and murder

[34] G Mettraux, *International Crimes and the Ad Hoc Tribunals* (Oxford, Oxford University Press, 2005) 332.

[35] *The Prosecutor v Alfred Musema* (Appeals Chamber Judgment) ICTR–96–13–A (16 November 2001) para 366. See however the *Krstić* case in which the Trial Chamber identified the similarities between grounds for commission in the context of crimes against humanity and in the context of genocide and in so doing arguably erred in operating a merging between the two types of crimes: 'the limitation to certain types of "group" as defined in the crime of genocide is far more specific than the "civilian population" defined in the crimes against humanity. The requirement in Article 5 that the crimes be part of a widespread or systematic attack against a civilian population is comprised within the genocide requirement that there be an intent to destroy a specified type of group.' *Krstić* Trial Judgment para 682.

[36] This is all the more surprising in light of the definition of genocide now included in art 211-1 of the New Penal Code (France), which expressly protects from genocide 'a group determined by reference to any other arbitrary criterion' ['un groupe déterminé à partir de tout autre caractère arbitraire'], thereby precisely acknowledging the specificity of genocidal victimisation.

a Jew because the law states that he is a Jew. It is not an issue of hierarchy of crimes; it is simply an issue of different crimes. The crucial distinction between the crimes was poignantly captured and expressed by André Frossard:

> The arrested opponent went alone to Dachau. Alone with his greatness, with his nobility.
>
> The little boy marked with the yellow star went to Auschwitz with his family . . .
>
> No, it is not the same violence to track down the Resistance fighter and the child from Izieu, who is still hope and promise of life.
>
> The clandestine fighter knew the risks he was taking.
>
> The child from Izieu did not know he was unwelcome on the Earth where he had, for a while, the authorisation to play. . .
>
> The opponent could cease his opposition.
>
> The Jew could not cease to be Jewish.[37]

Could it be precisely here that the true distinction between genocide and crimes against humanity actually lies? Could it be that rather than targeting a group, which may have no existence in reality and which can only be subjectively assessed by judicial instances to the detriment of the principle of legality, genocide in fact aims at destroying the family?

[37] A Frossard, *Le Crime Contre l'Humanité* (Paris, Editions Robert Laffont, 1987, reprint 1997) 68–69. Translation by the author. The original version reads as follows:

> 'L'opposant arrêté allait seul à Dachau. Seul avec sa grandeur, avec sa noblesse.
>
> Le petit garçon marqué de l'étoile jaune allait à Auschwitz avec sa famille . . .
>
> Non, ce n'est pas la même violence de traquer le résistant et l'enfant d'Izieu, qui n'est encore qu'espérance et promesse de vie.
>
> Le combattant clandestin savait à quoi il s'exposait.
>
> L'enfant d'Izieu ne savait pas qu'il était de trop sur la terre où il avait eu, quelque temps, la permission de jouer . . .
>
> L'opposant pouvait cesser de s'opposer.
>
> Le Juif ne pouvait cesser d'être juif.'

11

Genocide: A Crime Against the Family?

The suggestion that the crime of genocide might be understood as a crime aimed at destroying families as components of a group would not only bring back objectivity into the judicial assessment of the crime – the existence of a family arguably being easier to assess objectively than a group arbitrarily defined – it would also reflect more accurately the reality of the facts. Indeed, a close look at all genocidal instances reveals that the first and direct target of genociders is the family unit. As explained by Catherine Coquio,

> Genocide proceeds to both a horizontal and a vertical cut into the population: it targets births and filiations to eliminate all descendants, to genealogically eradicate a sub-humanity. This operation does not need to be justified to be efficient: the criminal invents a race. And he can do so with respect to any group as long as it is fictionalised not only as an enemy to be eradicated, but also as a sub-human to exterminate for eternity . . . The specificity of the genocidal crime must not be defined in terms of the racial *identity* of the target-group, this identity being generated by a delirium, but in terms of an annihilating *identification* process.[1]

This 'annihilating *identification* process', which relies on a 'hereditarisation' of certain features and which targets families, is the essence of genocide. In this respect, considering genocide as a crime perpetrated against families would also put an end to the debates and controversies raised by the Genocide Convention's selective protection of groups, as it would allow for a more accurate understanding of the crime of genocide, while refraining from trivialising or unduly stretching it. This would indeed not amount to adding further groups to the conventional list, but rather to acknowledging – by relying on an objective criterion – the subjectivity of the perpetrators who might have relied on other features than national, ethnic, racial or religious ones to define a group targeted for destruction. For instance, while the Convention famously excludes political and social groups from its scope of application, History has shown that political opinion or belong-

[1] Coquio, 'Du Malentendu' 48–49. Translation by the author. The original version reads as follows: 'Le génocide opère dans la population une coupe non seulement horizontale, mais verticale, c'est-à-dire vise les naissances et les filiations pour éliminer une lignée, éradiquer généalogiquement une sous-humanité. Cette opération n'a pas à être fondée pour être efficiente: le criminel invente une race. Et il peut le faire à l'égard de n'importe quel groupe dès lors que celui-ci est fictionnalisé non seulement comme ennemi à éradiquer, mais comme sous-homme à exterminer pour l'éternité . . . La spécificité du crime génocidaire ne doit pas être définie en termes d'*identité* raciale du groupe-cible, cette identité relevant d'un délire, mais en termes de processus d'*identification* annihilante.' Emphasis in original.

ing to a social group could be seen as a permanent feature of individuals based on family lineage, who could thus be transformed into a 'race' slated for destruction, amounting to a genocide which would however fall outside the conventional definitional scope. The case of Cambodia is perfectly illustrative of this situation, as the Khmer Rouge believed that some social groups were globally criminal, that they were criminal by nature, per se, and that this 'crime' was transmitted to spouses as well as to descendants,[2] through a 'hereditarisation' of the acquired social features. As Leo Kuper wrote, this instance revealed that 'past political affiliation can be as ineradicable a stigma, and as irrevocable a warrant for murder as racial or ethnic origin'.[3] Yet, insofar as the groups targeted were not among those expressly listed in the Genocide Convention, the event is not legally considered as genocide.

Just as it has been recognised that 'any act committed with the intent to destroy a part of a group, as such, constitutes an act of genocide within the meaning of the [Genocide] Convention',[4] it could be acknowledged that any group, defined through a 'hereditarisation' of arbitrarily defined features, constitutes a group protected within the meaning of the Genocide Convention. It is indeed not the belonging to a national, ethnic, racial or religious group which is the distinctive feature of the crime of genocide, but rather the 'hereditarisation' of certain characteristics – regardless of their qualification by the genociders. As recognised by the international criminal tribunals, 'for the purposes of applying the Genocide Convention, membership of a group is, in essence, a subjective rather than an objective concept. The victim is perceived by the perpetrator of genocide as belonging to a group slated for destruction'.[5] The group as such might thus not exist in reality and might be a pure invention on the part of the genociders who proceeded to a 'hereditarisation' of individual characteristics to create a group and target it for destruction. By taking as a focal point the families composing the group rather than the group as such, the law of genocide would acknowledge this 'hereditarisation' and thus the specificity of the crime of genocide.

11.1 The Legal Destruction of the Family

The enactment of the 1935 Nuremberg Race Laws will tragically remain as one of the darkest events in history. The first law comprising this despicable legal *corpus* was the Law for the Protection of German Blood and German Honour,[6]

[2] Children were deemed to be 'dangerous' until the third generation.

[3] L Kuper, *The Prevention of Genocide* (New Haven, Yale University Press, 1985) 127.

[4] *Krstić* Trial Judgment para 584.

[5] *Rutaganda* Trial Judgment para 56. See also *Musema* Trial Judgment para 161; *Kajelijeli,*Trial Judgment 811; *Gacumbtsi* Trial Judgment para 254.

[6] 15 September 1935.

promulgated to preserve 'the purity of German blood',[7] which notably regulated the right to marriage. Symptomatically for the purposes of the present development, the prohibition of marriages between Jews and 'citizens of German or some related blood' was deemed so important that it was encapsulated in the very first section of the law. The first Nazi anti-Semitic legal measure was thus directly aimed at outlawing supposedly mixed families.

The second law to be enacted was the Law on Citizenship and Race,[8] soon complemented by the First Supplementary Decree of 14 November 1935, which gave a definition of who was to be considered as Jewish under the Nazi regime; a definition precisely based on family linkage:

> (1) A Jew is an individual who is descended from at least three grandparents who were, racially, full Jews.
> (2) A Jew is also an individual who is descended from two full-Jewish grandparents if:
>
> (a) he was a member of the Jewish religious community when this law was issued, or joined the community later;
> (b) when the law was issued, he was married to a person who was a Jew, or was subsequently married to a Jew;
> (c) he is the issue from a marriage with a Jew, in the sense of Section I, which was contracted after the coming into effect of the Law for the Protection of German Blood and Honour of September 15, 1935;
> (d) he is the issue of an extramarital relationship with a Jew, in the sense of Section I, and was born out of wedlock after July 31, 1936.[9]

The identification of an individual as Jewish – crucial for the implementation of the genocidal plan and policy – thus relied on the family attachments and heritage of the individual.

Mirroring the Nuremberg Race Laws, the two *Statuts des Juifs* enacted by the Vichy government in 1940 also defined who was to be considered a Jew according to ascendance. Article 1 of the first Statute of 3 October 1940 indeed defined a Jew as 'one who has three grandparents of the Jewish race; or who has two grandparents of that race, if his or her spouse is Jewish'[10] while the second Statute of 2 June 1941 provided that

> A Jew is: He or she, of whatever faith, who is an issue of at least three grandparents of the Jewish race, or simply two if his/her spouse is an issue herself/himself of two grandparents of the Jewish race. A grandparent having belonged to the Jewish religion is considered to be of the Jewish race.[11]

[7] Law for the Protection of German Blood and German Honour, Preamble.

[8] 15 September 1935.

[9] Art 5, First Supplementary Decree (14 November 1935).

[10] See Loi portant statut des juifs (3 October 1940) *Journal officiel*, 18 October 1940, 5323: 'Art. 1er. Est regardé comme juif, pour l'application de la présente loi, toute personne issue de trois grands-parents de race juive ou de deux grands-parents de la même race, si son conjoint lui-même est juif.' Translation available in Beigbeder, *Judging War Crimes and Torture*145.

[11] See Loi portant second statut des juifs (2 June 1941) *Journal officiel*, 14 June 1941, 2475–76.

Not only did these infamous pieces of legislation pervert the legal importance of 'the family' into a legal category on which to found their anti-Semitism, they also used it as a means of identifying and qualifying the victims of exclusion and of destruction. As put by Benoît Descoubes,

> What exactly is to become of the Jewish family subjected to the harshness of the anti-Semitic legislation? The father is dismissed of the administration of the family capital, consigned with an administrator. Until 1942, this dismissal had no remedy: in France, the married woman had no legal capacity and thus no power to manage the matrimonial capital before the law of 22 September 1942.[12]

If, from 22 September 1942, the married woman was awarded legal capacity and could therefore replace her husband in the management of the family capital and resources, Benoît Descoubes rightly recalled that 'this remedy [was] unavailable for families in which both spouses [were] Jewish'[13] and that 'when the wife [was] not "Jewish" according to the Vichy laws, the legislator [had] foreseen the possibility of a separation of goods (law of 22 July 1941, article 20). The purpose of this article [was] to *provoke the divorce* of mixed couples'.[14] Vichy's legislation thus incorporated a fierce legislative attack on the family unit. The aim of the Vichy legislator was undoubtedly to target and destroy the family as a component of the group designated for exclusion and, subsequently, for destruction.

Rather symptomatically, when the Vichy authorities– predictably – filed all the information obtained on Jews living in France, they did so under five distinct headings[15] with the general file (*fichier général*) also tellingly labelled *family* file (*fichier familial*). It was indexed under the name of the father and it listed the names of the children below 15 years of age, thereby facilitating the subsequent arrest of the family as a whole. In fact, the victimisation of the family by the Vichy regime probably reached its apex in President Laval's decision to deport the children with their parents. As previously mentioned, Laval had indeed asked that 'in the course of the evacuation of Jewish families from the unoccupied zone, children under sixteen years of age be taken with them. As for the children who

[12] B Descoubes, 'Le juge, la famille juive et les dispositions antisémites' in Le genre humain (collectif), *Juger sous Vichy* (Paris, Éditions du Seuil, 1994) 53, 53. Translation by the author. The original version reads as follows: 'Que devient précisément une famille juive qui subit la rigueur de la législation antisémite? Le père de famille est dessaisi de l'administration du patrimoine familial, qui est confiée à un administrateur. Ce dessaisissement n'a, jusqu'en 1942, aucun remède: la femme mariée est juridiquement incapable en France jusqu'à la loi du 22 septembre 1942. L'épouse n'a donc aucun pouvoir normal de gestion sur le patrimoine familial jusqu'à cette date.'

[13] ibid. Translation by the author. The original version reads as follows: 'ce remède ne concerne pas les familles dont les deux époux sont juifs'.

[14] ibid. Translation by the author. The original version reads as follows: 'Lorsque l'épouse n'est pas «juive» au sens des dispositions de Vichy, le législateur a prévu la possibilité d'une séparation de biens (loi du 22 juillet 1941, article 20). La finalité de cet article est de *provoquer le divorce* des couples mixtes' (emphasis in original).

[15] The five headings were: general file, individual adult file, individual child file, the file of the camps at Pithiviers and Beaune-la-Rolande and the file of the camp at Drancy (available at the Mémorial de la Shoah). See E Conan, *Sans oublier les enfants – Les camps de Pithiviers et de Beaune-la-Rolande, 19 juillet–16 septembre 1942* (Paris, Editions Grasset & Fasquelle, 1991).

would stay in the occupied zone, the matter [did] not interest him.'[16] The family file thus constituted a precise gathering of information on each Jewish family – and a prelude to their annihilation.

11.2 The Physical Destruction of the Family

Not only does the genocide perpetrated against the European Jews illustrate how the family was initially used as a legal category to be excluded and discriminated against, it also reveals how it was the family unit which was subsequently targeted for destruction. In this respect, Elisa Joeden-Forgey defined genocidal violence as 'relational violence' and suggested that 'the assault on families is central to genocide':

> Since families are central for the on-going life of societies, they also become targets for attacks on this life. Joeden-Forgey notes that the targeting of families in genocidal violence has typically been overlooked by researchers, who focus either on harms to individuals or harms to groups. But genocidal violence is relational violence. She notes: 'Men are killed to expose women and children, women are raped to humiliate men, children are tortured to destroy parents – this relational logic is the core of genocidal violence against families.[17]

Indeed it was not a group that the genociders arrested and sent to its death, but rather the families that formed part of this group. It was the families which were arrested during the outrageous round-ups and, even if some were separated at the transit camp or upon arrival at the extermination camp, it was because of their family linkage and heritage that they were the targets of the genocidal machinery. The existence in Auschwitz of the *Familienlager*, ('family camp') – described by Henriette Asséo as 'families rounded up, all destroyed together, in one night'[18] – is perfectly illustrative of the genocidal *modus operandi.* Forcing parents to helplessly witness the atrocious suffering and fate of their children was also part of the Nazi dehumanisation enterprise – how could parents ever overcome the abject treatment imposed on their children? [19]

[16] Report of SS Hauptsturmführer Theodor Dannecker to Adolf Eichmann, 6 July 1942. See Rousso, *Le régime de Vichy* 91. See also S Klarsfeld *La Shoah en France – Vichy-Auschwitz, La « solution finale » de la question juive en France* (Paris, Librairie Arthème Fayard, 1983–1985, reprint 2001) 116. Translation by the author. The French version reads as follows: 'Le Président Laval a proposé que, lors de l'évacuation de familles juives de la zone non occupée, les enfants de moins de 16 ans soient emmenés eux aussi. Quant aux enfants juifs qui resteraient en zone occupée, la question ne l'intéresse pas.'

[17] E von Joeden-Forgey, 'The devil in the details: "life force atrocities" and the assault on the family in times on conflict' (2010) 5 *Genocide Studies and Prevention* 13. Cited in RM Schott 'War rape, natality and genocide' (2011) 13 *Journal of Genocide Research* 5, 14.

[18] H Asséo, 'Le sort des Tsiganes en Europe sous le régime nazi' in *Les Tsiganes dans l'Europe allemande* (1999) *Revue d'Histoire de la Shoah* 17. Cited in C Coquio et A Kalisky, A. *L'Enfant et le Génocide – Témoignages sur l'enfance pendant la Shoah* (Paris, Editions Robert Laffont, Collection Bouquins, 2007) xxviii. Translation by the author. The original version reads as follows: 'familles rassemblées, détruites toutes ensemble, en une seule nuit'.

[19] In this respect, see notably N Cohen, 'Manuscrits des Sonderkommandos d'Auschwitz: tenir face au destin et contre la réalité' in Centre de documentation juive contemporaine, *Des voix sous la cendre*

In his analysis of the Nazi genocide, Feliks Tych defined '[t]he war waged by Adolf Hitler against the majority of European countries to impose the "Nazi order" to the old continent, to submit Europe to Nazi Germany and ensure a "vital space" to the Germanic race of "übermenschen"' as 'the first war in History consciously waged against children'.[20] Catherine Coquio and Aurélia Kalisky subsequently asked: 'Could genocide be a "war consciously waged against children"?':[21]

> The physical extermination of children, at the heart of the annihilation project, presupposes control over births and descent as well as the criminalization of children. It gives the best illustration of the radical violence of genocide: a violence ultimately 'without reason' and which, by targeting the 'roots' and the future of a community, destroys the generational chain and attacks with unprecedented fierceness the elderly and the children. This is a purely genocidal feature, which is not exclusive to the history of Nazism, but which we also find in other widespread and massive family exterminations.[22]

Acts of genocide all aim at destroying a group through the systematic targeting of the families composing it. Genocide vertically perforates the population; it targets children, births and filiations to eliminate all ascent and descent, and destroys the generational chain to genealogically eradicate a group.[23] This understanding of the crime of genocide as a crime directed against the family as a component of the group rather than against the group itself would arguably remain respectful of the spirit of the Genocide Convention. It would in fact find some credence in the conventional text which includes, within the exhaustive list of prohibited genocidal acts, two acts unequivocally aimed at the destruction of the family via the victimisation of children, namely 'imposing measures intended to prevent births within the group' and 'forcibly transferring children of the group to another group'.[24] This conventional acknowledgement of the vulnerability of families and of children in genocidal occurrences finds a chilling echo in the phrase of *Reichsführer SS* Heinrich Himmler, which has lost nothing of its terrible resonance: 'The problem of the chil-

– *Manuscrits des* Sonderkommandos *d'Auschwitz-Birkenau* (Paris, Mémorial de la Shoah/Calmann-Lévy, 2005) 465–515. See, in particular, the analysis therein of Gradowski's manuscript, 501–502.

[20] Cited in Coquio et Kalisky, *L'Enfant et le Génocide* xv. Translation by the author. The original version reads as follows: 'La guerre que fit Adolf Hitler à la plupart des pays européens pour imposer l' «ordre nazi» au vieux continent, pour soumettre l'Europe à l'Allemagne fasciste et assurer un «espace vital» à la race germanique des «surhommes» fut également la première guerre de l'histoire consciemment livrée aux enfants.'

[21] ibid. Translation by the author. The original version reads as follows: 'Le génocide serait-il une «guerre consciemment livrée aux enfants» ?'

[22] ibid, xix–xx. Footnotes omitted. Translation by the author. The original version reads as follows: 'L'extermination physique des enfants, au cœur du projet d'anéantissement, suppose la maîtrise de l'enfantement et de la descendance ainsi que la criminalisation des enfants. Elle illustre le mieux la violence radicale du génocide: une violence ultimement «sans raison» et qui, s'en prenant aux «racines» et à l'avenir d'une collectivité, brise la chaîne des générations et s'attaque avec une férocité inédite aux vieillards et aux enfants. C'est là un trait proprement génocidaire, qu'on retrouve, au-delà de l'histoire du nazisme, dans les grandes exterminations familiales de masse.'

[23] See Coquio 48–49.

[24] See art II(d) and art II(e) of the Genocide Convention.

dren is the nation's vital problem';[25] a problem to which the Nazis devised a solution that proved final.

By considering the crimes perpetrated against the Jews as crimes perpetrated against individuals, part of a civilian population, French courts erred in both law and fact: they failed to acknowledge the fact that the atrocities were in reality perpetrated against a group and, perhaps more precisely, against the families composing this group. At the very beginning of the *Barbie* trial, *procureur général* Pierre Truche stated:

> On one hand there is the resistance fighter, aware of the consequences his arrest would have on his physical integrity and on his life and who bravely accepted the dangers . . . On the other hand, there is a two-year old Jewish child, like the one deported on 11 August by the last convoy, who does not yet quite know what it means to be Jewish.[26]

There is the difference between a crime against humanity and a genocide.

[25] Speech of 2 September 1938. H Himmler, *Discours secrets* (Paris, Gallimard, 1978) 73. Translation by the author. The French version reads as follows: 'Le problème des enfants est le problème vital de la nation.'

[26] P Truche 'Le crime contre l'Humanité' in A Kaspi (eds), *Les Cahiers de la Shoah* (Paris, Liana Levi, 1994) 39. Cited in Wieviorka, 'La France et le Procès de Nuremberg' 121–22. Translation by the author. The original version reads as follows: 'Il y a, d'une part, le résistant informé des conséquences sur son intégrité physique et sa vie d'une arrestation et qui a accepté courageusement les dangers encourus . . . D'autre part, il y a un enfant juif de deux ans, comme celui qui a été déporté le 11 août par le dernier convoi et qui ne sait pas encore vraiment ce qu'est être Juif.'

12

Conclusion

This book has attempted to answer a fairly straightforward question: why – in the French context – have individuals involved in the destruction of the European Jews been prosecuted for crimes against humanity and not for genocide? Taking as its focal points of analysis the respective trials of Klaus Barbie, Paul Touvier, Maurice Papon and Aloïs Brunner, this research has explored the French judicial understanding of crimes against humanity which proved to be not only correct in light of international criminal law norms in force at the time the verdicts were issued, but also to be rather visionary. It is highly revealing in this respect that, decades later, the definition of crimes against humanity provided by the French Cour de cassation in the *Barbie* case remains a valid and useful precedent for the two ad hoc international criminal tribunals.

If the French judiciary demonstrated an undoubtedly expert command of the law of crimes against humanity in these highly complex cases, there was however an inexplicable failure to consider the incrimination of genocide. This research has reviewed all the potential legal impediments to the application of the law of genocide to such cases without being able to determine the existence of any such obstacle, or to reach a definitive answer.

The only convincing – even if unsatisfactory – reason that could be invoked to justify the use of the law of crimes against humanity to the detriment of the law of genocide might simply be a very French conception of the crime of genocide as a crime against humanity. The French judicial embodiment of genocide within crimes against humanity indeed found a legislative confirmation with the enactment of the New Penal Code which expressly includes genocide within its section on 'Crimes against humanity and against persons' ('des crimes contre l'humanité et contre l'espèce humaine').[1]

If it could be argued that the entry into force of the New Penal Code has made the matter quasi-obsolete, such an understanding of the crime of genocide however remains problematic, not only because French law and case law would questionably depart from international criminal law, which clearly distinguishes between genocide and crimes against humanity, but also because they would be bound to keep on failing to capture the uniqueness of genocide.

[1] See Art 211-1 of the New Penal Code (France).

Or is the problem a more fundamental one? Is it that 'justice [in matters of genocide] is both necessary and impossible'?[2] Is it that such crimes 'explode the limits of the law'?[3]

Ultimately, if the respective trials of Klaus Barbie, Paul Touvier, Maurice Papon and Aloïs Brunner failed to unequivocally establish the specificity of the crime of genocide, they nonetheless brought to light the crimes perpetrated and allowed the victims to be remembered.[4] If French courts undoubtedly missed several opportunities to grasp the very essence of the crime of genocide, survivors were nonetheless called to testify and be heard, and the defendants were charged and convicted of the atrocities they had committed decades before.

Could it be that this is all that actually matters? After all, thanks to the *Barbie* and *Brunner* trials, further aspects of Nazi barbarism and genocidal enterprise came under the spotlight. The forty-four children of Izieu who, on 6 April 1944, were arrested by Barbie and his henchmen and sent to their death came out of anonymity. In this respect, the legacy of the *Barbie* trial owes a lot to the work and infallible dedication of lawyer Maître Serge Klarsfeld who, before the court,

> does not plead. He does not throw his sleeves towards the ceiling, he does not use any vocal effect, he talks with sadness, he does not even seem to be a lawyer. No, Maître Klarsfeld reads. And this reading, certainly more than everything which is to be said during eight days by the thirty-nine lawyers of the partie civile, distresses. Klarsfeld, who escaped from the raid, hidden by the thin rampart of a partitioned wardrobe. Klarsfeld the historian, the militant, the Nazi hunter, the auxiliary of justice haunted since 1971 by the memory of the forty-four Jewish children of Izieu. Klarsfeld, who only pronounces the name of these children, as if he was on the verge of beginning a teaching class. Forty-four names, one after the other, recited in a deathly silence.[5]

Thanks to the *Touvier* and *Papon* trials, and regardless of the final verdicts reached, France had to face its past and the crimes perpetrated in its name. As President Chirac eloquently stated, while opening the French Pavilion in Auschwitz in 2005,

> Jews of all ages, all conditions, all origins, who have brought so much to our country, our culture, our civilisation, annihilated by the Nazi criminal madness: your children,

[2] Rousso, *Vichy – L'événement, la mémoire, l'histoire* 677. Translation by the author. The original version reads as follows: 'la justice en la matière est à la fois nécessaire et impossible'.

[3] L Köhler and H Saner (eds), *Hannah Arendt/Karl Jaspers: Correspondence, 1926–1969* (New York, Harcourt Brace Jovanovich, 1992) 275.

[4] In this sense, see Wieviorka, *Le Procès Eichmann* 148. See also R Badinter, 'Préface: Un acquis de justice' in Chalandon and Nivelle, *Crimes contre l'Humanité* VI.

[5] Chalandon in Chalandon and Nivelle, *Crimes contre l'Humanité* 111–12. Translation by the author. The original version reads as follows: 'Me Serge Klarsfeld ne plaide pas. Il ne jette pas ses manches vers les moulures du plafond, n'use d'aucun effet de voix, parle avec tristesse, ne semble pas même être avocat. Non. Me Klarsfeld lit. Et cette lecture, plus que, certainement, tout ce qui doit être dit durant huit jours par les trente-neuf avocats de la partie civile, bouleverse. Klarsfeld, qui a échappé à la rafle, masqué par le mince rempart d'une armoire à double fond. Klarsfeld l'historien, le militant, le chasseur de nazis, l'auxiliaire de justice hanté depuis 1971 par le souvenir des quarante-quatre enfants juifs d'Izieu. Klarsfeld, qui se contente de prononcer le nom de ces enfants, à la manière d'un appel de début de classe. Quarante-quatre noms, l'un après l'autre, récités dans un silence de mort'.

> your families, your compatriots remember you. Your memory, the memory of this 'world which was', is for France more than sorrow. It is the conscience of a sin. It is a requirement of responsibility.[6]

With the zealous help and contribution of the Vichy authorities, the Nazis were able to carry out their bestial destruction plan on the French territory in a more efficient and murderous way. And this is what the fact of seeing Paul Touvier the *milicien* and Maurice Papon the high civil servant sitting in the dock meant and recognised.

One victim of the abject collaboration between Vichy France and Nazi Germany, Hélène Berr, a gifted 23-year-old student at the Sorbonne, died in April 1945 in Bergen-Belsen, just five days before the camp was liberated. Ill with typhus, she was beaten to death by one of the guards because she was unable to get up for the morning call.[7] What can one possibly add to this? Nothing. Or maybe an extract from her *Diary*, which contains within itself the 'unimaginable atrocity'[8] of genocide. Reflecting on the detention of a family in the camp at Drancy, she wrote:

> Thirteen children and parents, *what are they going to do with these little ones*? If they deport them to make them work, of what use can the little ones be? Is it true that they are put within the care of German welfare services? *The other workmen sent to Germany, their wives and children are not taken away*. The monstrous incomprehensibility, the horrible illogic of all this tortures one's mind. There is probably nothing to think about because the Germans don't even look for a reason or a purpose. They have one goal, exterminate.[9]

'What are they going to do with these little ones?' . . .

[6] Translation by the author. The French version reads as follows: 'Juifs de tous âges, de toutes conditions, de toutes origines, qui ont tant apporté à notre pays, à notre culture, à notre civilisation, happés par la folie criminelle des nazis: vos enfants, vos familles, vos compatriotes se souviennent de vous. Votre souvenir, celui de ce "monde qui fut", est pour la France plus qu'une douleur. Il est la conscience d'une faute. Il est une exigence de responsabilité'. J Chirac 'Discours prononcé lors de l'inauguration de la nouvelle exposition du pavillon d'Auschwitz le 27 janvier 2005', *Libération* (27 January 2005).

[7] See M Job, 'Hélène Berr, une vie confisquée' in H Berr, *Journal 1942–1944* (Paris: Editions Tallandier, 2008) 299, 304.

[8] See Preamble of the Rome Statute. See also Schabas, *Unimaginable Atrocities*.

[9] Berr, *Journal 1942–1944* 292. Translation by the author. The original version reads as follows: 'Treize enfants et parents, que vont-ils faire de ces petits? S'ils déportent pour faire travailler, à quoi servent les petits ? Est-ce vrai qu'on les met à l'assistance publique allemande ? *Les autres ouvriers qu'on envoie en Allemagne, on ne prend pas leurs femmes et leurs enfants*. La monstrueuse incompréhensibilité, l'horrible illogisme de tout cela vous torture l'esprit. Il n'y a sans doute pas à réfléchir, car les Allemands ne cherchent même pas de raison, ou d'utilité. Ils ont un but, exterminer.' (Emphasis added.)

BIBLIOGRAPHY

Alland D et Ferrand F, 'Jurisprudence Française en matière de Droit International Public, Cour de Cassation, chambre criminelle, 6 janvier 1998' (1998) 102 *RGDIP* 825.

Ambos K, 'What does "intent to destroy" in genocide mean?' (2009) 91: 876 *International Review of the Red Cross* 833.

Améry J, *Par-delà le crime et le châtiment – Essai pour surmonter l'insurmontable*, Traduit de l'allemand par Françoise Wuilmart (Arles, Actes Sud, (1966) 1995).

Aroneanu E, 'Le crime contre l'humanité', Document établi par M. Eugène Aroneanu, auteur de « Camps de concentration », (Dc. F321 au T.M.I.) et déposé au Tribunal Militaire International, sous le chiffre Dc. F775 (Paris, La documentation Française, 2 September 1946).

——, 'Le crime contre l'humanité', Doc. F. 775 au T.M.I. [1946] 2 *La Nouvelle Revue de Droit International Privé* 1.

——, 'Les droits de l'homme et le crime contre l'humanité' [1947] 3 *La Revue de Droit International, de Sciences Diplomatiques et Politiques* 1.

——, 'Responsabilités pénales pour crime contre l'humanité' [1948] 2 *La Revue de Droit International, de Sciences Diplomatiques et Politiques* 1.

——, 'Le crime contre l'humanité et la juridiction pénale internationale' [1950] 2 *La Revue de Droit International, de Sciences Diplomatiques et Politiques* 1.

Association française pour l'histoire de la Justice, Commission nationale consultative des droits de l'homme, Ecole nationale de la magistrature, *Colloque La lutte contre le négationnisme Bilan et perspectives de la loi du 13 juillet 1990 tendant à réprimer tout acte raciste, antisémite ou xénophobe* (Paris, La Documentation française, 2003).

Azéma J-P, 'Cessez de jouer avec les mémoires', *Libération* (10 May 2006).

Badinter R, *Un antisémitisme ordinaire – Vichy et les avocats juifs (1940–1944)* (Paris, Librairie Arthème Fayard, 1997).

Barbas J-C (ed), *Philippe Pétain – Discours aux Français, 17 juin 1940–20 août 1944* (Paris, Éditions Albin Michel, 1989).

Bassiouni MC (ed), *International Criminal Law, Volume III: Enforcement* (Ardsley, Transnational Publishers, 1987).

——, *Crimes Against Humanity in International Criminal Law*, 2nd edn (The Hague, Kluwer Law International, 1999).

—— (ed), *International Criminal Law, Volume I: Crimes*, 2nd edn (Ardsley, Transnational Publishers, 1999).

—— (ed), *International Criminal Law, Volume III: Enforcement*, 2nd edn (Ardsley, Transnational Publishers, 1999) 556.

Beigbeder Y, *Judging War Crimes and Torture – French Justice and International Criminal Tribunals and Commissions (1940-2005)* (Leiden, Martinus Nijhoff Publishers, 2006).

Berr H, *Journal 1942–1944* (Paris, Editions Tallandier, 2008).

Bertrand O, 'Pour les juges, Gollinisch est négationniste', *Libération* (19 January 2007).

Binder G, 'Representing Nazism: Advocacy and Identity at the Trial of Klaus Barbie' (1989) 98 *Yale LJ* 1324.

Bloxham D, *Genocide on Trial – War Crimes Trials and the Formation of Holocaust History and Memory* (Oxford, Oxford University Press, 2005).

Boltanski C, 'Faurisson, négationniste impénitent face à Badinter', *Libération* (13 March 2007).

Brayard F (ed), *Le Génocide des Juifs entre procès et histoire 1943-2000* (Paris, Editions Complexe, Collection « Histoire du Temps Présent », 2000).

——, *La « solution finale de la question juive » – La technique, le temps et les catégories de la décision* (Paris, Librairie Arthème Fayard, 2004).

Bryant B, 'Comment: The United States and the 1948 Genocide Convention, Part I' (1975) 16 *HILJ* 692.

Burgorgue-Larsen L (ed), *La répression internationale du génocide rwandais* (Brussels, Bruylant, Collection du CREDHO, 2003)

Burrin P, *La France à l'heure allemande 1940–1944* (Paris, Editions du Seuil, Collection Points Histoire, 1995).

Cammilleri-Subrenat A, 'L'incitation à la haine et la Constitution' [2002] 2 *Revue Internationale de Droit Comparé* 513.

Cassese A, 'Balancing the Prosecution of Crimes against Humanity and Non-Retroactivity of Criminal Law – The *Kolk and Kislyiy v. Estonia* Case before the ECHR' (2006) 4 *JICJ* 410.

Centre de documentation juive contemporaine, *Des voix sous la cendre – Manuscrits des* Sonderkommandos *d'Auschwitz-Birkenau* (Paris, Mémorial de la Shoah/Calmann-Lévy, 2005).

Centre de droit international de l'Institut de Sociologie de l'Université Libre de Bruxelles (Centre Henri Rolin), Fondation Auschwitz-Stichting (Centre d'Etudes et de Documentation), *Le Procès de Nuremberg – Conséquences et actualisation, Actes du Colloque International, Université Libre de Bruxelles, Brussels, le 27 mars 1987* (Brussels, Editions Bruylant, Editions de l'Université de Bruxelles, 1988).

Chalandon S et Nivelle P, *Crimes contre l'humanité – Barbie, Touvier, Bousquet, Papon* (Paris, Plon/Libération, 1998).

Chaumont J-M, *La concurrence des victimes – Génocide, identité, reconnaissance* (Paris, La Découverte & Syros, 2002).

Chirac J, *Discours et Messages de Jacques Chirac, Maire de Paris, Premier Ministre, Président de la République, En hommage aux Juifs de France victimes de la collaboration de l'Etat français de Vichy avec l'occupant allemand* (Paris, Fédération des Fils et Filles des Déportés Juifs de France, 1998).

——, 'Discours prononcé lors de l'inauguration de la nouvelle exposition du pavillon d'Auschwitz le 27 janvier 2005', *Libération* (27 January 2005).

Choisnel E, *L'Assemblée Consultative Provisoire (1943–1945) – Le sursaut républicain* (Paris, L'Harmattan, 2007).

Cohen-Jonathan G, 'Négationnisme et droits de l'homme' [1997] *Revue Trimestrielle des Droits de l'Homme* 573.

——, 'Le droit de l'homme à la non-discrimination raciale' [2001] *Revue Trimestrielle des Droits de l'Homme* 665.

Coignard J, 'Le négationniste Faurisson à nouveau traité de « faussaire »', *Libération* (3 April 2007).

Conan E, *Sans oublier les enfants – Les camps de Pithiviers et de Beaune-la-Rolande, 19 juillet – 16 septembre 1942* (Paris, Editions Grasset & Fasquelle, 1991).

——, 'Touvier: Un profond malaise', *L'Express* (28 April 1994).

——, 'Papon, Les Français et Vichy', *L'Express* (2 October 1997).

——, *Le Procès Papon – Un journal d'audience* (Paris, Editions Gallimard, 1998).

Conan E and Rousso H, *Vichy – An Ever-Present Past*, translated and annotated by Nathan Bracher (Hanover, University Press of New England, 1998).

Coquio C (ed), *Parler des camps, penser les génocides* (Paris, Editions Albin Michel, Bibliothèque Albin Michel Idées, 1999).

Coquio C and Kalisky A, *L'enfant et le génocide – Témoignages sur l'enfance pendant la Shoah* (Paris, Editions Robert Laffont, Collection Bouquins, 2007).

D'Almeida F, *La vie mondaine sous le nazisme* (Paris, Editions Perrin, Collection tempus, 2008).

Dayan Rosenman A, *Les alphabets de la Shoah – survivre. témoigner. Écrire, Préface d'Annette Wieviorka* (Paris, CNRS Editions, 2007).

Delmas Saint-Hilaire JP, 'La définition juridique de la complicité de crime contre l'humanité au lendemain de l'arrêt de la Chambre criminelle du 23 janvier 1997 (affaire *Maurice Papon*)' [1997] *Recueil Dalloz* 249.

Delperrie de Bayac J, *Histoire de la* Milice *1918–1945* (Paris, Le Cercle du Nouveau Livre d'Histoire, Arthème Fayard, 1969).

De Montvalon JB, 'Des historiens ont jugé «affligeant» la proposition de loi socialiste', *Le Monde* (11 October 2006).

De Saint-Exupéry P, *L'inavouable – La France au Rwanda* (Paris, Editions des Arènes, 2004).

Destexhe A, *Rwanda and Genocide in the Twentieth Century* (London, Pluto Press, 1995).

Duhamel O, *Histoire constitutionnelle de la France* (Paris, Editions du Seuil, 1997).

Drost PN, *The Crime of State – Penal Protection for Fundamental Freedoms of Persons and Peoples, Book II: Genocide,* United Nations Legislation on International Criminal Law (Leyden, A.W. Sythoff, 1959).

Dupaquier JF (ed), *La justice internationale face au drame rwandais* (Paris, Editions Karthala, 1996).

Earl H, *The Nuremberg SS-Einsatzgruppen Trial, 1945–1958 – Atrocity, Law, and History* (Cambridge, Cambridge University Press, 2009).

Ecole Cathédrale – Institut de Formation Continue du Barreau de Paris, *Le Crime Contre l'Humanité, mesure de la responsabilité ? Actes du cycle des conférences « Droit, Liberté et Foi », Juin 1997* (Paris, CERP, 1998).

Epstein S, *Un paradoxe français – Antiracistes dans la Collaboration, antisémites dans la Résistance* (Paris, Éditions Albin Michel, Bibliothèque Histoire, 2008).

Fédération Internationale des ligues des Droits de l'Homme, 'La répression des présumés génocidaires rwandais devant les juridictions françaises: Etat des lieux 2004', www.fidh.org.

Fédération Internationale des ligues des Droits de l'Homme, *France – Compétence universelle: État des lieux de la mise en œuvre du principe de compétence universelle* (October 2005) www.fidh.org.

Ferenczi T, 'Les Vingt-Sept pénalisent le racisme et le négationnisme', *Le Monde* (19 April 2007).

Frossard A, *Le crime contre l'humanité* (Paris, Editions Robert Laffont, 1987).

Friedländer S, *Nazi Germany and the Jews 1933–1939 – The Years of Persecution* (London, Phoenix, 2007).

——, *Nazi Germany and the Jews 1939–1945 – The Years of Extermination* (New York, HarperCollins Publishers, 2007).

Garapon A, *Des crimes qu'on ne peut ni punir ni pardonner – Pour une justice internationale* (Paris, Éditions Odile Jacob, 2002).

——, *Peut-on réparer l'histoire ? Colonisation, esclavage, Shoah* (Paris, Editions Odile Jacob, 2008).

Gendrel M et Lafarge P, *Eléments d'une bibliographie mondiale du droit pénal militaire des crimes et délits contre la sûre té de l'Etat et du droit pénal international (Crimes de guerre – Génocide – Crimes contre l'Humanité) – arrêtée au 31 décembre 1961* (Paris, Librairie générale de droit et de jurisprudence, 1965).

Le Genre humain (collectif), *Juger sous Vichy* (Paris, Editions du Seuil, November 1994).

——, *Le droit antisémite de Vichy* (Paris, Editions du Seuil, Mai 1996).

Govciyan A, *24 Avril, Témoignage sur la reconnaissance par la France du génocide arménien de 1915* (Paris, le cherche midi, 2003).

Grosser A, *Le crime et la mémoire* (Paris, Flammarion, Collection Champs, 1989).

Guéno J-P (ed.), *Paroles d'étoiles, Mémoire d'enfants cachés (1939–1945)* (Paris, Librio, 2002).

Hertz H, 'Le drame juif à Nuremberg', [1946] *Le Monde juif* in Klarsfeld S (ed), *Mémoire du Génocide* (Paris, Le Centre de Documentation Juive Contemporaine et l'association « Les Fils et Filles des Déportés Juifs de France », 1987) 348.

Igounet V, *Histoire du négationnisme en France* (Paris, Editions du Seuil, Collection XXè Siècle, 2000).

Joly L, *Vichy dans la 'Solution Finale' – Histoire du Commissariat général aux Questions juives (1941–1944)* (Paris, Editions Grasset & Fasquelle, 2006).

Jouanneau B, *La justice et l'histoire face au négationnisme – Au cœur d'un procès* (Paris, Librairie Arthème Fayard, 2008).

Juratowitch B, 'Retroactive Criminal Liability and International Human Rights Law', [2004] LXXV BYBIL 337.

Kessel J, *Jugements derniers – Les procès Pétain, de Nuremberg et Eichmann* (Paris, Editions Tallandier, Collection Texto, 2007).

Klarsfeld A, *Touvier, Un crime français* (Paris, Librairie Arthème Fayard, 1994).

——, *Papon, Un verdict français* (Paris, Editions Ramsay, 1998).

——, La *Cour, les Nains et le Bouffon* (Paris, Editions Robert Laffont, 1998).

Klarsfeld S, *Vichy-Auschwitz, Le Rôle de Vichy dans la Solution Finale de la Question Juive en France – 1942* (Paris, Librairie Arthème Fayard, 1983).

——, *Les enfants d'Izieu, une tragédie juive, Documentation réunie et publiée par Serge Klarsfeld, Président de l'Association « Les Fils et Filles des Déportés Juifs de France »* (Paris, AZ Repro, 1984).

——, *Vichy-Auschwitz, Le Rôle de Vichy dans la Solution Finale de la Question Juive en France – 1943–1944* (Paris, Librairie Arthème Fayard, 1985).

——, *La Shoah en France – Vichy-Auschwitz, La « solution finale » de la question juive en France* (Paris, Librairie Arthème Fayard (1983–1985) reprint 2001).

——, *La Shoah en France – Le calendrier de la persécution des Juifs de France, juillet 1940 – août 1942* (Paris, Librairie Arthème Fayard, 2001).

——, *La Shoah en France – Le calendrier de la persécution des Juifs de France, septembre 1942 – août 1944* (Paris, Librairie Arthème Fayard, 2001).

——, *La Shoah en France – Le mémorial des enfants juifs déportés de France* (Paris, Librairie Arthème Fayard, 2001).

——, *Adieu les enfants (1942–1944)* (Paris, Mille et une nuits, 2005).

Köhler L and Saner H (eds), Hannah Arendt/Karl Jaspers: Correspondence, 1926–1969, Translated by Robert Kimber and Rita Kimber (New York, Harcourt Brace Jovanovich, 1992).

Kuper L, *The Prevention of Genocide* (New Haven, Yale University Press, 1985).

Laborie P, *L'opinion française sous Vichy – Les Français et la crise d'identité nationale 1936–1944* (Paris, Editions du Seuil, Collection Points Histoire, 1990).

Lambert B, *Dossiers d'Accusation: Bousquet, Papon, Touvier – Inculpés de crimes contre l'humanité* (Paris, Editions de la Fédération Nationale des Déportés et Internés Résistants et Patriotes, 1998).

Landrin S, 'Peine confirmée en appel pour Bruno Gollnisch, poursuivi pour négationnisme', *Le Monde* (28 February 2008).

Lauterwein A and Strauss-Hiva C (eds), *Rire, Mémoire, Shoah* (Paris/Tel Aviv, Éditions de l'éclat, 2009).

LeBlanc LJ, 'The United Nations Genocide Convention and Political Groups: Should the United States Propose an Amendment?' (1988) 13 *YJIL* 268.

Lemkin R, *Axis Rule in Occupied Europe – Laws of Occupation, Analysis of Government, Proposals for Redress* (Washington, Carnegie Endowment for International Peace, Division of International Law, 1944).

Libération, 'Faurisson, négationniste débouté' (2 April 2007).

——, 'L'Europe sanctionne le racisme' (19 April 2007).

——, 'Faurisson perd son procès contre Badinter' (21 May 2007).

——, 'Cinq mois de prison avec sursis requis contre Jean-Marie Le Pen' (14 December 2007).

Lindeperg S et Wieviorka A, *Univers concentrationnaire et génocide – Voir, savoir, comprendre* (Paris, Mille et une nuits, 2008).

Lochak D, 'Le Conseil d'Etat sous Vichy et le Consiglio Di Stato sous le Fascisme – Eléments pour une comparaison' in Centre universitaire de recherches administratives et politiques de Picardie (C.U.R.A.P.P.), *Le Droit Administratif en Mutation* (Paris, Presses universitaires de France, 1993) 51.

Longerich P, *« Nous ne savions pas » Les Allemands et la Solution finale 1933–1945*, Essai traduit de l'allemand par Raymond Clarinard (Paris, Éditions Héloïse d'Ormesson, 2008).

Lottman HR, *L'épuration, 1943–1953*, Traduction de l'anglais par Béatrice Vierne (Paris, Librairie Arthème Fayard, Editions du Seuil, 1986).

Maeck J, *Montrer la Shoah à la télévision, de 1960 à nos jours* (Paris, Nouveau Monde éditions, 2009).

Marcou L, 'Ils ont déporté les Juifs de France', *La Tribune Juive* (October 1979) 12.

Marrus MR and Paxton RO, *Vichy France and the Jews*, with a new Foreword by Stanley Hoffmann (Stanford, Stanford University Press, 1995).

Massias F, 'La Liberté d'Expression et le Discours Raciste ou Révisionniste' [1993] RTDH 183.

Maupas S, 'Perpétuité pour Aloïs Brunner', (2 March 2001) *Diplomatie Judiciaire*, www.diplomatiejudiciare.com.

Maupas S, 'Le TPIR demande à la France d'arrêter et de juger deux Rwandais, un prêtre et un ex-préfet, accusés de génocide', *Le Monde* (4 July 2007).

——, 'Deux Rwandais accusés de génocide ont été arrêtés en France', *Le Monde* (21 July 2007).

May L, *Genocide – A Normative Account* (Cambridge, Cambridge University Press, 2010).

McAuliffe deGuzman M, 'The Road from Rome: The Developing Law of Crimes against Humanity' (2000) 22 *HRQ* 335.

McCormack TLM Simpson GJ (eds), *The Law of War Crimes, National and International Approaches* (The Hague, Kluwer Law International, 1997).
Meier Wang M, 'The International Tribunal for Rwanda: Opportunities for Clarification, Opportunities for Impact' (1995) 27 *Columbia Human Rights Law Review* 177.
Meron T, 'International Criminalization of Internal Atrocities' (1995) 89 *AJIL* 554.
——, 'War Crimes Law Comes of Age' (1998) 92 *AJIL* 462.
Mertens P, *L'imprescriptibilité des crimes de guerre et contre l'humanité* (Brussels, Editions de l'Université de Bruxelles, 1974).
Mettraux G, *International Crimes and the* ad hoc *Tribunals* (Oxford, Oxford University Press, 2005).
Mission d'étude sur la spoliation des Juifs de France, *Guide des Recherches dans les Archives des Spoliations et des Restitutions* (Paris, La documentation Française, 2000).
——, *La Persécution des Juifs de France 1940–1944 et le Rétablissement de la Légalité Républicaine – Recueil des textes officiels 1940–1999* (Paris, La documentation Française, 2000).
——, *Le pillage des appartements et son indemnisation,* Rapport rédigé par Annette Wieviorka et Floriane Azoulay (Paris, La documentation Française, 2000).
——, *Rapport Général* (Paris, La documentation Française, 2000).
Moix Y, 'Une nouvelle ère de l'humanité', *Libération* (14 September 2001).
Le Monde, 'A l'Assemblée, le débat sur la loi sur le génocide arménien reporté après des incidents' (18 May 2006).
——, 'La négation du génocide arménien débattue à l'Assemblée' (18 May 2006).
——, 'Gollnisch condamné à 3 mois de prison avec sursis pour des propos sur les chambres à gaz' (18 January 2007).
——, 'Robert Faurisson a été débouté de ses poursuites contre Robert Badinter' (21 May 2007).
——, 'La justice française libère deux Rwandais accusés de génocide' (1 August 2007).
——, 'Deux Rwandais inculpés pour génocide ont été à nouveau interpellés en France' (8 September 2007).
——, 'La cour d'appel reporte sa décision sur les deux Rwandais réclamés par le TPIR' (26 September 2007).
——, 'Le TPIR se dessaisit au profit de la France pour juger deux Rwandais' (21 November 2007).
——, 'M. Le Pen devant la justice pour avoir jugé l'Occupation allemande « pas particulièrement inhumaine' (14 December 2007).
——, 'Suisse: condamnation pour négation du génocide arménien confirmée' (19 December 2007).
——, 'La Cour de cassation casse la décision d'extrader un Rwandais vers le TPIR' (16 January 2008).
——, 'Un Rwandais recherché pour génocide arrêté à Annecy et écroué' (27 February 2008).
Monneray H, *Rapport*, Session du Conseil Economique et Social (Genève, août 1948 – Microfiches, Centre de Documentation Juive Contemporaine, Ref. CCCLXVI-34).
Montagnon P, *La France dans la guerre de 39–45* (Paris, Pygmalion, 2009).
Némirovsky I, *Suite française* (Paris, Editions Denoël, 2004).
Nicolaïdis D, *Oublier nos crimes – L'amnésie nationale: une spécificité française* (Paris, Editions Autrement, Collection Mémoires, 2002).
Le Nouvel Observateur, 'La cour d'appel de Paris ordonne la remise au TPIR d'un génocidaire présumé' (14 November 2007).

Novick P, *L'épuration française, 1944–1949*, Traduction de l'anglais par Hélène Ternois (Paris, Editions Balland, Collection Points Histoire, (1968) 1985).

Nowak M, *UN Covenant on Civil and Political Rights: CCPR Commentary* (Kehl am Rhein, NP Engel Publishers, 1993).

Ory P, *Les collaborateurs, 1940–1945* (Paris, Editions du Seuil, Collection Points Histoire, 1976).

Osiel M, *Mass Atrocity, Collective Memory, and the Law* (London, Transaction Publishers, 2000).

Paxton RO, *Vichy France – Old Guard and New Order, 1940–1944* (New York, Columbia University Press, (1972) 2001).

Pendas DP, *The Frankfurt Auschwitz Trial, 1963–1965 – Genocide, History, and the Limits of the Law* (Cambridge, Cambridge University Press, 2010).

Poliakov L, *Le Procès de Jérusalem – Juger Adolf Eichmann* (Paris, Calmann-Lévy, 1963).

——, *Sur les traces du crimes* (Paris, Berg International Éditeurs, 2003).

——, *Auschwitz* (Paris, Editions Gallimard/Julliard, Collection folio histoire, (1964) 2006).

Poznanski R, *Propagandes et persécutions – La Résistance et le 'problème juif', 1940–1944* (Paris, Librairie Arthème Fayard, 2008).

Quigley J, *The Genocide Convention – An International Law Analysis*, International and Comparative Criminal Justice (Aldershot, Ashgate, 2006).

Rémy D, *Les lois de Vichy – Actes dits 'lois' de l'autorité de fait se prétendant 'gouvernement de l'État français'* (Paris, Éditions romillat, 1992).

Ricard P, 'Bruxelles juge la loi française 'contre-productive', *Le Monde* (13 October 2006).

Robert-Diard P, 'Robert Badinter, poursuivi par le négationniste Robert Faurisson, a fustigé « l'une des pires entreprises de faussaires de l'histoire »', *Le Monde* (13 mars 2007).

Robinson J, 'The International Military Tribunal and the Holocaust, Some Legal Reflections', (1972) 7 *Israel Law Review* 1.

Robinson N, *The Genocide Convention – A Commentary* (New York, Institute of Jewish Affairs, 1960).

Roth SJ, 'Denial of the Holocaust as an Issue of Law' (1993) 23 *Israel Yearbook of Human Rights* 215.

Rousso H, *Le syndrome de Vichy de 1944 à nos jours*, 2nd edn (Paris, Editions du Seuil, Collection Points Histoire, 1990).

——, *The Vichy Syndrome – History and Memory in France since 1944*, Translated by Arthur Goldhammer (Cambridge, Harvard University Press, 1991).

——, *Vichy – L'événement, la mémoire, l'histoire* (Paris, Éditions Gallimard, Collection folio histoire, 2001).

——, *Le dossier Lyon III – Le rapport sur le racisme t le négationnisme à l'université Jean-Moulin* (Paris, Librairie Arthème Fayard, 2004).

——, *Le régime de Vichy* (Paris, Presses Universitaires de France, Collection Que sais-je?, 2007).

Salas D, 'Le droit peut-il contribuer au travail de mémoire?' in Association française pour l'histoire de la Justice, Commission nationale consultative des droits de l'homme, Ecole nationale de la magistrature , *Colloque La lutte contre le négationnisme Bilan et perspectives de la loi du 13 juillet 1990 tendant à réprimer tout acte raciste, antisémite ou xénophobe* (Paris, La Documentation française, 2003) 36.

Sadat Wexler L, 'The Interpretation of the Nuremberg Principles by the French Court of Cassation: From Touvier to Barbie and Back Again' (1994) 32 *Columbia Journal of Transnational Law* 289.

Schabas WA, *Genocide in International Law – The Crimes of Crimes*, 2nd edn (Cambridge, Cambridge University Press, 2009).

——, *The International Criminal Court: A Commentary on the Rome Statute*, (Oxford, Oxford University Press, 2010).

——, *An Introduction to the International Criminal Court*, 4th edn (Cambridge, Cambridge University Press, 2011).

——, *Unimaginable Atrocities – Justice, Politics, and Rights at the War Crimes Tribunals* (Oxford, Oxford University Press, 2012).

Schott RM, 'War Rape, Natality and Genocide' (2011) 13 *Journal of Genocide Research* 5.

Schwelb E, 'Crimes Against Humanity' [1946] *BYBIL* 178.

Sémelin J, *Purifier et Détruire – Usages politiques des massacres et génocides* (Paris, Editions du Seuil, 2005).

Seymour DM, *Law, Antisemitism and the Holocaust* (Oxon: Routledge-Cavendish, 2007).

Simpson AWB, 'Britain and the Genocide Convention' [2002] LXXIII BYBIL 5.

Simpson G, 'Objective Responsibility: Show Trials and War Crimes Trials (2006), 4 *International Commentary on Evidence* 1.

Smith KE., *Genocide and the Europeans* (Cambridge, Cambridge University Press, 2010).

Stern B, 'Universal jurisdiction over crimes against humanity under French law' (1999) 93 *AJIL* 525.

Taieb K (ed), *Je vous écris du Vel d'Hiv – Les lettres retrouvées* (Paris, Editions Robert Laffont, 2011).

Ternisien X, 'Les 62 000 dossiers de la honte', *Le Monde* (17 avril 2000).

Todorov T, *Une tragédie française – Été 1944: scènes de guerre civile*, Edition revue et corrigée (Paris, Editions du Seuil, Collection Points Essais, 2004).

Todorov T, 'Memory as Remedy for Evil' (2009) 7 *Journal of International Criminal Justice* 447.

Tomuschat C, 'International Criminal Prosecution: The Precedent of Nuremberg Confirmed' (1994) 5 *Criminal Law Forum* 237.

Van Schaack B, 'The Definition of Crimes Against Humanity: Resolving the Incoherence' (1999) 37 *Columbia Journal of Transnational Law* 787.

van Sliedregt E, 'Joint Criminal Enterprise as a Pathway to Convicting Individuals for Genocide' (2007) 5 *JICJ* 184.

Verschave F-X, *Complicité de Génocide? La politique de la France au Rwanda* (Paris, Editions La Découverte, 1994).

Vidal-Naquet P, *Les assassins de la mémoire – « Un Eichmann de papier » et autres essais sur le révisionnisme* (Paris, Editions La Découverte, Collection Points Essais, 1987).

Wald PM, 'Running the Trial of the Century: The Nuremberg Legacy' (2006) 27 *Cardozo Law Review* 1559.

Wanhong Z, 'From Nuremberg to Tokyo: Some Reflections on the Tokyo Trial (on the sixtieth anniversary of the Nuremberg Trials)' (2006) 27 *Cardozo Law Review* 1673.

Wechsler H, 'The Issues of the Nuremberg Trial' (1947) LXII *Political Science Quarterly* 11.

Wieviorka A (ed), *Les procès de Nuremberg et de Tokyo* (Paris, Editions Complexe, 1996).

Wieviorka A, *Auschwitz – La mémoire d'un lieu* (Paris, Robert Laffont, Hachette Littératures, Collection Pluriel Histoire, 2005).

—— (ed), *Auschwitz La Solution finale* (Paris, Editions Tallandier, 2005).

Wieviorka O, *La Mémoire Désunie – Le souvenir politique des années sombres, de la Libération à nos jours* (Paris, Editions du seuil, 2010).

Wirth S, 'Germany's New International Crimes Code: Bringing a Case to Court' (2003) *JICJ* 151.
Woetzel RK, *The Nuremberg Trials in International Law with a Postlude on the Eichmann Case* (London, Stevens & Sons Limited, 1960).
Wolfe R, 'Flaws in the Nuremberg Legacy: An Impediment to International War Crimes Tribunals' Prosecution of Crimes Against Humanity' (1998) 12 *Holocaust and Genocide Studies* 434.
Wright Q, 'The Law of the Nuremberg Trial', (1947) XLI *AJIL* 38.
Zaoui M, *Mémoires de Justice – Barbie, Touvier, Papon* (Paris, Editions du Seuil, 2009).
Zappala S, '*Do Heads of State in Office Enjoy Immunity from Jurisdiction for International Crimes? The* Ghaddafi *Case Before the French* Cour de Cassation' (2001) 12 *EJIL* 595.

INDEX